Abbé (Alexandre) Leguay

The path of perfection in religious life

A work intended for persons consecrated to God

Abbé (Alexandre) Leguay

The path of perfection in religious life
A work intended for persons consecrated to God

ISBN/EAN: 9783741175718

Manufactured in Europe, USA, Canada, Australia, Japa

Cover: Foto ©Lupo / pixelio.de

Manufactured and distributed by brebook publishing software (www.brebook.com)

Abbé (Alexandre) Leguay

The path of perfection in religious life

THE PATH

OF

PERFECTION IN RELIGIOUS LIFE.

A Work

INTENDED FOR PERSONS CONSECRATED TO GO

BY M. L'ABBE LEGUAY,

VICAR-GENERAL OF PERPIGNAN;
DIRECTOR OF SEVERAL RELIGIOUS COMMUNITIES.

With the Approbation of Mgr. the Archbishop of Paris, and the Bishop of Bayeux.

"Teach me, O Lord! the way in which I should walk, for I have lifted up my soul to You."—Ps. cxlii.

TRANSLATED FROM THE FRENCH.

DUBLIN:
JAMES DUFFY, WELLINGTON-QUAY, AND
22, PATERNOSTER ROW, LONDON.
1869

DUBLIN:
Printed by Moore and Murphy,
2, CRAMPTON-QUAY.

CONTENTS.

	Page.
Translator's Preface,	vii
Author's Preface,	ix

PART FIRST.

The Religious State considered as a Life of Separation from the World and its false and transitory Goods, . . 1

CHAPTER I.

The Nature and Extent of the Separation that the Religious Life imposes on those who embrace it. This separation is conformable to the designs of God, . . . 1

CHAPTER II.

Of Vows in general, ... 4
Section I.—Nature of vows.—Their different kinds.—They are agreeable to God, ... 4
Section II.—Vows are the essence of the religious state, . 9
Section III.—On the emission of religious vows, . . 12

CHAPTER III.

Of the Vow of Poverty, ... 16
Section I.—Nature and extent of this vow, . . 16
Section II.—Perfection of poverty; its different degrees, 21

CHAPTER IV.

Of the Vow of Chastity, ... 26
Section I.—The extent and excellence of this vow, . 26
Section II.—The gravity of faults against chastity, . 28
Section III.—That which alarms timid souls is no sin, . 33
Section IV.—Perfection of chastity, . . . 36

CHAPTER V.

Of Obedience, ... 40
Section I.—The law of obedience is a free contract which the religious makes at her profession, . . . 40

CONTENTS.

Page.

SECTION II.—The vow of obedience is the most important of the religious vows, ... 43
SECTION III.—The obligation imposed by the vow of obedience is most reasonable, and conduces to the happiness of a religious, ... 45
SECTION IV.—Indifference with regard to offices is a necessary consequence of the vow of obedience, . . 49
SECTION V.—Perfection of obedience, . . . 53
SECTION VI.—Religious obedience excludes all murmuring against superiors, ... 59

CHAPTER VI.

Of Enclosure and of the Parlour, ... 63
SECTION I.—Of enclosure and the duties it imposes on religious, ... 63
SECTION II.—Of the parlour, ... 66

CHAPTER VII.

Of the Rules and Constitutions, ... 70
SECTION I.—Rules and constitutions are indispensably necessary for religious communities, ... 70
SECTION II.—Religious are obliged to observe their rules and constitutions, ... 75
SECTION III.—How we should interpret this principle,—The rules and constitutions do not bind under pain of sin, ... 79
SECTION IV.—In what circumstances the violation of the rules and constitutions is a sin, and of what nature the sin is, ... 82

PART SECOND.

The Religious Life considered as a Life of Union with God, 85

CHAPTER I.

Of the Interior Life, ... 85
SECTION I.—In what the interior life consists, . . 85
SECTION II.—Of the control which the soul who aspires to an interior life should have over her passions, . 90
SECTION III.—Second means of arriving at an interior life—humility, ... 90
SECTION IV.—Third means to arrive at an interior life—the love of God, ... 96
SECTION V.—Fourth means for arriving at the interior life—conformity to the will of God, ... 103
SECTION VI.—Fidelity to grace, the fifth means of arriving at the interior life, ... 110

CONTENTS.

Page.

SECTION VII.—Fraternal charity, the sixth means of arriving at the interior life, ... 113
SECTION VIII.—Of private friendships, how opposed they are to fraternal charity, ... 121
SECTION IX.—Of antipathies—their source, dangers, and remedies, ... 127
SECTION X.—Of rash judgment—how opposed it is to charity, ... 131
SECTION XI.—On silence, which is the safeguard of the interior life, ... 136

CHAPTER II.

Of the Practices of the Interior Life, ... 141
SECTION I.—Of mental prayer, ... 141
SECTION II.—Prayer is the first and most important exercise of the religious life, ... 145
SECTION III.—Mental prayer is an exercise easy and natural to the creature, ... 148
SECTION IV.—An abridged method for making mental prayer, ... 152
SECTION V.—Some hints taken from spiritual writers in order to make mental prayer profitable, . . . 155
SECTION VI.—Of distractions in prayer, . . . 159
SECTION VII.—Of the void and insensibility we sometimes experience in prayer, ... 162
SECTION VIII.—Of different kinds of prayer, . . 167

CHAPTER III.

Of the Divine Office, ... 170
SECTION I.—Definition and origin of the divine office, . 170
SECTION II.—Of the recitation of the divine office, . 174

CHAPTER IV.

Of the Examen of Conscience, ... 179

CHAPTER V.

Of Spiritual Reading, ... 185

CHAPTER VI.

Of the Holy Sacrifice of the Mass, ... 189

CHAPTER VII.

Of Visiting the Blessed Sacrament, ... 196

CHAPTER VIII.

Of Confession, ... 202

CHAPTER IX.

Of Frequent Communion, ... 206

CHAPTER X.

Of Spiritual Direction, its Necessity and Advantages, . 211

CHAPTER XI.

Of the Chapter of Faults, ... 215

CHAPTER XII.

Of the Sanctification of our Actions in general, . . 220
SECTION I.—Necessity of sanctifying our ordinary actions, . 220
SECTION II.—Of purity of intention in our ordinary actions, 223
SECTION III.—Of retiring to rest, and of sleep, . . 226
SECTION IV.—Of rising, and the manner of sanctifying it, . 230
SECTION IV.*—Of our meals, ... 233
SECTION V.—Of recreation, ... 237
SECTION VI.—Of chapters or assemblies which take place to deliberate on the affairs of the community, . . 241

CHAPTER XIII.

Of the Trials of the Interior Life, ... 246
SECTION I.—Of interior pains in general, . . . 247
SECTION II.—Of scruples, ... 253

CHAPTER XIV.

SECTION I.—Of tepidity, ... 258
SECTION II.—Of abuse of grace, ... 263
SECTION III.—Of illusions of the interior life, . . 267

CHAPTER XV.

Of some works of charity which are united in several religious orders to the practices of an interior life, . . 272
SECTION I.—Of the instruction of youth, . . . 272
SECTION II.—Of some defects we ought to avoid in the instruction of youth, ... 279
SECTION III.—Of the method which may be successfully followed in the instruction of youth, . . . 287
SECTION IV.—Of the care of the sick, . . . 292

TRANSLATOR'S PREFACE.

THE object of this work, as sufficiently indicated by the title, is to enable those souls that have consecrated themselves to God, to attain that perfection to which they are bound to aspire. The religieuses of Ireland, being generally obliged to add the active to the contemplative life, have not sufficient leisure to devote themselves to the study of the voluminous treatises that have been written on the subject of religious perfection. Most of these productions, too, locked up as they are in a foreign tongue, are inaccessible to the greater number of those who, in our country, embrace this state of life. Nor has much been done until recently to place these works within the reach of the many by the medium of translation. It has been only within the last few years that the wonderful works and letters of St. Teresa have appeared in an English shape; and the "Mystic City of God," of Sister Mary of Jesus of Agreda, is still emtombed in its Spanish original, or has been but partially revived the other day in a garbled French version. The present work, indeed, has no such pretensions as those we have mentioned, being a plain and methodical exposition of the every day life and duties of the religieuse. To instruct in the essential duties of their state those chosen souls whom God has withdrawn from the allurements of the world to an union with Himself, is the aim that the Author has had in view throughout. In pursuing this aim he has sedulously avoided the two extremes of rigor and laxity; and seldom speaks in his own person, but draws his most valuable materials from the great approved masters of the spiritual life. The work has received the highest approbation from distinguished Prelates of the French Church, and has run rapidly through four editions; no ordinary proof, in these days, of its solid merit and excellence. The Translator deems, accordingly, that in giving an English version of this work to the light, she is conferring a boon upon those who, like herself, have embraced the holy state of religion. It may also lead to the republication amongst us of works of a still higher and more ascetical character.

PREFACE.

GOD, having destined man to partake of His immortal glory, points out to him two paths by which he may attain this end: the common life, and the religious life. These two paths are equally founded on the doctrine and precepts of our Divine Redeemer, but differ in the manner of arriving at the promised goal. The common life implies the observance of the commandments and the precepts; the religious life supposes, in addition to these, the accomplishment of the evangelical counsels, under the sway of a rule more or less austere.

In the common life, the faithful Christian lives amid the riches, honours, and pleasures of the world, which are the very food of concupiscence; but, directed by the precepts of the Lord, he governs his passions, he stifles in his heart every inordinate attachment to these perishable goods; according to the Apostle, "he enjoys them as if he enjoyed them not." In the religious life the Christian does more; following the counsels of the Saviour, he vows an eternal separation from all worldly goods: we may then look on the religious life as a life of separation.

In the common life, the faithful Christian copies in his exterior the holy life of our Saviour, and establishes in his interior the reign of Christ, as far as is possible amidst the distractions of the world. But, the Christian in religious life goes yet farther; separated from all that is vain and transitory, freed from every earthly care and solicitude, he unites himself exclusively to God, and, in a state almost celestial, consecrates to Him every faculty of body and soul; hence, religious life is also a life of union. Religious life, then, implies a total separation from the transitory goods of this world, and an intimate union of the soul with God. The holy vows of religion are the mystic sword which separates from the earth, and those same vows are the mysterious bond which unites the soul to its God.

Following the order observed by mystic theologians, we have divided this work into two parts. In the first, we have considered the religious life as one of separation, by the practice of vows, rules, and constitutions. The second part treats of the religious life as one of union with God, by the exercises of an interior life, prayer, meditation, &c.

It is true, nothing new can be said on these subjects, which have already been so ably handled by many spiritual writers, whose immortal works fill the libraries of monasteries. It would even grieve us to be suspected of adding anything to a theme to which the holiest of God's servants have devoted their brilliant talents. Ours is the humbler task of gleaning from their multitudinous and heaven-inspired writings, such passages as may form a compendium of the principal duties of the religious state. Having directed religious communities for forty years, we have found there are few ascetical works in which are united all the instructions necessary for religious, regarding their vows, rules, constitutions, the difficulties and trials of an interior life, and the various works of mercy, corporal and spiritual, to which they are devoted. Instructions on these matters may be had at great length in separate works, but few persons in religion have leisure to peruse so many volumes. Hence, to supply the deficiency, it has been our endeavour to make this work an abridgment of the doctrine of the most learned ascetics on the duties of the religious state. Relying little on our own experience, we have copied literally, or in substance, many passages from Rodriguez, Nouet, Guilloré, Surin, Bellecius, &c.

In presenting this small volume to the public, we hope to render some slight service to the chosen portion of Christ's flock, His consecrated spouses, and to merit their suffrages.

THE PATH

OF

PERFECTION IN RELIGIOUS LIFE.

PART FIRST.

THE RELIGIOUS STATE CONSIDERED AS A LIFE OF SEPARATION FROM THE WORLD AND ITS FALSE AND TRANSITORY GOODS.

CHAPTER I.

NATURE AND EXTENT OF THE SEPARATION THAT THE RELIGIOUS LIFE IMPOSES ON THOSE WHO EMBRACE IT. THIS SEPARATION IS CONFORMABLE TO THE DESIGNS OF GOD.

It is peculiarly to the souls whom God calls to religious life that the seoracles of Scripture are addressed: "Arise from the midst of Babylon, and let each one think of the salvation of his soul. Go out from this people, separate yourself from them; come to Me; I will be your father, and you will be My people; If any one comes to Me and does not hate his father, his mother, his brother and his sister, he is not worthy of Me. Leave to the dead the care of burying the dead. Renounce yourself, carry your cross and follow Me."

The saints perfectly understood the import of these maxims. Thus, we behold many of them who were called to a perfect life, renounce the honours with which they were surrounded, the riches they possessed, and the most legitimate pleasures; we behold them abandon parents, friends, and relatives, and bury themselves in the deepest solitudes, to be occupied with God alone, with heaven and eternity. And if the place of their retreat were discovered, if the concourse of people, attracted by the odour of their virtues and the desire of claiming the assistance of their prayers or their counsels, came to trouble their solitude, they sought one more profound and obscure.

The first founders of religious orders selected the most inaccessible deserts, to build the monasteries in which they assembled their disciples; and the renunciation of all the perishable goods of this world formed the basis of the angelical life to which they were formed.

Later, when monasteries began to multiply, and to be built even in the midst of populous cities, either to diffuse the good odour of religious virtues, and to attract the benedictions of heaven, or to form youth to social virtues by a Christian education, or to exercise the works of mercy to the poor, sick, and infirm, the Church, ever penetrated with the same spirit, established within these sacred dwellings a similar renunciation, and a religious enclosure at least passive, in order that, although in the midst of the world, those who were consecrated to God should be separated from all that is foreign to the holy works to which they are devoted.

This holy separation, which is in full vigour in our days in religious communities, rests on the same basis, and contains four points, prescribed in a manner more or less austere, according to the spirit of different orders. The first is poverty, the second chastity, the third obedience, the fourth religious enclosure, or separation from the world. These important obligations are the matter of the vows of religion about which we will speak in the following chapters; they are, in a manner, the mystic sword which separates the soul of the religious from the world and its perishable goods, and immolates to God all that is corrupt in nature.

Nothing can be more conformable to the designs of the Almighty Creator, than the separation to which the religious soul is vowed. By the vow of poverty, she restricts herself to what is necessary for lodging, clothing, and nourishment. And, did God propose to Himself any other end in placing at the disposal of man the things of this earth? By the vow of chastity, she obliges herself to lead, in a sinful body, an angelical life—a life of innocence and of sanctity—such as the Son of God Himself led on earth—on which He pronounced so many eulogiums, and the practice of which has been so eminently recommended by the Apostle. Now, can aught be more conformable to the views of a God of infinite sanctity than a holy life?

By the vow of obedience, the religious soul renounces her will, which is perverted by original sin—which is often opposed to good and inclined to evil; she renounces the free disposal of that will to follow the will of God, intimated to her by her rules, constitutions, and the voice of her Superioress. Again, can anything be more conformable to the designs of God? Has He not created man to be subject to Him and to obey Him?

In fine, by religious enclosure the consecrated soul separates herself from a corrupted and corrupting world, and shuns its contagion, to pray for the sinful, or to devote herself to the instruction of youth, or to the consolation of the afflicted. What can be more agreeable to the God of charity, who commands us to love one another, as He has loved us?

To reason and true wisdom, nothing is more conformable than the separation which religious life imposes. For what can be more wise than to renounce those perishable goods, those moth-eaten treasures, which we must eventually quit at the portal of the tomb? What more foolish than to be attached to insipid pleasures, which disappear with the rapidity of lightning, frequently leaving but remorse and despair? Can anything be more reasonable than to renounce a perverted will, which often leads us astray—than to separate ourselves from a contagious world, in the midst of which it is so difficult to preserve innocence, and to attain salvation?

Again, nothing can be more wise and reasonable, above all when the religious soul has in perspective a solid, a perfect, an infinite good, and an unfading glory, than to renounce the false wisdom of the world, to submit to Infinite Wisdom;—than to renounce a perverted will, to follow the holy will of God;—than to forsake a polluted world, to be united in the most intimate manner to a God of goodness, whose delight is to be with the children of men, and to render them participators of His happiness.

CHAPTER II.

OF VOWS IN GENERAL.

SECTION I.—*Nature of Vows.—Their different Kinds.—They are agreeable to God.*

THE Vow is the sword destined to accomplish the separation which takes place between the world and the soul consecrated to her God in religious life. What then is a vow?

A vow is a deliberate promise that is made to God—a promise by which the soul engages to do a thing that is better to do than to omit, and which is not incompatible with a greater good.

A vow is a promise. It must not then be confounded with those *resolutions* we make so easily; and which, unfortunately, we violate with a deplorable facility. It is a *deliberate promise*, that is, a promise made with reflection, not with carelessness, and without having calculated its responsibilities. It is a *promise, by which we engage to do a thing that would be better to do, than to omit;* or rather, as some theologians say, it is a promise to *do a greater good;* according to Saint Antoninus, it *is to do a greater good than is requisite in order to be saved.*

In fine, it *is a promise to do something which is not incompatible with a greater good;* thus, to make a vow to engage in the married state, would be null, because, in effect, the married state is less perfect than the state of virginity.

Vows may be considered either as simple or solemn.

A simple vow is a promise made to God without solemnity, or rather without a certain kind of solemnity: such are the vows made in certain secular communities, either in private and without witness, or in public and before those who wish to assist.

A solemn vow is one made in an order approved by the Church, and with the formalities she prescribes; it binds the soul in the most strict manner to her God.

The holy vows of religion, either simple or solemn, are superior in force and in effect to private vows which are made in the world; thus they annihilate all previous vows that have been made, so that the religious is no longer obliged to accomplish them; for Saint Thomas says, with Fromagean, Samel, Pantase, &c., the vows of religion contain the substance of all private vows, as that which is universal comprehends all that is particular. We make private vows in the world, continues Saint Thomas, but in consecrating ourselves to God in religion, we renounce and die to this life of the world, to devote entirely to Him our body, soul, and will—a sacrifice, which includes all that has been previously promised to God by private vows.

This doctrine is founded on reason. Take the example of a debtor, who, to liquidate some trifling debts, would abandon all his wealth to his creditor, and besides, would engage himself to his service for the remainder of his life, would he not be perfectly free?—Now, this is what the person does who consecrates herself to God by religious vows; by her holy profession, she despoils herself, for God, of all she possesses, and consecrates herself irrevocably to His service; thus, she amply pays all debts she may have contracted by simple vows. Besides, add these holy doctors, the peculiar practices and singularity, which accompany these private vows, never suit a religious community, in which perfect uniformity should reign.

With much greater reason, then, should the vows of religion supersede all practices imposed by associations in which we have been enrolled in the world, as well as all others that might be contrary to the spirit of the order we have embraced. Thus Saint Francis de Sales obliged Sister Saint Michael, first Superioress of the Visitation of Besançon (as we read in the Life of this holy religious), to quit the cord and scapular of Saint Francis, addressing to her these remarkable words: "My daughter, the Mount of Calvary, on which this Congregation is formed, is a place of renunciation; the meek Jesus was there stripped of the seamless robe, which Mary had made for Him. Why are you grieved? The habit of the children of the Visitation is a holy and blessed habit; their cross, on which are engraved the names of Jesus and Mary, is to them as a scapular, and the fastening of this cross is the chain of sacred love which unites them to God. You see, then, my daughter, that you lose nothing in quitting these things; the religious habit holds to you the place of all beside."

The vows, and particularly that of obedience, render equally void every private vow made after religious profession, without permission of the Superioress. It is an acknowledged principle, at least generally, that any one who by her state is subject to another, cannot contract any obligations without permission of the person to whom she is subject; thus, according to Saint Thomas, a religious, in virtue of her vow of obedience, has subjected herself in all things to her Superioress; consequently, she is not permitted to form any engagement, or make any vow without her consent. If this were not the case, that perfect uniformity and harmony of religious communities, would often be disturbed by indiscreet vows; such as to make a vow to fast and abstain, on days not appointed by the rules, to recite certain prayers, or to perform mortifications which would incapacitate the religious from fulfilling her other duties. In all vows made by the religious after profession, it must be understood, that they only oblige in case the Superioress approve of them.

Fromagean says, that vows made after profession do not suit in communities, whose exercises ought to be uniform; that the yoke of religion is sufficiently onerous, without being augmented. We should, then, regard these vows as not being of *a greater good*, because incompatible with the rule, and consequently not obliging the person who made them.

It is an incontestible truth that the vows of religion, made with deliberation and the necessary conditions, are most meritorious and agreeable to God. The Royal Prophet seemed to take pleasure in reminding God of those he had made, as of something capable of conciliating His favour. " Lord," said he, " I have made vows to You, and I will faithfully execute them." The Holy Ghost tells us, by the mouth of the Wise Man, in the book of Proverbs, " That the vows of the just are acceptable in the eyes of God." They are so agreeable to Him, that He declares, by the prophet Isaiah, that those will be days of benediction, when the people, rising from the darkness of error, will make vows and observe them. " Then," said He, " the Lord will be known in Egypt, and the Egyptians will know the Lord. They will make unto Him vows, and they will keep them."

Thus, the Church, the ever faithful interpreter of the will and oracles of God, has always considered vows as an act of religion the most holy, the most agreeable to God, and the most meritorious. She has pronounced the most magnificent eulogiums on those who, to honour the Lord, to acknowledge more perfectly His sovereign dominion over everything, and over themselves in particular, consecrate to Him, by vow, whatever they have most precious, by the religious profession. She has ever encouraged by her exhortations, and ever consecrated by her ceremonies, these heroic sacrifices.

Reason itself teaches us that it is with an eye of complacency God regards those sacrifices, and that in His infinite goodness, He cannot fail to recompense, by abundant blessings, the generous conduct of those who, through His love, or zeal for His glory, propose to themselves not only to offer some general or particular sacrifice, but to deliver up the victim; immolate it to Him all entire, by the vows which irrevocably bind the soul.

SECTION II.—*Vows are the Essence of the Religious State.*

Vows are the essence of the religious state. It is of importance to define the difference between perfection and the state of perfection; between a religious life and the religious state.

Religious perfection, in general, consists in the actual and entire execution of the evangelical counsels. This accomplishment may exist without any other bond than the will—a will that is liable to change, a bond that we are free to dissolve when we please.

The state of perfection, on the contrary, consists not in the actual accomplishment of the counsels, but in the actual, permanent, stable obligation of forming ourselves to the practice of the counsels; as the word "state" means; so that we may be perfect, without being in a state of perfection; and we may be in a state of perfection, without being perfect.

Religious life, to be a state of perfection, implies the obligation of tending constantly to perfection, otherwise it could not be a state of perfection, just as a person may have deep religious feelings and sentiments, yet not be in a religious state.

Vows are an excellent preservative against the fragility and inconstancy of man, for nothing can be more inconstant than the human mind. This inconstancy is independent of the will of man, and, aided by grace, he can resist it, and persevere in the resolution of walking in the path of rectitude. But experience sadly demonstrates he is not always equally faithful to grace, he does not always resist the deplorable inconstancy of his mind and heart. Thus the man of the world in the beginning zealously embraces virtue and the practices of an interior life; he frequently approaches the sacraments; he devotes himself with fervour to prayer, withdraws from all dangerous occasions, follows with docility the precepts and evangelical counsels; but, not being habitually directed or restrained by any powerful bond, or stimulated by any perpetual obligation, except the commandments, and meeting at each step new obstacles, to-day he will omit one exercise, to-morrow another, until, eventually, he will abandon all his practices of piety, and, led astray by the torrent of bad example, he will be hurled into the abyss. The religious soul, on the contrary, a captive by her holy vows, stimulated by good example, encouraged by her superiors, to whom she has made a vow of obedience, will be preserved from a similar fall, and will persevere in the path of virtue. According to Rodriguez, a holy man being interrogated if perfection could be attained in the world, replied that it could, but that he would rather have one degree of grace in religion, than ten in the world; because in religion, where we are separated from the world, which is a capital enemy of grace, and where we are continually excited to virtue by good example, grace is easily preserved and augmented; whereas, in the world it is very easily lost, and preserved with much difficulty.

Vows perfect liberty in place of destroying it; in effect, true liberty does not consist in following the unrestrained fancies of the imagination, and the disorderly inclinations of the mind and heart. Such liberty, says St. Anselm, is a mark of true slavery. Those who follow their passions may glory in their liberty, yet they are only the miserable slaves of sin. St. Augustine says, that before his conversion he was bound, not by the fetters of a captive, but by his own will, perverted by passion and vice; a will more difficult to bend than the strongest metal.

True liberty consists in freedom from the slavery of the passions, and in being confirmed in the virtues opposed to them. When we are arrived at this happy term, we are in our centre,—in our element; then we are truly free; hence, it is, that the holy vows of religion lead to true liberty. The effect of these vows is to confirm and strengthen the will in what is good, and to hinder it from allowing itself to be drawn to what is evil. And this no more destroys liberty in us, than the perfect liberty which God and the saints enjoy in heaven, is destroyed by their incapacity of sinning.

Do not think, says St. Ignatius, that it is a small advantage for your free will, to be able to restore it entirely into the hands of Him who gave it; for by this means you do not destroy it, but render it far more perfect by conforming it to the sovereign rule of all perfection, who is God, of whom your superioress is the substitute and the interpreter.

In fine, the vows produce another effect—that of augmenting, in a wonderful manner, the merit of our virtues and good works;—for which St. Thomas gives three excellent reasons:—

The first is: That a vow is an act of religion, which enhances the value of all the acts of virtue that depend on it. These acts have a double merit, that of the virtue, and that of obedience. Thus poverty, chastity, and obedience have their intrinsic merit as virtues, and when vowed, their merit as acts of religion.

Secondly: By the actions we perform in virtue of our vows, we give much more to God, than by those we perform without vow; because we not only offer God what we do, but also the impossibility of doing otherwise; we offer Him our liberty, which is the greatest oblation and sacrifice we can make Him. Now, by the vow of poverty, we not only deprive ourselves of what we possess, but what is still more, we deprive ourselves of the power of ever possessing anything; as St. Anselm says, we give to God the tree together with the fruit. "We give Him at once," says St. Bonaventure, "the interest and the principal."

The third reason why vows render our actions more meritorious is, that these actions contain a more copious merit, because they spring from a more constant and determined will; and no will can be more perfect and constant than that which is attached to God by the indissoluble vows of religion; consequently no acts can be more meritorious than those which result from this attachment.

Section III.—*On the Emission of Religious Vows.*

After having maturely reflected on their vocation, consulted God, and received the decision of the director of their conscience, those who believe themselves called to the religious life should assiduously prepare for profession. It is for them a step of the highest importance, since the engagement they contract binds them in an irrevocable manner, and their eternal salvation depends on it. They should endeavour to have their profession accompanied by all the conditions necessary for its validity; and they should themselves be in the dispositions, which would render it holy and agreeable to God.

In order that the religious profession may be valid, it is required:

First. That she who presents herself to make the vows should have received baptism. This condition is indispensable; and if, after profession, there arises any serious doubt on the subject, she should recur to conditional baptism; then renew the vows conditionally. The sacrament of confirmation is not absolutely necessary, but it is suitable to receive it before profession, as some rules expressly demand.

Second. According to the Council of Trent, the person must have made a year's probation. This year must be complete, and as theologians agree, if it wanted an hour, or even a quarter of an hour, the profession would be invalid. The year of probation must be also uninterrupted.

Third. She who presents herself should be of the age prescribed by the canons. The decree of the Council of Trent is, that none should enter the Noviceship under the age of twelve, nor be admitted to profession until the candidate has completed her sixteenth year. In some communities they are not allowed to make the vows until eighteen years of age.

Fourth. The candidate for profession should be free; she should not be led to this step through fear, nor should any artifice or violence be used to determine her; God will never accept of forced service, the heart must accompany any oblation that is presented to Him; consequently, vows made in other dispositions are null and void in the eyes of God.

Fifth. The profession should be made in the hands of a person legitimately authorized. Such is the formal decision of the canon law; and the reason is evident; profession is a reciprocal contract, which obliges the professed to the observance of the rule, and religion to maintain her according to the constitutions of the order she has embraced. Thus, as the Church requires her consent, she must have the consent of the Church; and that can only be had from the Superiors of the community, or from some one who, according to the constitutions of the Institute, is capable of representing them.

Sixth. The person who aspires to profession should be exempt from certain impediments, such as being born of infidel parents, or of an outlawed family; she should be free from debt, and from having done anything that would defame her. She must not be epileptic, nor liable to certain maladies of body or mind. Of these defects, some render profession illicit and criminal, others absolutely void. For these subjects we must refer to the constitutions and customs of the different orders.

Seventh. Persons whose parents are in indigence should not be admitted as members of communities; because, it is only a counsel to embrace religious life, but the support of a parent is of precept; and the precepts naturally go before the counsels. Collet makes three observations on this point; first, it is not necessary that this poverty be present, it suffices if it be imminent. Secondly, a young person is not really obliged to remain in the world, when she finds she cannot assist her parents, although they may be in want. In the third place, no necessity, however great, can retain a person in the world, when her parents are the first to lead her to evil: or when, from her own weakness, she is in danger of yielding to violent temptation; then she must remember the counsel of the Saviour: "If any one does not hate father, and mother, even his own life, he cannot be My disciple." She must leave to " the dead the care of burying the dead."

The dispositions necessary to make profession holy and agreeable to God are: First, the state of grace. She who presents herself for profession demands to be admitted into the number of the Spouses of a thrice-holy God—of a God in whose presence the angels are not pure. How carefully, then, should the creature purify herself from all stain of sin to become worthy of the espousals of a Being whose special attribute is sinlessness. How culpable would she be, did she offer herself for the divine alliance with a conscience sullied with mortal sin. She would be guilty of fearful hypocrisy, and would attract on her reprobate soul the maledictions of heaven ! !

Second. She must be penetrated with a profound sentiment of humility, and look on herself as unworthy of the sublime alliance she is to contract.

Third. She must be animated with lively gratitude for the goodness of God, who, by gratuitous predilection, has preferred her to a thousand others more faithful and more worthy. She should frequently reflect that "He hath not done so to every nation."

Fourth. She should be determined to serve God as He wishes, in the new state she purposes embracing, without any other desire than that of glorifying Him all the days of her life.

CHAPTER III.

OF THE VOW OF POVERTY.

SECTION I.—*Nature and Extent of this Vow.*

THE vow of poverty may be considered either as simple or solemn. The solemn vow of poverty, such as is made in orders approved by the Church, according to the rules prescribed by the ecclesiastical canons, is an act by which we renounce solemnly and for the love of God, not only the faculty of disposing of anything as if it were our own, but even all proprietorship over the things we do possess, and all right and pretension to those we do not possess.

The simple vow of poverty is an act, by which we renounce the liberty of *using* any of our goods without permission of our own Superior, reserving to ourselves the dominion of them, and the faculty of possessing new ones. The simple vow of poverty is in use in many religious congregations, such as those of the Lazarites, the Sisters of Charity, established by St. Vincent de Paul, the Brothers of the Christian Schools, &c. Many persons in the world, zealous for their perfection, make this vow, and deprive themselves of the power of using their goods without permission of their confessor, or any superior they may select.

The essential difference between the simple and solemn vow is, that by the solemn vow we deprive ourselves of the faculty of possessing or acquiring any temporal goods; but by the simple vow we retain that liberty, and only forbid ourselves the use of our riches without a legitimate permission. Consequently, she who is bound by a solemn vow, in violating poverty commits a much more grievous sin, than she who has only made a simple vow. In fact, she commits a double fault. First, against the virtue of religion, since she violates a vow she has made to God, —a vow which obliges her as strictly as those of chastity and obedience. Secondly, against justice; for having freely despoiled herself of all in favour of her monastery, even of the power of possessing or of receiving, she cannot of herself possess, give, or receive without being guilty of theft.

But the person who has only made the simple vow, having reserved to herself the right of possessing and acquiring, in possessing or disposing of what she possesses, or in receiving without permission, evidently does not sin against justice, but only against the virtue of religion, by the violation of the vow she has made of acting with dependence.

Now, the question proposes itself, can we consider as solemn those vows now made in France, in the orders in which these solemn vows were usual? It is doubtful, as some theologians say, because the civil law of this kingdom does not permit religious to renounce the dominion of their property, nor the power of adding to it. Hence, the vows that are made are not conformable to the canons, and can only be considered as simple vows.

The holy Council of Trent points out to religious how they should conduct themselves with regard to poverty. " Religious are not permitted to possess or to retain any private property, nor can they ever keep in the name of their monastery any property, moveable or immoveable, no matter of what quality, or in what manner acquired; all such property is to be placed in the hands of the Superior without restriction, that he may dispose of it as he pleases." Monsigneur Bouvier says, that there can be no exception to this rule, and that every act of proprietorship is a violation of the vow of poverty, more or less serious according to the matter. Whence it results:

First. That a religious cannot, without violating poverty, retain a sum of money, however small it may be.

Second. That she cannot receive a deposit, because such an act implies a contract, by which the religious would render herself accountable for the thing deposited if it were lost or injured—an obligation, which a person who possesses nothing could not contract.

Third. That she cannot accept of anything in her own name, either from her parents, friends, or any person else; and that everything she receives should be put with the goods of the community, without permitting the religious to have any right over it, or to be favoured on that account more than the other members of the community.

Fourth. That she cannot give to the poor what she retrenches from her own nourishment, because what she does not consume belongs not to her, but to her community; and unless she has the express permission of the Superioress, she cannot give to others what is allotted for her own use.

Fifth. She cannot conceal her clothes, books, work materials, or anything else which is allowed for her use, fearing her Superioress should take them from her; because, as Rodriguez says, by such conduct it would appear she desired to appropriate to herself these objects, and retain them against the will of the Superioress, or, at least, she would display an affection for them, which is contrary to the spirit of poverty.

Sixth. She cannot, without permission, make exchanges with the sisters of the things that are for her own use, which would be an act of proprietorship.

Seventh. She cannot dispose of the things it is her office to distribute, but according to the wishes and instructions of the Superioress; for if, knowing the will of the Superioress, she gave more or less, better or worse, than had been appointed, she would act as if she were the proprietress, and would sin against poverty. It is not uncommon to find in monasteries religious holding offices, such as procuratrix, dispenser, infirmarian, keeper of garments, &c., who, too sensibly attracted to some sisters, anticipate their wants, whilst other sisters, for whom they have not the same affection, or for whom they have an antipathy, are left without what is necessary.

Eighth. She cannot destroy, either voluntarily or through negligence, the objects which are given to her for her use, or which are confided to her care, because it only belongs to a person who is proprietor to destroy.

Ninth. The religious cannot renounce, without permission, any legacy or inheritance; because this property may turn to the advantage of the community, and the renunciation would be an act of proprietorship. All these decisions are applicable to religious who are only bound by the simple vow of poverty, as well as to those who have made solemn vows, with this double difference, that those who are under the obligation of simple vows require a more grievous violation of their vow to constitute a mortal sin, and that any disposal against poverty made by them is illicit but valid, whilst any disposal made by those who have contracted solemn vows is illicit and null.

She who embraces the monastic life, if she wishes to restrict herself within the limits of religious poverty in the disposal of temporal goods, ought to observe the following rules :—

First. She should neither use nor dispose of anything as proprietress.

Second. She should neither use nor dispose of anything, without having received from the Superioress a legitimate permission. A legitimate permission is that which the Superioress freely gives, and which has not been extorted by fear, cunning, fraud, or importunity.

Third. She ought only to use these goods in the manner indicated in the rules and constitutions of her order, for each one is obliged to practise poverty, as she has promised; and in making her vows she promised to observe them conformably to the rules and constitutions of the order she embraced.

Fourth. She ought, in the use of temporal goods, confine herself to what is absolutely necessary; that is to say, she should carefully avoid in necessary things every appearance of superfluity, and every desire of possessing objects of curiosity; if she notably offended on this point she would be grievously culpable.

Of what nature, then, is the sin of which the religious is guilty, when she violates her vow of poverty? As theft is only a mortal sin when the matter stolen is considerable, and venial when it is less, so the transgression of the vow of poverty is only mortal when what the religious gives, keeps, or receives is of value. Thus, what constitutes a mortal sin in theft, suffices equally to make a violation of the vow of poverty mortal.

In order to understand perfectly the grievousness of the sin, some matters must be examined, such as whether the monastery is rich or poor; whether it be to a stranger or to one of the house the religious has given; also, what degree of scandal resulted from the violation of the vow.

Section II.—*Perfection of Poverty; its Different Degrees.*

Among those who make profession of poverty, three classes may be distinguished. First, those who exteriorly quit all temporal goods, but who love them interiorly, and detach not the heart from them. The second comprehends all those who have left the world in heart and affection, who seek not after superfluities, but who are attached to what is necessary. The third class includes those who are truly detached from all, even from the necessaries of life, and who love poverty in deed and in effect.

First. Those who exteriorly quit all temporal goods, but who love them interiorly, and detach not the heart from them. This first class may be divided into two degrees: those who are attached to them merely for the gratification of self, and those who are attached to them for the sake of their community.

To renounce exteriorly earthly possessions, but to be interiorly attached to them, as to a thing we esteem and love, is to mock God, to deceive our superiors and ourselves; it is to imitate the blindness and hypocrisy of the Scribes and Pharisees, who, according to our divine Redeemer, "Make clean the outside of the cup, whilst inside they are full of rapine and uncleanness." It is to resemble sepulchral monuments, whose exterior is magnificently adorned with sculpture and colouring, but whose interior is the dwelling of worms and corruption; it is to impose on one's self sacrifices and privations which are unworthy of recompense. The poverty counselled by our Saviour, and which the religious promises to observe, is not purely exterior; it is poverty in heart and mind, as the Son of God has declared,

"Blessed are the poor in spirit," that is, those who are detached in heart and mind from everything terrestrial, whose only treasure is God, and whose heart is incessantly echoing the sentiments of the Royal Prophet, "What have I in heaven, but thee my God, and on earth what do I desire?"

Saint Peter, addressing himself to Jesus Christ, said, "Behold, Lord, we have left all to follow Thee, what will be our recompense?" "Verily," answered our Redeemer, "I say to you, you have followed Me;" remark, says St. Jerome, that our Saviour does not say you have left all, but *you have followed Me;* because it does not suffice to leave all, it is still necessary to follow Christ by poverty of spirit and detachment of heart. To abandon all is not the essential point; several Pagan philosophers have renounced all through human motives, such as Diogenes, Antisthenes, &c. But what is absolutely required, in order to merit the recompense of evangelical poverty, is to detach the mind and heart from everything terrestrial, and, with a generous contempt, to trample under foot every created object, believing, with the Apostle, that *provided we gain Jesus Christ, all the rest is but dust and ordure.* It is thus, those act who are truly poor in spirit, and who are declared "blessed" by the Son of God.

There is another snare to shun, and concerning which, persons do not sufficiently distrust themselves in religion. We meet souls sincerely detached in all that concerns their temporal interests, but who are too solicitous as to what regards the welfare of their community; they too earnestly desire the temporal prosperity of their monasteries, and all their labours seem devoted to that end; and if adversity happen they are inordinately grieved, and forget that the same God who has dispensed temporal goods to them can withdraw them at pleasure. The reason persons do not distrust this inclination is, that it is so perfectly divested of self, and they pretend their object is solely to advance God's glory. Deceived by the artifices of the demon, who thus hides his venom under the veil of a noble and generous sentiment, they complain, they exaggerate the wants of the convent, and very frequently cast aside truth, and the duties imposed by their vow of poverty, which made a learned and holy religious say : "There are some convents which, without necessity, continually allege want: such are those which, from a principle of avarice, fancy they will never have sufficient; which, with too great solicitude, regard as present some trying pecuniary circumstances that are hardly possible, and may never happen; or such as never having known the strict bonds of religious poverty, place in the number of necessary things, objects that are absolutely superfluous."

Second. There is another class of persons whose minds and hearts are perfectly disengaged from everything superfluous, who are content with what is necessary, as determined by the rules and constitutions of their order, but who have a disorderly affection for these necessary things; they are exacting; they often murmur when they want anything, or when what is given for their wants does not suit them. They examine what is given to others, and allow jealousy to govern them.

This defect is more common than is generally thought, and religious do not sufficiently reproach themselves with it; nevertheless, it is evidently contrary to the spirit of poverty. There are in religion, says Rodriguez, persons who have generously abandoned the world, who have no attachment to what is superfluous, but who are extremely careful to have all things necessary: who wish to have good nourishment, good clothing, convenient lodgings, and such like, and are much troubled and complain when they are denied what they desire. This is not true poverty, and, as St. Bernard says, it is strange that so many at present should glory in being the poor of Christ, at the same time be unwilling to bear any inconvenience. This is to be rich rather than poor, and such as these surpass secular persons, who are not always provided with necessaries; some, because they have not the means to procure them, and others who would rather be without conveniences than incur the expense of procuring them, so that a thrifty disposition does in them what virtue should do in us; others, in fine, though they have much, and put themselves to vast expense, yet are never served according to their will. Yet you, who are religious, and have made a vow of poverty, would have everything you want, and suffer no inconvenience. This shows no desire of poverty, but rather a desire to live in ease and plenty. Had you been in the world still, perhaps you would have suffered a great deal more in this point; is it, therefore, just that you who entered religion in order to mortify your passions, and to lead a penitential life, should be solicitous for those very conveniences which you should not have had in the world?

Third. In fine, there is a third class of persons, and God grant they may be the most numerous, who are truly detached in mind and heart even from what is necessary, who sincerely love poverty in the most indispensable things of life:—these are truly the poor, whom our divine Saviour has blessed.

Again we quote Rodriguez: "It is not enough to be detached from unprofitable and superfluous things, but we must destroy all affection to those that are necessary, and show our love of poverty by an absolute want of all. Unable, however, to do without what is necessary to sustain life, we must take no more than is strictly required and necessary, and by keeping this necessity within narrow bounds, rather than by extending it, we must show that we are glad of any occasion to give testimony to our love of poverty." It is nothing to be poor, says St. Vincent, unless we love to be so, and even rejoice to suffer for Jesus Christ all the inconveniences of poverty. If, then, you would wish to know if you are poor in spirit, reflect whether you love the effects and the inevitable consequences of poverty, as hunger, thirst, cold, fatigue, and a real want of all. See if you are glad to wear an old habit, worn out and mended, or that you rejoice when you want part of your dinner, when the server forgets or gives you what you do not like, or when your cell is changed for a most incommodious one. If you are not satisfied when these things happen, or that you endeavour to shun them, you may be assured you have not arrived at true poverty of spirit.

We may distinguish four degrees of poverty of spirit. The first is to be perfectly detached from what is necessary; the second, to be satisfied with any privation, either in quantity or quality; the third, to rejoice in privation, because it would imply another trait of resemblance with the poor Jesus; the fourth, to seek, for the love of Jesus Christ, to suffer a complete privation of all.

Any soul which has a sincere desire of her perfection, will not rest content with the two first degrees we have indicated; she will pass on to the fourth, and will become daily more conformable to her spouse Jesus; and is it not just that the spirit of privation should be that of the spouse of a God, who was born in a stable, lived in extreme indigence, and died on a cross despoiled of all? Let the religious, then, be generous in the sacrifice she has made to God in professing poverty. Let there be no rapine in her holocaust, let her glory in being among those faithful spouses of the poor Jesus, who put no reserve to their offering.

CHAPTER IV.

OF THE VOW OF CHASTITY.

SECTION I.—*Extent and Excellence of this Vow.*

THE vow of chastity in religion is a promise made to God, and accepted by a Superior,—a promise by which the religious consecrates to God the integrity of her mind, her body, and her heart.

This vow obliges her who has made it, not only to shun with care every exterior disorder, every stain which could sully or tarnish the purity of her body, consecrated to an exact and rigorous continence, but also to preserve her heart and soul exempt from every thought and desire opposed to this sublime virtue. Thus, all should be chaste in the spouse of Jesus Christ, the mind in its thoughts, the heart in its affections, the eyes in what they look on, the ears in what they hear, the lips in what they say, the hands in what they do, and, in fine, every step should breathe but this angelic virtue.

The life of the religious should be a continual warfare to defend the virtue of chastity against the attacks of concupiscence and of the demon, and to preserve stainless in a fragile vase so precious a treasure, remembering that every fault against this virtue increases its enormity, in consequence of the vow which binds her to observe it in perfection.

This virtue is so agreeable to God, that His only Son wishing to assume human nature, would have a virginal mother, and selected as His favourite a virgin disciple, and promises to recompense with His ineffable vision the clean of heart. "Blessed are the clean of heart, for they shall see God." Again in the Proverbs, God declares that "she who loves purity will have the king for a friend;" and as creatures glory in the friendship of an earthly prince, so should the religious exult in the friendship of Him whom the angels adore. How assiduously should she cultivate the virtue that will procure for her this happiness! The religious is called not alone to be His friend, but His consecrated spouse, therefore she should aspire to the very highest perfection in this holy virtue, and exclude from her heart every desire and affection opposed to the fidelity she owes Him. She must never forget that her God is a jealous God, who dwells reluctantly in a heart which is not wholly His. His chosen dwelling is amid the lilies of chaste souls. They are "the forty-four thousand, who sung, as it were, a new canticle, which none else could sing, but these forty-four thousand, who had been redeemed from the earth." It is they who "follow the Lamb withersoever He goeth."

This virtue raises the creature to the nature of angels, and makes her a citizen of heaven. "O chastity," exclaims Saint Ephrem, "thou art that glorious flower, whose beauty adorns both body and soul, and whose fragrance diffuses over both the odour of celestial perfume." "Virgins of Jesus Christ," says Saint Jerome, "know and cherish all the advantages of your state of innocence; it is one of exalted greatness, of spiritual and chaste delights, which are far more precious than all you have sacrificed. You have for Spouse even the Son of God, who selected as His Mother, the only unstained one among the daughters of Eve, and who chooses His beloved ones from among pure and chaste souls. Correspond with the honour bestowed on you. The more you love chastity, so much the more intimate will be the bonds that unite you to your Spouse; in proportion as you purify your heart, the more capable will it be of loving God."

"O holy virginity," cries the pious Fenelon, "happy the chaste doves who on the wings of divine love seek your delights in the desert! O chosen and well-beloved souls, to whom it is given to live independent of the flesh! They have a Spouse who can never die, in whom they will never see a shadow of imperfection, who loves them, who renders them happy through His love; they have nothing to fear, but not loving Him sufficiently, or loving what He does not love." We may here remark that all the practices of religious life tend to establish this virtue in the heart; separation from the world, poverty, humiliations, austerities, watchings, prayers, confessions, frequent communions, &c. How is it possible that this treasure would not be preserved with assistance so powerful and so varied.

SECTION II.—*Gravity of Faults contrary to Vow of Chastity; that we should make account of the least things on this delicate point; particularly in Confession.*

If there be a sin which God has in horror, and which he pardons with difficulty, it is that which is opposed to the virtue of purity. It is truly "the abomination of desolation" in the holy place of which the Prophet speaks, and which excites the indignation of a thrice-holy God. But if this vice is hideous and enormous in a simple Christian, what must it be in a religious, in a spouse of Jesus Christ; who not only tramples under foot the most beautiful of all virtues, but violates the sacred vow by which she has made to God the sacrifice of her being, and joins to the horror of vice the blackness of sacrilege! Ah! if it be a horrible profanation, to employ in common use the vases destined to the service of God, may we not say it is much more revolting for a religious, who has consecrated herself to the Lord, to defile what has been vowed to Him at the foot of the altar, in the presence of heaven and earth? No, there is no vice which so dishonours the sanctity of the religious state, as that opposed to the holy virtue of which we speak; it is to sin against the Incarnate God, since of a spouse of Jesus Christ it makes an adultress, a slave of satan, a victim of hell; from a living temple, where the Divine Spouse dwells, it makes her the habitation of unclean spirits.

Saint Basil wrote thus to an unfaithful virgin: "Has not God reason to complain of you," said he to her, "and to address to you the reproaches which He formerly put into the mouth of the prophet Jeremias? Have you seen what the daughter of Israel has done to Me? I had, by an effect of My goodness and mercy, chosen her for My spouse; I have accomplished with liberality My promises towards her; nevertheless, she has abandoned Me to attach herself to strangers; she has left an immortal Spouse to devote herself to creatures who are perishable and full of imperfections! Yes," adds the Saint, "I had made you know the merit of virginity; I had told you that you were the temple of God,—and your body has been shipwrecked with your mind; you have profaned your members; you have made them those of a prostitute; behold the height of iniquity, there is no crime that can equal it!"

In faults opposed to the vow of chastity, theologians say, there is no lightness of matter; as soon as we consent voluntarily to a sensual pleasure, the sin is always entire, and in all its inward malignity, in whatever way it is committed. They add, there may be small thefts, trifling lies, inconsiderable detractions, but there are no small faults against chastity, *as soon as there is a complete consent;* above all, in a person who has made a vow to practise this virtue: although some of these faults are more enormous than others, they are all forbidden under pain of damnation; consequently, they are never simple venial sins.

This is the opinion of Saint Thomas, and of all other theologians; Saint Anthony even decides that it is heresy to maintain the contrary.

"In this matter," says the casuist of Angers, "sins are always mortal, unless the want of consent diminishes the fault. The lightness of the matter cannot render them venial, because, although the thing may appear light in itself, it is notwithstanding always of consequence, since persons thus expose themselves rashly to the danger of falling into greater disorders, without being able to prevent themselves, after having exposed themselves voluntarily."

"The exterior action," says Collet, "is not necessary to make the sin mortal; as the desire of vengeance can destroy a man, so a desire can damn him eternally, and to sin mortally in this kind, it is not necessary to go even to the desire of crime; a voluntary impure thought suffices, although entertained *voluntarily* only for an instant; and this thought, even separated from the desire, is more or less criminal, according as its object is more or less forbidden.

Second. It is then necessary, above all at the sacred

tribunal, to make account of the least things, fearing illusion in a point where the salvation of our souls may easily be compromised.

Saint Bonaventure, treating of confession, gives a very important instruction. "However light the things may be which occur against chastity, we must," says he, " take care not to conceal them in confession, under pretext either that they are not sins, or are only venial ones; for this has been the cause of innumerable disorders; the loss of many souls has commenced by it. And may God preserve you from giving this entrance to the demon, or from opening to him this door! he would not require anything more to destroy you. Soon shame, joined to the little account you make of those things, will persuade you that even those things which are sins, or at least whose culpability is doubtful, are not so in effect; and thus you will dispense yourself from saying anything about them in your confessions."

Persons naturally inclined to virtue, and whose conscience is not ordinarily burdened with mortal sin, are subject to this false shame when anything of this kind happens to them; for then, pride, and the desire of being esteemed, so natural to man, and so rooted in our nature, awake, and make them dread to lose credit in the mind of their confessor; so they seek for reasons to persuade themselves, that the thing they are ashamed to tell is not in reality a mortal sin, and that, consequently, they are not obliged to speak of it; but supposing even that they do accuse themselves of it, it is sometimes in such terms, and with such extenuations, as diminish and weaken it, so that it seems almost nothing, and the confessor can scarcely comprehend what they mean; this is almost the same as if they did not confess it at all, for an accusation of those things in confession, ought to be so clear, that the confessor may know immediately the grievousness of them.

What hinders penitents from explaining themselves as clearly as they ought is, that shame or rather their pride blinds and deceives them; they have not a true sorrow for their sins, since they have not courage to declare them exactly to their confessor. If they had true sorrow, they would offer this shame in satisfaction for their faults.

I say more, I say, that the very repugnance they feel to accuse themselves of a thing ought to suffice to make them suspect all the reasons they think they have not to mention it, and to make them see that it is useful to speak of it, though it were only to overcome this repugnance, to mortify themselves, and to hinder the flesh and the devil from domineering over the spirit.

But what renders the accusation still more necessary is, that in the matter of chastity there are many things which ignorant persons do not think to be mortal, though they really are so. There are other things so doubtful, that it is not easy to decide positively of their gravity, and there is the same obligation to confess these, as there is to confess those which are certainly mortal; so that the simple doubt of it being a mortal sin is sufficient to oblige the penitent to accuse himself of it.

It often happens, that the confessor himself, although very skilful, cannot decide whether the sin is mortal or not: how, then, dare the penitent constitute himself a judge in his own cause? This is too great a risk, particularly when there is an inclination to conceal it, and a wish to lessen the fault in order to diminish the shame. I would not answer for a penitent in this disposition.

I act thus, some say, to prevent myself from being too scrupulous; and this is another artifice the devil uses to deceive us; for it is not being scrupulous to accuse one's self of these things, since those who make profession of piety ordinarily accuse themselves of much lighter faults, and this not through necessity or scruple, but from respect towards the august sacrament they are afterwards to receive: so great purity is required to approach it, that certain masters of the spiritual life counsel in matters of chastity to accuse one's self even of things which are not sins.

Section III.—*That which sometimes alarms timid Souls not a Sin.*

Amongst persons who are consecrated to God by the vows of religion, there are some who, although perfectly detached from creatures and sensual pleasures, though full of esteem and veneration for the sacred vow by which they have consecrated to God their body, their mind, and their heart, yet find in themselves certain dispositions which trouble them, disquiet them, sometimes even cast them into so fatal a discouragement, that a prudent director can scarcely calm them.

We will place before those poor souls some principles which the Saints and Doctors have suggested to us. Happy, if by this means, we enlighten them and restore to them the peace they have lost!

In the first place the dispositions which *during sleep* manifest themselves in the mind, heart, or otherwise in opposition to the virtue of which we speak, may be considered, says St. Thomas, both in themselves and in their cause.

If they are considered only in themselves, they ought not to be regarded as a sin, because to commit sin it is necessary to be capable of discerning, and to have sufficient liberty: now, a person is not capable of discerning, and has not sufficient liberty in this case; consequently, adds the holy Doctor, all that happens during this time is no offence against God, because a person in this position has no more liberty than those who are in a frenzy and foolish, and who have not at all the use of their reason.

Persons who are prudent and habitually reserved may form the same judgment on what happens to them when they are, as they say, half awake.

If we consider these dispositions, illusions, &c., *in the different causes which may produce them*, continues the same Doctor, it is necessary to distinguish three kinds:

1st. Some proceed from temperament, and we must then trace them to their source, and examine in what we may have given occasion to them, because this is what decides if there is sin or not. If this disposition of temperament proceed *from a culpable cause*, for example, if it comes from excess in eating or drinking, then the effects which are the consequence of it, take all their malice from the cause which produces them; but if there is no culpability in the cause, then the effect is in itself exempted from fault; and this particularly happens when those things occur in consequence of *debility of temperament*, or rather, as other Doctors say, *from strength* and *natural vigour*.

2nd. Sometimes these painful dispositions *proceed from the mind*: when voluntarily, and without legitimate reason, it is occupied during the day in thoughts capable of irritating concupiscence, there is sin, because these painful dispositions are voluntary in the cause.

3rd. Others in fine proceed *from the malice of the devil*, who disturbs the imagination; and, as there is no occasion given for them they must be contemned; there is not any fault in having them.

Although these sorts of dispositions bring with them a certain sentiment of pleasure, sometimes decided enough, we must take care not to conclude from that that they are criminal, since these sentiments may also be involuntary; as it happens in those which are experienced in spite of one's self when awake, and even when resisted with the greatest generosity and courage. All that it is necessary to do is: 1st. As soon as awake to raise the mind and heart to God. 2nd. To humble one's self. 3rd. To remain calm. 4th. To beware of making an examination, under any pretext whatever, about what we may have felt; the only examination that is permitted to be made, is on the occasion which may have given cause to what we have experienced in ourselves.

This advice is of the greatest importance, because often, in seeking if we consented to sin, we expose ourselves very much to the demon, who tries to plunge us again into those thoughts which have already been so dangerous, and thus make us yield to the temptation.

But timorous souls are particularly inclined to be troubled when they think they have given occasion to those dispositions by some disorders of their past life, the remembrance of which torments them during sleep: this remembrance ought to lead them to great humility, to great contempt of themselves, and to a renewed contrition for their sins, but ought not at all to trouble them; for having sincerely confessed those weaknesses, they have been pardoned, they are effaced, God has entirely forgotten them, the cause being thus destroyed; these dispositions are no more imputable to them (from the time they cease to take complacency in them, and do not give any other occasion to them) than if they had never committed them.

St. Augustine, a long time even after his conversion, and already arrived at the highest degree of sanctity, still experienced these sorts of illusions. He speaks thus of himself: "The images of my past weakness," says he, "are still living in my memory; they present themselves to me, and although when I am awake they have no power over my mind, yet in my dreams they have so much that they incline me not only to take pleasure in them, but even to a kind of consent and of action; and the illusions of these vain phantoms have so much power over me, that these false visions persuade me when I sleep to that which real objects could not persuade me to when I am awake."

The principles I have just laid down are applicable to all inclinations of whatever kind they may be, which we have to grieve over as occurring whilst awake and during the day. When we cannot reproach ourselves with having given voluntary occasion to them, when we grieve over them, when they are resisted and God invoked against them, there is no sin. The best means of being delivered from them, is to despise them, and to produce contrary acts, by renewing often in the depth of the heart the vow which is opposed to them.

Section IV.—*Perfection of Chastity.*

That there is no virtue more delicate, more fragile, and consequently more difficult to preserve in its integrity than Christian chastity, is the opinion of all the saints and masters of spiritual life. But if the preservation of the integrity of this virtue exacts many precautions on the part of ordinary Christians, it demands much more from virgins consecrated to God, because they are obliged to practise this virtue in a more eminent and more perfect manner.

By the vows of religion they have renounced, not only all that is opposed to the precept of God on this point, but they have even sworn to Him to shun all that would wound the most delicate modesty. Spiritual writers have regarded, as opposed to the perfection of religious chastity, all sensual affection for the creature. The heart has been created to love; but as God does not always act sensibly upon it, and as it cannot feel God in a sensible manner, it seeks a substitute in the creature; sometimes it surprises and carries away, in its wanderings, the most upright and innocent souls. This inclination of the heart is commonly directed towards persons in whom are discernible remarkable talents, or in whom there is a similarity of character, or from whom we have received some mark of sympathy, charity, or affection. The heart chooses, in a blind manner, the object of its affections; it seeks it in all ranks and in all ages, but more frequently it gives a decided preference to persons with whom we have the most habitual intercourse—even the most holy and spiritual intercourse; then the snare is only the more dangerous, because less suspected. In communities, sisters associated in office, mistresses of novices, and superioresses, are usually the objects of its undue predilection.

A religious, who wishes to remain faithful to the sacred promises she has made to God, should guard against this snare, and resist it from its first manifestation in the heart. A skilful ascetic speaks to us in the following terms of the nature of these dangerous inclinations: " The marks by which we recognize them, is to think often of the person, even to recall her to mind during prayer; to love the society of this person, to converse with her with more freedom and less gravity than an exact modesty requires;

to be pained at separation from her; to seek to please her by little acts of condescension, not always conformable to the rule; to be offended if she receives our advances coolly. These inclinations, if not promptly resisted, withdraw the light of grace, which would discover to us our danger, and we do not perceive that there is but a short step between natural affection and sensual love. We say there is no danger, because we do not wish there should be any, we even persuade ourselves of it; those who love thus do not believe themselves capable of committing any fault by so doing. Neverless, the danger is not less imminent, and although we may not reflect on it, the words of Jesus Christ should make us tremble: " He who loves the danger shall perish." Thus, a heart which has resisted every other passion, yields to human affections. Let us suppose such an affection to exist without any injury to virtue, how can we exculpate ourselves from the offence offered to God, to whom we are unreservedly consecrated? A throne will not suffer two kings, and the heart cannot contain two rival lovers. We serve a jealous God, who will have neither competitor nor associate; He reigns with regret in a heart of which He is not absolute master. The grace which He gives to a soul who loves Him undividedly He withdraws from the ungenerous soul. Then the spirit of prayer, which demands interior tranquillity, is lost; the soul goes to prayer with a heart agitated by remorse, trouble, and inquietude, which are the usual consequences of an attachment with which God is dissatisfied; it makes useless efforts to overcome the distractions which it can no longer master; it seeks in vain, because it seeks with indifference, the presence of a God who is no longer loved as formerly, and who, on His side, hides Himself from a heart of which He is not the only treasure. It is with indignation He beholds the creature occupy a place in the affections which should be entirely His!

The saints also consider too great familiarity, which is sometimes to be found between the members of a community, as quite opposed to religious chastity. Thus, in the constitutions of some orders, all shaking of hands, embraces, &c., are rigorously forbidden. All unnecessary familiarity is much more strictly to be discountenanced between religious and the pensioners in their establishments or the secular persons with whom they come in contact. Such conduct would be most scandalous in a religious, and would clearly show that the affections are not given to God.

It may be useful here to remark, that light words, immodest conversations, scandalous anecdotes, are quite out of place on the lips of virgins consecrated to God,—lips, which are so often purpled with the blood of the Lamb without stain, which should only be employed in prayer, and in chanting sacred hymns. These conversations are most dangerous for persons of a lively imagination. We may say the same of certain lectures persons are tempted to make through sensual curiosity, or under plea of being instructed; too much is generally known on this point, wherein the least remembrance is capable of enkindling an unholy flame in the heart and senses.

The saints regard as being as much opposed to the perfection of chastity as to the perfection of humility, a certain refinement of sensuality, truly shameful, quite unworthy of the spouse of a crucified God, which makes the religious consider with complacency her features in a mirror, use perfumes, or arrange in a worldly manner her holy habit, which should breathe but penance and death. This would be an index of a soul enslaved by the senses, and more jealous to please the creature than her celestial Spouse: to please Jesus Christ it is not the body we must adorn or ornament, it is the soul; its clothing, and most beautiful ornament, are the austere virtues of which the Sod of God has given the example.

CHAPTER V.

OF OBEDIENCE.

SECTION I.—*The Vow of Obedience is a free Contract which the Religious makes at her Profession.*

THE vow of obedience is a promise that is made to God, by which the religious engages herself to obey her superioress, in all that she commands conformably to the rules and constitutions of the order.

Nothing is more solemn than this sacred engagement. On the day appointed, she who is to make her profession assembles her friends and relatives; she calls them together, in the most holy and sacred place, even at the foot of the altar; she invites the ministers of the Lord to consecrate, by prayers and the benedictions of the Church, the step she is about to take, and to receive in the name of God, of whom they are the representatives, the engagements she is to contract. And what are these engagements? and what is the promise she is to make with so much display? She promises to obey her superioress, as God Himself, in all that she may prescribe for the good of the community, the observance and maintenance of the rules,—a promise without reserve, as far as obedience is concerned; it should extend to all that is not evidently contrary to the commandments of God and of the Church, and to the constitutions of the order; a promise, without reserve, in respect to duration, which should have no other term than life: a promise free and entirely voluntary. In effect, the religious, of her own impulse, has presented herself to the convent, in which she is about to pronounce her vows; she has solicited with entreaties to be received. During more than a year, she has studied the rules and constitutions and the obligations she is about to contract; she has reflected leisurely on all.

Frequently, during this time of trial, she has reiterated her entreaties, after having consulted God in prayer, and received the advice of her director. Having come to the foot of the altar, still free to return to the world, where she could preserve her liberty, her superiors interrogate her with regard to her dispositions, and ask her if she is sufficiently instructed on the extent of the obligations she is to contract; if she feels she has strength to accomplish them; and if she perseveres in the resolution of renouncing herself for the love of God. She replies without hesitation, " that she fully comprehends the extent of the duties she wishes to impose on herself; that with the assistance of divine grace, she hopes to accomplish them faithfully; that she perseveres in demanding admission into the community in which she has made her probation, and that she wishes to oblige herself by vow to obey the superioress who directs it."

How many precautions on the part of superiors, before allowing the novice to take this important step! How many means for the novice to appreciate its importance and its consequences! What perseverance in her solicitations to be admitted! What spontaneity in the engagement she wishes to assume! She advances: "I promise, and I vow to God, in the presence of heaven and earth, Obedience."

She *was* free, but she is no longer so;—she has renounced her liberty,—she has vowed and immolated it. She *had* a will, she could use it to direct her actions,—but now, it is no longer hers;—she has sacrificed it,—she has renounced the liberty of directing herself. And to whom has she vowed and immolated her liberty and will? To God: "I vow and promise to God, Obedience," were her words. And this vow is a solemn contract, by which she has freely abandoned the entire dominion of her will and liberty; a dominion over which God will rule, by the medium of her superioress, who will be His vicegerent in her regard, and whom she must obey at all times and in all places, as if it were God Himself.

The professed religious, by a vow, by the most solemn of contracts, has obliged herself to obey God in the person of her superioress; the superioress is truly for her the representative of God; in obeying her, it is God she obeys; in disobeying her, it is God she disobeys; in murmuring against her, it is against God she murmurs; in resisting her, it is God she resists, according to the words of St. Paul, "He who resists power, resists the order of God."

St. Francis de Sales, so penetrated with the spirit of God, orders, in his constitutions, the religious of the Visitation to have the greatest veneration and respect for the superioress; he orders them to regard God in her, and to reverence her as the organ of the Holy Ghost. "In effect," says he, "it is in His name and on His part she conducts and commands you. To disobey her, is to withdraw from God the will you sacrificed to Him at the foot of the altar; it is to violate the sacred compact you made in giving yourself to Him by your profession; it is to burst asunder the sacred ties which attach you to religion, and which make you a religious; so that disobedience, according to Holy Writ, is a kind of idolatry. If you disobey, you are idolaters, who prefer your will to your God; or apostates, violating as you do the most essential of your engagements; or adulterers, who fail in the fidelity you owe your Divine Spouse."

St. Thomas decides, that in general, disobedience is a mortal sin. However, he says, to make it so grievous it is requisite that it be voluntary, deliberate and in a serious matter, or if the matter is light, if it be accompanied with contempt. When the disobedience is in a matter of little import, not entirely voluntary, or unaccompanied with contempt, the sin is not so grievous.

SECTION II.—*The Vow of Obedience is the most important of the Religious Vows.*

St. Fulgentius was so convinced of the necessity of obedience in religious life, that he affirms, that those only are true religious who, mortifying their will, are always in a state to have no will of their own, but to follow implicitly that of their superiors. It was from this same conviction, that St. Teresa, in her Path of Perfection, says, "That we are religious in proportion as we are obedient;" and St. F. de Chantal: "If we are not submissive and obedient, we will be but false religious." St. Thomas, equally convinced of the necessity of obedience, asserts that it is the most essential and important of the vows of religion, for three reasons: the first, because by this vow the religious offers more to God than by the others. By the vow of poverty, the religious sacrifices all earthly goods; by the vow of chastity, she immolates her body; whilst by the vow of obedience, she sacrifices that which the creature cherishes most, her will and judgment, to be in religion such as God and her superiors wish her to be. This vow is as the sacrifice of Holocaust, which was the most perfect sacrifice of the Ancient Law. By this vow, as by holocaust, we reserve nothing of the victim immolated; we sacrifice, we give it entirely to God; and this is the reason, "Obedience is more agreeable than sacrifice," as Samuel said to Saul.

The second reason St. Thomas assigns, why the vow of obedience is the most important and essential of the vows of religion is, that it includes the others, whilst it is not included in any; a religious may oblige herself by particular vows to practise poverty and chastity, yet these two obligations are included within the vow of obedience, by which she obliges herself to observe all that will be commanded. For example, the Benedictines and Carthusians make no other vow than that of obedience. "I promise obedience according to the rule," says the religious at his profession, and in this promise, the vows of poverty and chastity are comprised.

The third reason is, because obedience is the vow which unites the religious most perfectly to the end of her Institute, which is death to self, the imitation of Jesus Christ, the glory of God;—a sublime end, to which obedience infallibly conducts. St. Jerome adds, "That obedience is an abridgment of all virtue; and that we only require to follow its guidance to arrive at the highest perfection." All the saints and masters of a spiritual life are of the same opinion. St. Ignatius, addressing himself to his religious, says, "Whilst obedience will flourish amongst you, all other virtues will equally flourish, and produce in your soul the fruit that I desire." "Obedience," says St. Augustine, "is one of the greatest of virtues, and the source and mother of all others." It is it which imprints all others in the soul, and nourishes them when once planted. St. Bernard, explaining this passage of Holy Scripture, "The obedient man will speak victories" affirms, that the obedient man will not only gain a victory, but that he will acquire every virtue.

SECTION III.—*The Obligation imposed by the Vow of Obedience is most reasonable, and conduces to the happiness of the Religious.*

Nothing can be more just than religious obedience. What could be more reasonable, than to accomplish an obligation which we have freely imposed on ourselves, after having weighed it with scrupulous attention,—an obligation of which we have measured the extent and calculated the consequences, which we have willingly accomplished beforehand, for a considerable time, to try our strength, and which we have solicited with eagerness?

Let us consider obedience in itself. Is it not indispensable for all men who live united in society? See, said St. Jerome, to some religious, on whom he wished to impress the necessity of obedience, see in the political order, all are submissive to kings, emperors, and those who govern in their name. Hardly was Rome founded, when Romulus, slaying his brother, indicated that the government of two kings was impossible. Do we not read in Scripture, that Jacob and Esau disputed their birthright even from their mother's womb? In the ecclesiastical hierarchy, all submit to the Bishops in each diocese; Bishops are subject to a chief Superior, who is the Vicar of Jesus Christ; in fine there exists no state, in which the subordination of the multitude to one head is not necessary and established. It is also indispensable that in every community of the servants of God, who have the same object in view, there should be a chief to guide and direct them in their path, whom they should obey with submission and docility.

This obedience is so much the more reasonable in religion, because in the convent into which we have solicited entrance, where we have freely made a vow of obedience, we have chosen the superioress to whom we submit. She only governs those over whom she is placed, according to the rules and constitutions of the order, to which she herself is obliged to submit in the most perfect manner, in order to be a model to her inferiors. The superioress, being obliged to provide for the wants of her sisters, to direct them in the painful path of perfection, to aid them to carry their burthens, to overcome their temptations, to surmount the obstacles they encounter, in fine, "to make herself all to all," according to the expression of the Apostle, in order to gain all to Jesus Christ; she is rather the servant than the superioress, and the yoke of superiority is more painful for her, than obedience for her subjects.

Obedience has nothing burthensome for a religious, who, enlightened by faith, perceives Jesus Christ in the person of her superioress, having incessantly before her eyes this Divine Model, who, for love of her, became obedient even to the death of the cross; never ceasing to conform her thoughts to those of her Divine Spouse, her desires to His desires, her actions to His adorable will, she considers every command given to her as coming from the lips of Jesus Christ, and lovingly submits.

"Ah," says Fenelon, "what comparison between what is painful in the yoke of religious obedience, and what we would have suffered in the world from family trials? What comparison between the service of Jesus Christ and that of the world? Between the innumerable restraints imposed by society, and those of community life?

" In religious life, solitude, silence, and exact obedience to the rules and constitutions, shelter you from almost all you would have to suffer from the caprice of superiors or equals. All is well regulated, and in following the rule you are safe. The rules and constitutions are not burthens added to the Gospel; they are only the Gospel explained in detail, and applied to community life. If the rule is only an explanation of the Gospel for religious life, superiors are only the stewards to make this evangelical rule be practised: thus all can be reduced to the Gospel."

" Let us suppose even that superiors, going beyond their limits, should treat harshly their inferiors, what in reality can they do to them? In fact, almost nothing. They may mortify their inclinations in trifling things, retrench some vain consolations, reprehend them sharply; but these trials cannot go as far as in the world. Here there is a written Rule; each thing has its notified and prescribed limits. The daily exercises leave nothing undecided; you have but to chant the praises of God, labour, be punctual at every duty, not interfere in the duties of others, keep silence, lead a hidden life, seek your support in God alone, not in private friendships, and the worst, then, superiors can do is not to trust you with confidential offices, which are troublesome and dangerous, and which you should rejoice to escape; or again, they may humble you by putting you in penance, as if such should never be the case, as if Christian and religious life should not be a sacrifice of love, humiliation, and continual penance."

" How, then, is obedience so very severe? Alas! should I not fear my self-will more than the will of any other. *My will*, no matter how good, reasonable, or virtuous it may be, is still *my own self-will*, which delivers me to my own desires, and renders me independent of the will of God. On the other hand, the will of those who have authority over me, however unjust it may be, is still in my regard the holy Will of God. The superioress may command what is wrong, but I obey, happy in only having to obey; and amongst so many occupations which distract me, I have in the eyes of God but one, that of having neither will nor judgment, but to allow myself to be led like a little child, without reasoning, foreseeing, or asking questions. If I obey, I can say with my Divine Model, "Consummatum est," "All is consummated." In a spirit of candour and infantine simplicity, I have only to forbid my curious mind from reasoning on the motives of my superioress, and leave to her conscience the responsibility of all."

"O sweet peace! O happy self-abnegation! O liberty of the children of God, who go like Abraham without knowing whither! O poverty of spirit, by which we despoil ourselves of self-judgment and self-will, as we do of our riches and patrimony! In it is found the perfection of the other vows; the same purity of love, which makes us renounce ourselves unreservedly, renders the soul virginal as well as the body, impoverishes the creature, even to take from her, her own will; in fine, so deprives her of self-dominion, that she can no longer conduct herself, but must submit to the guidance of others. Happy she who does those things! Happy she who relishes them! Happy even she who begins to understand them, and to open her heart to their meaning."

"Let it no longer be said that obedience is painful; on the contrary, no pain can be compared to that which is felt by the slave of passion and of irregular desires. Woe to him who thinks he is free, when he is not restrained by others! he does not feel that he is urged onwards by a tyrannical pride, by insatiable passions, and even by a wisdom which, under a deceitful appearance, is often worse than the basest of passions. No, let it not be said that obedience is painful! How consoling it is to belong no longer to self, this blind and unjust master! How gladly do I exclaim with St. Bernard, 'who will give me a hundred superiors, in place of one, to govern me? It is no restraint, it is an assistance; the more I depend on my superiors, the less I expose myself. superiors are like cloisters, which are not a prison for captives, but a rampart which defends a feeble soul against a deceitful world and her own fragility.'"

SECTION IV.—*Indifference with regard to Offices is a necessary Consequence of the Vow of Obedience.*

There are in every order and community two classes of duties, which correspond to the spiritual and temporal wants of the religious who are members. The duties corresponding to the spiritual necessities of the members are, prayer, meditation, the office, &c. These occupations are common to each religious of the community, and no one can neglect them, without a particular dispensation. These duties are the very essence of a religious life, which is a life of recollection and prayer; a special command from the superioress is not necessary in order to apply to them.

The duties corresponding to the material wants of communities are, the administration of temporal affairs, the different employments which concern the food and clothing of the sisters, &c. We may range in the same category those duties which bring the religious into intercourse with seculars; works of charity, such as the instruction of youth, visiting the sick, comforting the afflicted, &c. All religious, members of the same community, are not indiscriminately called to these occupations, which in future we will designate under the name of Employments or Offices; each, in order to apply to them, requires a special command from the superioress; and we affirm that the acceptance of these employments and offices without refusal or murmur, is for the religious a rigorous consequence of her vow of obedience.

In effect, from the moment the religious has renounced her will, and that she has promised to obey her superioress without restriction, it is evident she ought to obey her in all, to submit to whatever she commands, devote herself to any employment she may prescribe, accept any office she wishes to entrust to her; to act otherwise is to be guilty of disobedience and of revolt. If it happen that the employment to which obedience calls is important, the religious should accept it; whatever sentiment she may have of her unworthiness, whatever distrust she may have of her own experience, or however convinced she may be of her incapacity, let her remember that God had chosen, to preach the Gospel, ignorant, imperfect men, and that He Himself has supplied for their insufficiency. When God chooses her, as He has chosen and called His apostles, like them she should obey; she cannot refuse without sinning.

If the office is inferior or unimportant, she should accept it joyfully, no matter what may be her capacity or talents, for she has entered religion, not to do all the exterior good which she is able to perform, but to accomplish the will of God. She has entered religion, not to excel by the brilliancy of her talents, but to imitate Jesus Christ, " meek and humble of heart," and lead with Him a hidden life. If the employment confided to her is obscure, she will learn more successfully to love, to be ignored and regarded as nothing, which is, according to the author of the Imitation, the most important point of a perfect life.

If the employment assigned to her is easy of execution, she should accept it, blessing her Lord for His indulgence to her, and try to enhance the merit of her works by her ardent love and zeal: if it is difficult or painful, let her execute it eagerly, recollecting that she has only embraced religious life as a life of sacrifice; that she has only renounced the comforts of life to immolate herself to God and to carry the Cross with Jesus Christ. Let her courageously walk in the path trodden by the martyrs, apostles, confessors, and an infinite number of generous souls, who have undertaken so many labours, supported so much fatigue, and endured countless torments with joy for the love of Jesus Christ. Let her remember how painful are the labours and sacrifices that persons in the world impose on themselves for perishable interests, and let her be animated by the contemplation of the eternal recompense which will be the reward of her labours.

If the employment to which she is appointed suits her desires or inclinations, let her accept it, in blessing the Good God who has compassion on her weakness; ever bearing in mind, that there is less merit in actions done through natural inclinations, because they cost us less; she will then try to elevate all she will do by supernatural motives, proposing only to please God, to act purely for His love, and with the desire of accomplishing His holy will.

If it is opposed to her desires, or her inclinations, let her accept it with so much the more eagerness and joy, because her actions will be most meritorious in each one of them; she will immolate to God her inclinations and the repugnances of nature; she will execute them, not from human or carnal motives, but from motives infinitely more noble; submission to the will of God in a spirit of mortification and love. Let her reflect then on the generosity of the saints: on that of an Aloysius Gonzaga for example, who, born of an illustrious family, brought up in the most delicate manner, accustomed from infancy to receive from his domestics every assistance he required, and who, after becoming a religious, took the greatest delight in serving others, in discharging towards them the lowest offices, whose ambition it was to receive the most humiliating employments, and those which were most repugnant to nature, such as sweeping the house, washing the kitchen utensils, &c.

In fine, if the employment assigned to her is favourable to recollection, she should receive it gratefully, and corresponding to grace, she should labour to make rapid progress in an interior life. If it is dissipating, if it obliges her to have much intercourse with the other members of the community, or with seculars, she ought to accept it with submission and confidence in God, who always proportions His graces to the difficulties we may meet in the various situations in which His providence places us. Let her then take for her model a Catherine of Sienna, a Francis de Sales, a Vincent de Paul, and so many others, who, embarrassed with a multitude of distracting occupations, discovered the secret of never losing sight of God. Like them, she should form an interior solitude in her heart, where she may entertain herself with her Heavenly Spouse, whilst treating with creatures of exterior affairs. In fine, like them, she should endeavour by her sincere piety, by her wisdom, and by her modesty, to diffuse around the good odour of Jesus Christ.

And if, in consequence of her numerous exterior

occupations, she is sometimes obliged to interrupt or omit her spiritual exercises, she ought not be uneasy, complain, lament, nor show any sadness on that account. She does the will of God, that alone should suffice; this divine will is ever wise, ever adorable, ever amiable, and it is always the best, the most salutary, and the most perfect. She may then recal those words of St. Francis de Sales, so full of heavenly wisdom, " To quit God for God."

After having examined what the vow of obedience rigorously demands, we will now consider its perfection.

Section V.—*Perfection of Obedience.*

Obedience, that it may be conformable to the spirit of the vow which is made in religion, and agreeable to God, ought to be *blind, affectionate, prompt,* and *persevering.*

Obedience should be blind; blind in regard of the person who commands, of the manner in which she commands, and of what she commands. First, blind in regard of the person who commands. A superioress, legitimately elected, and approved by the requisite authority, is the representative of God for the religious who compose the community over which Providence has placed her; and this is, in the light of faith, the only reason for which the obedience that is vowed to God is due to her. In fact, were she descended from the most illustrious family; were she enriched with every gift of nature and grace; did she possess all the sciences, human and divine; had she arrived at the highest degree of sanctity and perfection; if, at the same time, she were not legitimately elected, if she were not the representative of God, the obedience the sisters have vowed to God alone, is not due to her. But, if she is the representative of God, whatever else she may be, that alone is sufficient in the eyes of faith; all the sisters should obey her, as God Himself; if they refuse obedience to her, it is God whom they refuse to obey. They should obey her, whether she is young or old, of an illustrious or obscure birth; whether her mind be cultivated or not; whether God has lavished on her the gifts of nature, or that He has refused them; all that is but an exterior bark; religious, animated by the spirit of faith, should pay no attention to such things. She is the representative of God; that suffices; it is the only principle, the only foundation of their obedience.

Religious obedience should be blind, in regard of the manner in which the superioress commands. Let her command more or less wisely, with more or less discernment and precision; let her command with haughtiness or with humility, with firmness or indecision, with meekness or with sharpness, what matters it to souls who have embraced community life for the purpose of dying to self, and to carry their Cross after their Saviour. She is the representative of God, that is sufficient; they obey her with a generous heart.

Religious obedience should be blind in regard of what the superioress commands. The vow of obedience admits of no restriction; it is made to God with the intention of sacrificing to Him every faculty, every desire, every energy, every inclination, and every repugnance. Consequently, as we have said before, whether what the superioress commands is easy or difficult, painful or agreeable, necessary or useless, repugnant or flattering to nature, as long as what she commands contains nothing contrary to the laws of God and of the Church, or to the constitutions of the order, the religious must obey her as God Himself; she must execute what is ordered in the manner commanded, without examining if what the superioress commands, and if the manner indicated is the best, according to human reason; she must embrace the holy folly of the cross, remembering that it is God who commands, that He does everything for the best, and that the manner prescribed, although it should be accompanied with ridicule, humanly speaking, is the best and most agreeable to His heart, because it includes the sacrifice of our own ideas, our wisdom, our judgment, and our self-love—a sacrifice infinitely more acceptable to Him than anything suggested by human wisdom, which He reprobates, as having pride for its source and principle.

Thus Abraham obeys. God orders him to leave his country, and to go to the place He would point out. Abraham sets out, without reply and without knowing whither. God orders him to immolate his only son, and to sacrifice him with his own hands. What more difficult for a father! Nevertheless, without examining the motives of a command so severe, he obeys, in spite of all the repugnances of nature; he conducts Isaac, the tender object of all his hopes, to the destined spot. He binds, places him on the altar, and is in the act of immolating him, when God, satisfied with his obedience, arrests his hand.

Elias calls Eliseus, who is cultivating his land, and commands him to follow him. Eliseus immediately abandons his work, his plough, his cattle, although there was no one to whom he could entrust them, and follows Elias without reflecting either on the nature of the command, or the loss he would incur.

The angel of the Lord orders St. Joseph to take Jesus and Mary, and to withdraw into Egypt to shun the rage of Herod. Joseph obeys without reply. He sets out, without representing that the Divine Infant is too young for such a journey; that the road is unknown to him; that the mother and child were not able to support the fatigue of so long a journey; that the Egyptians are the enemies of the Israelites, and that the child Jesus, with them, would be as much exposed to death as at Bethlehem. Admirable examples of blind obedience!

Obedience should be prompt; this is the characteristic the Royal Prophet so much admires in the Heavenly Spirits, and which he uses as a motive to invite them to bless the Lord, and to chant His glory. "Angels of the Lord, bless the Lord, ye who are powerful in strength, doing His will, fulfilling His word." For that reason, Holy Scripture describes them with wings, ever ready to fly; in this the true children of obedience should imitate them. Such was the obedience of Abraham, when he received the order to leave his country, and to sacrifice his son. He set out without delay, rose in the night, (as the Scripture says,) to show his docility. Such was that of the Apostles when Jesus called them to be His followers;—at His first word, they leave their barks and nets. Such was that of Paul, when, thrown from his horse on the road to Damascus, he received an order to go to Annanias. Ah! how the least delay in obedience diminishes its merit and recompense!

Were the religious employed in the most holy occupations, were she even at the feet of Jesus Christ, abyssed in the most sublime contemplation, enjoying the most intimate communication with her heavenly Spouse; were she occupied shedding a torrent of tears over past sins, she should quit all at the call of obedience. Ever attentive to the will of her superioress, she should be always prompt and ready in executing it. Prompt obedience admits of no delay, no to-morrow; it is more disposed to anticipate the command than to await it; the eyes should be ever open; the ears attentive; the hands prepared to work, and the feet to walk, when obedience so ordains.

Such is the obedience St. Ignatius recommends to his religious. "At the sound of the bell, or the voice of the superior, you must be as ready to obey as if Jesus Christ himself spoke; you must leave all, even a letter unfinished;" otherwise there is immortification, and resistance to grace. Obedience should be affectionate and generous; if it does not come from the heart, if, far from being inspired by love and generosity, its only principle is necessity or fear, how could it be agreeable to God, who loves a cheerful giver? He will have no slaves in His service.

Obedience, says St. Gregory, ought not to be servile and inspired by fear, it should come from the fervour of charity, and the love of justice. To obey through fear, is to act rather as a slave than as a Spouse of Jesus Christ. A soul consecrated to God, says St. Ambrose, should submit to her duties voluntarily, not through necessity. She should obey not only exteriorly, her docility should be also interior; it should come from the heart as its source, and tend to God, as its end. Obedience without love is but a corpse. L'abbe Desvillars says, that "if we only submit with repugnance, with a melancholy expression of countenance, with a discontented air, it is but too evident that self-will is not subjected, that there are in the soul many revolts, that the mind and heart are not submissive." Like those vile animals which bore the holy Ark from the camp of the Philistines to that of Israel, continually lowing, we only bear the yoke of obedience in murmuring, complaining, seeking to lessen it; we carry it through constraint, not from love, and we displease God. When a religious obeys through love, it is easily perceived by the sobriety of her countenance; on it is depicted a profound peace, which proves that she submits her will and judgment without constraint; that she is habitually submissive to every one; having no other will than that of her superioress, whom she looks on as God, she fears nothing, she has no repugnances, no desires, but immolates her judgment to the holy joy of obeying in the sight of God for His love; then it is the religious is sure of pleasing Him.

In fine, obedience should be persevering. Of what use would it be to obey for a time, if afterwards we relax? According to our Divine Redeemer, "He only who perseveres to the end shall be saved." The obedience of this Man-God which commenced in His crib, only terminated with His life on Calvary; for, says the Sacred Text, "He was obedient even to death." The religious is the spouse of this same Divine Saviour; she should be His imitator, and consequently she should obey with constancy, without ever relaxing in the practice of this holy virtue, of which He has given an example to which she should conform.

Nothing can be more opposed to obedience and to the religious submission of which we have been treating, than the spirit of murmuring and criticising superiors: a spirit that glides imperceptibly into communities. In the following section we will try to make our readers comprehend how very injurious it is to God, and how fatal in its effects to those who are guilty of it.

SECTION VI.—*Religious Obedience excludes all murmuring against Superiors.*

It is not rare to meet in religious communities persons with a dissatisfied, discontented mind, who, at each moment, break out into complaints and murmurs against those who govern the monastery. They find in every determination which is come to, in everything which is prescribed or forbidden, some subject on which to exercise their criticism and censure, if not publicly, at least privately and in secret. Nothing is more opposed to the spirit of obedience than this conduct. In effect, by the vow that they have freely made, they have renounced their own will, their own rights, their own wisdom, and have sacrificed them to God; they have freely immolated the inclinations and desires of nature; they have sworn to act only by the impulse of grace, to be no longer conducted but by their superiors, who, in quality of vicegerents of Christ, should henceforward direct and govern all their thoughts, their desires, their actions, and their conduct. Then, behold, all at once, giving free scope to their unruly passions, they erect in their heart a tribunal, over which pride presides, whence they arrogantly review, judge, blame, condemn the thoughts, intentions, projects, actions, and entire conduct of their superiors. Now in such conduct is there not a deplorable blindness, a species of apostacy?

In vain do these religious seek as an excuse the conduct of their superioress. Let us repeat, it should be engraved on their hearts, that they have only entered religion, they have only assumed irrevocable engagements to obey, and to sacrifice themselves to God. If obedience sometimes includes what is painful, they are only the more strictly obliged to accomplish, in the most perfect manner, the engagements they have contracted of renouncing themselves, of following Jesus Christ, and of carrying their cross.

What should above all make us understand how grievous is all criticising of superiors, and murmuring against them, is the signal manner in which God has ever punished this crime. In obeying superiors, says Rodriguez, we obey God whom they represent, and whose place they hold; when we fail in respect to them, we fail in respect to God. Thus our Saviour, after having said, " He who hears you, hears Me," immediately adds, " He who despises you, despises Me." St. Paul says, " All power comes from God; he who resists the power resists the ordinance of God." Holy Writ contains many passages in confirmation of the truth we wish to establish. When the children of Israel arrived at the desert of Sinai, the fear of dying there of hunger made them regret having left Egypt, and caused them to murmur against Moses and Aaron, who said to them, "*We have heard your murmurs against the Lord; for we, who are we that you should murmur against us? Know ye not that your murmuring is not against us, but against God Himself.*" When the same people rejected Samuel, and wished to have a king like other nations, God said to Samuel, " *They have cast Me off, not you. They are unwilling that I should reign over them.*" Thus all murmuring and blaming of superiors fall on God Himself. The extraordinary chastisements with which God has punished offences against superiors, prove what interest He takes in all that concerns them, and that He makes their cause His own. Witness the punishment of Core, Dathan, and Abiron for murmuring against Moses. The earth opened and engulphed them, their families and their riches, and St. Thomas remarks, that God punished more severely those who murmured against superiors, than those who directly offended Himself in worshipping the golden calf. On another occasion the Israelites having murmured against Moses and Aaron, God sent serpents, that destroyed a great number of them. And again, God was on the point of exterminating this ungrateful people for murmuring against their leaders, on the return of those who had been sent to the promised land. He pardoned them at the prayer of Moses, but not those who had been the authors of the rebellion. "They were," says the Scripture, "struck dead before the Lord." Mary, the sister of Moses, was she not also severely punished for speaking against her brother? On the spot she became leprous, and God would not pardon her, nor cure her until she had remained seven days outside the camp separated from the people. It was not alone for the intimidation of the Jewish people, and the instruction of their great Law-giver, that God thus acted; He wished it should be a lesson to succeeding ages, and that religious who are His chosen people, governed by His chosen vicegerents, should have ever present to their minds how rigorously He punishes every offence offered to superiors. St. Basil, so enlightened on religious matters, ordains in his rule, that all murmurers should be separated from the rest, as persons affected with contagion. He would have nobody speak to them, nobody have any communication with them, either in eating, drinking, sleeping, working, or even in praying, in order that this great confusion might help to correct their fault, and cause an entire reformation in them.

Nevertheless, if obedience rigorously forbids all murmuring, it does not hinder us from representing our difficulties to our superioress; but we must carefully remark, that in making these representations

E

we should not be actuated by pride, attachment to
our own judgment, the spirit of opposition, the love
of our own ease and conveniences, the perverse inclinations or the repugnances of corrupt nature, as it too
often happens. These representations should be influenced by supernatural motives, or by motives of
utility or good. If, for example, anything be notably
useful or hurtful to our health, it is not only permitted, but it is even our duty to represent it to the
superioress.

If it is dangerous, says Rodriguez, to have too
much solicitude for things which regard the body, so
is it reasonable to preserve our health and strength
for the service of God; and this obligation is common
to all religious. Hence, if any one finds her diet,
clothing, lodging, or employment prejudicial to her
health, or judges something else to be necessary for
it, she ought to inform her superioress, or the person under whose care she is. For, though the principal care of our life and health belongs to our
superioress, yet, because they are not angels, and cannot know our particular wants, it is suitable we
should aid them in this point, by representing our
necessities to them, in order to have them supplied.
The principal thing is to make this representation in
a suitable manner; for it is much to be feared that
we are often actuated by self-love, or too much
guided by our own judgment. Hence St. Ignatius
requires that to be on our guard against ourselves
on this occasion, we observe two things:—

The first is, that before we make the application,
we apply ourselves to prayer, and examine in the presence of God if it be for His greater glory that we
should address ourselves to our superioress; if such
is the case, we must speak to her freely, respectfully,
and humbly; but if we find we are actuated by

carnal and human motives, we must abstain from making our representations.

The second is, totally to acquiesce in the determination of our superioress, after we have represented our case to her, either by word of mouth, or in writing to help her memory; and whether she grants or denies our request, not to make any reply to her orders, or renew our entreaties either by ourselves or others; since we ought to be persuaded that what she ordains will tend most to the service of God, and our spiritual advancement. We ought, therefore, so dispose ourselves, both before and after making the proposal, as to be equally ready, not only to obey what the superioress shall ordain, but also to receive it with joy, as being most advantageous for us.

CHAPTER VI.

OF ENCLOSURE AND OF THE PARLOUR.

SECTION I.—*Of Enclosure and the Duties it imposes on Religious.*

THE holy founders of religious orders have had in view different duties, some of which exact frequent, even habitual intercourse with the world, but all, conformably to the spirit of the Church, have recommended to those who become members of the congregations they have established, the love of solitude and estrangement from the world, in all that is foreign to the duties of their state. Religious not cloistered should be deeply imbued with this spirit, and imitate as much as they can the retired lives of religious who are cloistered.

It is certain, says Monsignor Bouvier in his Theology, that enclosure is not the essence of the religious state. Until the Pontificate of Boniface VII., it was not prescribed by any law; it was only recommended in an urgent manner. But the holy Popes, Boniface VIII. and Gregory XIII., have made a precept of it to all professed religious living in community, at least partially, according to their order, rule, and denomination.

The Council of Trent has confirmed the decree of the first of these Pontiffs, and has imposed on religious the obligation of enclosure in these terms:—

"The holy Council, in renewing the constitution of Boniface VIII., commands all Bishops, under the threat of the judgments of God, whom it takes to witness, and under pain of eternal malediction, that of their own authority with regard to the convents subject to them, and as delegates of the Holy See in regard of those who are exempt from their jurisdiction, they be most careful to see that religious enclosure be re-established in the houses in which it has been violated, and to maintain it entire in those convents where it has been faithfully preserved. Let them repress, by their ecclesiastical censures and penalties, every opposition, and for that purpose they may call in the assistance of secular force; and this assistance the holy Council exhorts all Christian princes to afford, also all magistrates to do the same, under the penalty of excommunication. No religious, therefore, is permitted to leave her monastery after her profession, even for a short time, under any pretext whatever, without a legitimate reason approved by the Bishop, notwithstanding any indults or privileges which would seem to authorize it."

"It is not lawful for any person, no matter of what rank, condition, age, or sex, to enter the enclosed precincts of a convent without a written permission from the Bishop or the Superior; whoever would do so would in the fact incur excommunication. Now, this permission the Bishop or Superior can only grant on necessary occasions, and no one else can grant this permission in consequence of any faculty or indult heretofore ordained, or obtained hereafter."

From these prescriptions of our holy Church result two obligations for all religious who belong to an approved order; the one passive, which is not to go out of their monastery; the other active, not to admit strangers without a legitimate reason. These obligations are virtually implied, says Bouvier, in the three vows of religion, and oblige equally those religious (of an approved order) who have made no vow of enclosure, or in whose rules it is not mentioned. But to correspond faithfully to the views of God over the souls He calls to perfection, and to imitate the first Christians who were docile to His voice, and to enter into the spirit of the founder of religious orders, it is not sufficient to observe materially, and even to the letter, the rules laid down by the Doctors of the Church on this subject. The religious must separate herself completely from the world; she must separate from it her looks, her hearing, her thoughts, her desires, her affections, in fine, her entire being, and under this consideration quite spiritual, enclosure imposes on the religious who wishes to live according to the spirit of her state two duties: the first is, to keep herself removed from the world; the second, to keep the world removed from her.

First, she ought to keep herself as far as possible removed from the world, and she fails in this duty:

1. In speaking to persons without the gate of the monastery, in showing herself at the window, &c.

2. If, yielding to curiosity, she carried her looks outside the precincts, to see what took place in the streets, fields, or neighbouring houses.

3. If she listened to what was done or said without the walls.

4. If she spoke without permission, without necessity, or, at least, when the duties of civility do not require, to persons of the world, in places not appointed for these communications.

5. If she allows her thoughts, affections, or desires to wander to the world.

6. If she corresponded on useless or worldly subjects.

Secondly. She ought to keep the world removed from her as far as she can, and she would fail in this duty if she solicited seculars to pay her frequent and useless visits, and lose her precious time listening to their worldly discourses; if she made inquiries about what was passing in the world: and she would commit a double fault if she communicated such views to the other members of the community.

Section II.—*Of the Parlour.*

What do we propose to ourselves in leaving the world, to embrace religious life, in separating ourselves from the rest of mankind, to shut ourselves up in a cloister? We have said it, we ought to propose to ourselves to forget the world and creatures, to be exclusively occupied with salvation and eternity. To attain this end we ought in the cloister to shun contact with the world; we ought to be detached from it, and only have necessary and useful intercourse with it. To act otherwise is to forget the end we have proposed to ourselves, and to look back.

Be not content that the wall of the cloister separate you from the world, says F. Marin; prevent as much as you can the world from coming, by frequent visits, to trouble your solitude and interrupt the tranquillity of your retreat. If charity lead you to receive with kindness and politeness those who come to visit you, your solemn renunciation of the world exacts that you do nothing to procure for yourselves useless visits.

It cannot be too strongly recommended to novices to testify to seculars, from the beginning, their dislike to these visits, and to accustom them to come but seldom. It is even necessary to show firmness in their resolution, without regarding their complaints or murmurs. If they do not hesitate to declare openly that they do not wish to appear in the parlour without necessity, they may be at first taxed with scrupulosity, and may have reproaches and railleries to undergo; but the world will soon cease to importune them, and then the esteem that will be entertained for them will be as great as the contempt in which a religious is held in whom is perceived too eager a desire for the conversation of worldlings. "If thou canst let men alone, they will let thee do what thou hast to do," says the author of the Imitation.

What opinion can be formed of a religious who runs in haste and dissipation to the parlour when called to it—who testifies to seculars an extreme joy to see them—profuse in compliments and frivolity, or reproaches them for their long absence—who asks a thousand questions on what passes in the world, and who takes an extraordinary pleasure in all the news she hears? Has a religious of this character sincerely renounced the world? Has she the true spirit of her state? A modest reserve, indifference for the occurrences of the age, and a constant love for retreat, would edify her visitors. Perhaps, by acting thus, she would fear to appear impolite or austere? No; on the contrary, her religious and retired appearance will render her most agreeable to God, and edifying to the world.

Before going to the Parlour. A religious, continues the same father (from whom we have quoted nearly all this chapter), ought never to appear in the parlour without first invoking the protection of her Divine Spouse and the Blessed Virgin. She ought to withdraw as soon as she can in politeness. She should leave it with as much delight as she ought to have had repugnance in going thither. Fidelity to these three points will prevent the parlour from being an obstacle to her perfection.

What more preposterous vanity than that of a religious, who appears in the parlour, to have her figure extolled, whose only aim is to inspire others with admiration for those graces which she should rather fear than value. There are some even who cannot descend without adjusting their habit and veil with *affectation;* we say that it is a preposterous vanity; but should it not be more justly qualified a profanation in a person who has been divorced from the world to be consecrated to Jesus Christ crucified?

During the time spent in the Parlour. A reasonable fear, a prudent distrust of self, ought always to accompany a religious to the parlour. She ought to preserve a grave and serious deportment, to avoid loud laughter, to repress the vivacity of her senses, particularly her eyes, by modestly casting them down. Her conversation should be calculated to inspire seculars with a respect for the sanctity of her state, very far from her receiving from them any worldly impression. Do not affect in the parlour too free an air, nor assume worldly manners. Do not pique yourselves on making smart repartees, like one who wishes to pass for a wit. Say nothing that may attract applause, elicited solely by worldly qualities.

Let us now listen to Pere Bourdaloue with regard to the intercourse religious should have with seculars.

"It is an error," says this Father, "by which some religious deceive themselves in thinking that by playful and unreserved conversation, they render themselves more agreeable to the world, and attract its esteem and confidence. The world is, on the contrary, the most enlightened and the most severe censor that religious persons have to fear; it knows perfectly how reserved they should be, and in what esteem they should hold the sanctity of their profession. The world reflects on this, and sinful and degenerate as it is, it exacts on their part a regularity and circumspection, amounting almost to scrupulosity."

Thus, in the conversation of a religious, the world expects to find gravity, recollection, moderation, discretion, and wisdom; and when it meets a religious possessing these qualities it is edified and attracted to her; any other behaviour only serves to amuse seculars.

"What is most deplorable," says the same Father, "is that religious sometimes keep up long conversations with seculars, without ever introducing any spiritual subject. They fear to repel or weary them by such discourses. It is true, prudence must be observed, but three things are certain. *First.* Seculars are not so easily repelled as we may imagine, by what a religious says to edify them and inspire them with Christian sentiments. *Secondly.* Not only they are not repelled, but sometimes they are touched and profit by the discourse; if they were scandalized, it would rather be that religious espoused to Jesus Christ would not make Him the subject of their conversation. *Thirdly.* Supposing such discourse was not relished by them, they will see them less frequently. This was the excellent maxim of St. Ignatius. "Either," said he, "persons of the world will listen to me willingly, when I speak to them on edifying subjects, then

God will be glorified and I will obtain what I desire; or, disgusted with such discourse they will leave me, and thus not make me lose my time."

When we leave the Parlour. When a religious retires from the parlour, she ought to endeavour to forget all the useless conversation she has heard. Would to God that she could even forget the visit! At least it should be observed as an inviolable law, never to repeat the worldly news she has heard, though she could not avoid listening to it.

A monastery, where parlours are seldom frequented, and the most public reports are unknown, where persons only go to receive instruction, to speak on necessary matters or edifying subjects, and depart improved, such a monastery is according to the heart of Jesus Christ; it must draw down the most abundant benedictions of heaven on the city in which it is situated. It depends on each religious to act so in regard to the parlour, that this encomium may be applied to her monastery.

Let no one deceive herself on this point; visits of seculars, when frequent, only serve to distract religious, to fill their minds with the spirit of the world, to withdraw them from their duties, and to lead ultimately to the ruin of a community.

CHAPTER VII.

OF THE RULES AND CONSTITUTIONS.

SECTION I.—*Rules and Constitutions are indispensably necessary for Religious Communities.*

THE physical world has its laws which govern it, and the wisdom which presided at their establishment, and which still presides at their faithful accomplishment, lends to the universe a wonderful lustre. It is in virtue of these laws, says the holy Scripture, that day succeeds to day, that the irritated waves of the sea stop with respect before the grain of sand which has been given them as a limit; rivers and streams, mountains and plains, the country and its rich harvest, the trees and the grass of the field, the domestic animal which serves man, and the ferocious beast which flies before him, hiding in its den at the first rays of the sun, all announce to us the wisdom of the Divine Legislator. As heralds, heaven and earth publish it, and there is no people who do not comprehend their eloquent language. But without these laws which God has given to the universe, what would the stars become? what would the earth become? what would the sea become? soon entire nature would return to its first chaos!

And without laws what would men become? among them we would find but confusion and disorder. The moral world has also its laws, which are its ornament and glory. Kingdoms and empires, cities and simple villages have theirs; general and particular societies are provided with theirs, and there is no one who does not acknowledge their utility. Religious communities, composed of members united in the formal design of aspiring to higher perfection than the rest of mankind—communities, whose members have so well understood the necessity of order and submission, that they have, by vow, renounced solemnly their will, their liberty, their tastes, their inclinations, to bend beneath the yoke of obedience, ought, with stronger reason, to have their laws and rules appropriated to the end they have proposed to themselves; otherwise, in these societies expressly formed to establish the reign of order, there would be less than in secular societies, or rather there would be but disorder and confusion.

Rules and constitutions are besides a very powerful assistance to arrive at perfection. In effect perfection consists in the accomplishment of the evangelical counsels; now, the rules and constitutions are the expression of the evangelical counsels; they are these counsels reduced to practice; they all tend to detach us from earth, and to raise us on high; they disengage the soul, give it flight, and elevate it to God, to Whom it should incessantly tend.

Thus, the Saints and Doctors compare the rules and constitutions of religious orders to the wings of birds and the wheels of chariots. Wings, say they, are not for the bird an embarrassing burthen, they render it, on the contrary, lighter, they sustain it in the air, and communicate to it the faculty of flying; nor do wheels add an inconvenient weight to the chariot, on the contrary, they are so great an assistance to the animals which move them, that without them they could not draw half the weight they do.

It is the same of the rules and constitutions; so far from being a load and an embarrassment, they are, for the religious, wings, which aid her to fly towards heaven; wheels, which help her to bear more easily the yoke of the Lord; whilst seculars, who have not the same advantages, drag it painfully along, sometimes even fall beneath it.

The Saints again compare the rules and constitutions to the exterior fortifications which are used for the defence of cities. In the same manner, say they, that a city is in a better state of defence, when it is environed with exterior fortifications, which concur with those of the interior, in arresting the enemy and paralyzing his efforts; so, religious, provided with rules and constitutions, are in a better state to resist the attacks of the demon; because these rules and constitutions concur with the commandments of God and the Church in paralyzing his efforts, and at the same time keep in a state of subjection any interior enemies who might be in league with him.

For example, the rules which regard the mortification of the senses, the mortification of the passions, of pride, envy, jealousy, hatred, sensuality, the love of perishable goods; the mortification of our inclinations, our desires, our will, all those rules, in a word, which keep us in watchfulness and perpetual activity, are solid walls which obstruct exterior enemies, and prevent those of the interior from holding any communication with them. The meditations, lectures, examens, pious aspirations, attention to the presence of God, which these rules prescribe, are as formidable artillery, made use of by warlike troops, and preceded by advanced sentinels, who watch continually around our heart, ready to give alarm at the first appearance of danger, and to fire on the enemy. In fine the saints say, that the rules and constitutions are remedies sovereignly efficacious for curing the diseases of the soul; that they are a mysterious ladder, which contains as many steps as they impose particular practices, and by which we elevate ourselves to the summit of perfection.

But do we wish more fully to understand their utility and their importance? Let us glance over the different monasteries which have existed, or which still exist. Which are those where were practised the most brilliant virtues? They are those in which the rules and constitutions are best observed. Besides the admirable spectacle which the whole presents, the order and harmony which reign in the exterior, that have so often struck strangers and excited their admiration; how many virtues bud there, and attain a marvellous increase! What profound humility! what recollection! what generosity! what fervour! what love of God! These convents are the most perfect image of heaven. Let us now glance at those where the rules and constitutions either are violated, or are not in vigour. What dissipation! what disorder! what confusion! what division and what scandal! what relaxation and what tepidity! Oh! why have so many convents, formerly so celebrated by the sublime virtues which were practised in them, fallen into such disorder? It is because the ramparts which defend them have been overturned, and the enemy has entered the place.

To that rigid poverty prescribed by the rules, abundance and luxury have succeeded; to mortification, effeminacy and sensuality; to recollection and silence, dissipation and worldly conversation; to holy meditation, terrestrial and carnal thoughts; to exactness and regularity, sloth and remissness; to fervour, carelessness and tepidity. The wheels have been broken, and the chariot can no longer continue its course. The wings have been torn, and they who formerly flew with so much swiftness, now crawl shamefully on the earth. The ladder has been destroyed, there is no longer any ascent; salutary remedies have fallen into disuse; wounds have not been healed, they are now envenomed, enlarged, and at last become incurable. These convents seem to be peopled with living members, although they are in reality but dead bodies.

When rules and constitutions are in vigour in monasteries, God is infinitely pleased, because He is the God of order and regularity, and principally because these rules are the expression of His will, their basis being the evangelical counsels emanating from Him, and because it was He who inspired the saints who wrote them. In effect, the admirable men to whom we are indebted for the establishment of religious orders, have only written their rules after having long meditated on them in the presence of God, after having by fervent prayer solicited His lights and graces, and after having obtained the approbation of the Church, which is in our regard the organ of the will of heaven. In concluding this section, let us pause and consider the eulogium given them by a great servant of God.

"What is there more holy and more consolatory than the doctrine contained in these divine rules? In them we clearly perceive the maxims and instructions of Jesus Christ. They are a precise abridgment of all that He has taught most high, most sublime, and most perfect. They teach men to despise this world, and to sigh after heaven; they raise them to the purity of angels; they place them near to God, and engage them in the royal road of self-renunciation and humiliation; they render them true imitators of a Man-God annihilated; and this is the true glory of His faithful servants. The good arising from these holy institutions is immense; it is they who have given birth to a new world in the midst of the world, that is to say, a world of grace in a world of iniquity; it is they who have formed to sanctity innumerable souls of every age and sex who, consecrated to Jesus Christ, have borne the glory of His name to every quarter of the earth, and who have rendered and daily render, by continual immolation, an immortal testimony to His greatness and His power."

SECTION II.—*Religious are obliged to observe their Rules and Constitutions.*

Religious are bound to the observance of the rules and constitutions established in their communities.

First, because by the vows of religion they are strictly obliged to tend to perfection; for, in effect, what object had they in view in entering a convent, and binding themselves by indissoluble vows? Was it not to arrive at a holy and perfect life, not merely at the first step, but to advance incessantly, that they have separated themselves from the world? Thus St. Jerome tells us that it is a prevarication for a religious not to aspire to perfection. St. Eusebius adds, that as the way to perfection is to retire into solitude, so the way to perdition is not to live holily in solitude.

St. Thomas is not less decisive on this point. The religious, says he, who does not aspire to perfection, and who does not exert every effort to become perfect, is not a true religious, since she neglects that for which she alone embraced religious life. Our life, adds he, should harmonise with our name, and our profession should be known by our works.

Now, as we have shown in the preceding section, the rules and constitutions are the most powerful means to arrive at perfection; they are, in fact, the sole means of perfection placed at the disposal of each member of religious communities, since they are in their regard the expression of the evangelical counsels, and that religious perfection can only be attained by the accomplishment of these counsels.

Thus St. Ignatius said to his religious: "Let all who enter into the Society propose to themselves to observe faithfully the rules, constitutions, and practices which are in force amongst us, and let them, with the grace of God, use every effort to accomplish them perfectly; for, behold in this their spiritual advancement and perfection consist; and we will be perfect religious if we observe our rules in their primitive fervour."

Religious are obliged to the observance of their rules and constitutions, because they have engaged themselves to them by a formal and often reiterated promise. From their entrance into the convent, they have been explained to them, and commented on; they have been made to feel their extent and importance; a thousand times they have been recommended to practise them exactly; when they have been unfaithful to them, they have been carefully reprehended; they have been made feel the dangers of such infractions; it has been intimated to them that they can only be agreeable to God, by fidelity to the smallest observances, and that they can only be admitted into holy religion by promising this fidelity. These instructions, renewed at the foot of the altar, where they consummated their sacrifice, have been followed by particular promises, and, in fine, by the public and solemn promise of living conformably to the rules and constitutions of the convent of which they have been admitted members; and without these promises they would never have been admitted to this step. And promises so solemn, and so often reiterated, do they imply no obligations?

Religious are obliged to the observance of their rules and constitutions, in virtue of the obedience they have vowed to their superioress. They have solemnly promised to obey her as Jesus Christ; and when they obey her it is Jesus Christ they obey, when they disobey her it is Jesus Christ they disobey. Their obedience should be universal, it should extend to all; to things of importance, as well as to others less considerable; their dependence should lead them to conform in all to the intentions and desires of their superioress, although not expressed; such is the doctrine of the Saints.

What more frequently and more strongly recommended; what more formally prescribed by superiors, than the exact and punctual observance of the rules and constitutions? To violate these rules and constitutions, is then to resist the desires, the intentions, and the orders of superiors, and it is consequently to resist the desires, intentions, and orders of God, and to transgress the vow of obedience.

Religious should fulfil their rules and constitutions for the edification of their convent. Nothing can be more advantageous or more fatal than example, according as it is good or bad. A pious, humble, exact, regular religious will diffuse among her sisters the good odour of her virtues; she will inspire them, by her example, with a love of piety, submission, exactness, and regularity, as did formerly among their brethren, an Aloysius Gonzaga, a Stanislaus Kotska, and so many others. But, on the contrary, a religious without piety, without submission, without exactness, without regularity, will diffuse all around disorder, and the contagion of her sad example, and with so much the more facility, as man is naturally more inclined to vice than to virtue. Thus she will become for her sisters a stumbling-block. Dissipation, relaxation, and the other disorders which are the principal of the disorganization and ruin of communities, will be communicated from one to another, and multiplying in a fearful manner, will at last fall with an overwhelming weight on the devoted head of her who first gave the bad example. What an awful account will not she have to render to God, who has pronounced in the Gospel such terrible anathemas against the authors of scandal.

The observations made in this chapter are applicable not only to the most important rules, but also to the least important observance of the community duties; for, besides that the promises we have made to lead a regular life, are without restriction, it is a recognised truth in spirituality, that infidelity in little things insensibly leads to the greatest faults, and the most deplorable falls have arisen from trifling infidelities; this is even an oracle emanating from the Holy Ghost. He who is faithful in little things will be so in greater, and he who is unfaithful in the least, will be so equally in the greatest. St. Jerome says, a soul truly devoted to God applies with equal zeal to avoid one as well as the other, knowing she must render an account to Him for every useless word, and that according to the doctrine of St. Thomas and all theologians, a little fault disposes the soul for the commission of a greater.

SECTION III.—*How we should interpret this Principle, — The Rules and Constitutions do not bind under pain of Sin.*

It is a principle universally received, it is to be found in the greater part of the books used by religious, and we have a thousand times heard it repeated in communities, that "The constitutions and rules do not bind under pain of sin, except in what regards the vows." But how are we to interpret this maxim?

To understand well its signification and its consequences, we must remark, that an action may be bad in several manners and for several reasons. It may be bad, First, in consequence of a divine or ecclesiastical precept which forbids it. Second, from a particular precept imposed by a society which has jurisdiction over us; as for example, by a congregation of which we are members, and which, in its constitutions, forbids the action under pain of sin. Third, on account of the imperfect motive from which we act. Fourth, on account of circumstances. Fifth, from the scandal which results, and which we could and should have prevented. We may remark an action may be bad from one of these causes, or from several, or from all combined.

The action which is bad from all these causes at once, is evidently a grievous sin, because each cause adds a peculiar character of grievousness to the action.

The action which is bad only on account of some of the causes indicated, is less grievous, and implies a fault less important, and only proportioned to the gravity of the reasons which render it sinful. In fine, the action defective from only one of the causes is in proportion less sinful.

We may make these principles more evident by adducing the example of a religious who omits assisting at the holy Sacrifice of the Mass.

1. This omission may include several causes of grievous sin. If it takes place on a Sunday, and the religious has no legitimate impediment, this omission contains a violation of the precept of the Church, the first cause of sin; if it has for motive contempt of rule and of the precept of the Church, this is a second cause; if from this omission great scandal results to the community, behold a third cause.

2. This omission may include fewer causes of sin, for example, if its principle is not contempt of the Church and of the rule, but simply negligence or want of foresight, and if there results no scandal, the fault is evidently less serious.

3. This omission may contain but one cause of sin, and that only of venial sin; thus, if it occurred on a week day, and implied no contempt of rule, but negligence; when it did not give scandal, and was not the result of habit, then the omission arising only from negligence which was its principle, has no cause of sin but the negligence, because the rule which

obliges to assist at Mass daily, does not in itself bind under pain of sin; consequently the omission in this case is but a slight fault of negligence.

There may then exist simultaneously in an action several causes of sin; the material fact of the violation of a point of the rules may be one of these causes, if holy founders had wished to impose them under pain of sin; but they have not wished it, and why? because the different observances, which the rules and constitutions contain, being innumerable, the occasions of sin would be too multiplied, too frequent, and would render salvation too difficult. This maxim, "The rules and constitutions do not oblige under pain of sin," is only meant to explain the intention of the legislator, and merely signifies that the material fact of the violation of the rules and constitutions, considered in itself, and abstracted from its circumstances, its motive, and its consequences, is not a particular cause of sin, and in itself does not constitute a sin; but it does not mean that the violation of the rules and constitutions, considered with reference to its motive, its circumstances, and its effects, is not a sin, since the most innocent action may become sinful, from its motive, its circumstances, or its effects.

Impressed with the vital importance of this point, and fearing we have not been sufficiently clear and intelligible to all, we repeat, that this maxim, "The rules and constitutions do not bind under pain of sin," signifies merely that the violation of rule, in those points which do not regard the vows, is not a sin, provided this violation is not preceded, accompanied, or followed by any cause which may render it culpable; which is rarely or ever the case.

SECTION V.—*In what Circumstances the Violation of the Rules and Constitutions is a Sin, and of what Nature the Sin is.*

We may here observe, with all theologians and spiritual writers, that the rules and constitutions regarding the vows oblige under pain of sin, more or less grievous, as the case may be. In other points, the rules and constitutions may be violated:

Firstly; through inadvertency and fragility: and then all agree, it is an imperfection not a sin, because there is neither the deliberation nor matter necessary for a sin.

Secondly; through negligence and tepidity: then it is a sin, because the motive of the transgression is vicious, but it is not a grievous sin. However, continues St. Thomas, if the transgression were often and deliberately repeated, the religious would expose herself eventually to violate the rule through contempt, which would be a mortal sin. Theologians even decide that the habit of transgressing, through negligence and tepidity, the principal points of the rule, although in themselves they do not bind under pain of sin, implies an interpretative contempt of rule. Now to transgress the rule through contempt, is, according to the opinion of theologians, and St. Thomas in particular, a grievous sin, because such a transgression overturns the foundation of the vow of obedience.

If this habitually negligent and tepid transgression, extends to a great many points of the rule, the fault is much more serious. Thus, Fromageau, in his "Dictionary of Cases of Conscience," decides that a religious, who dispenses herself habitually from nearly all the points of regular observance, is not in a state of salvation, because she violates the promise she made at her profession to lead a religious life, which consists in practising the means indicated in the rule to arrive at the perfection of the state which she has embraced.

St. Thomas says also, that a religious is not obliged to practise every means which lead to perfection, but that she is strictly bound to practise those specified in the rule she has promised to observe. Now, to live in a kind of neglect of rule, by habitual infractions of the points it prescribes, is in some manner to abandon a regular life, and to fail in her solemn promise. And in fact, did no other evil arise from these habitual transgressions, than a moral impossibility of accomplishing this sacred engagement, would not this be sufficiently serious?

Besides, according to St. Thomas, Cajetan, and others, a religious who does not propose to herself to tend to perfection according to her rule is in a state of mortal sin; and a religious who fails habitually in regular observance, can it be imagined her design is to arrive at the perfection of her state? And if not, we must conclude she is in a state of mortal sin. Such a religious is a burthen to her community, and hurtful to religion, by the scandal she gives and the annoyance she causes in her convent, by habitually violating her rule, and in the eyes of God she is guilty of a most grievous sin by the injury she does her sisters.

What prejudice does not this religious do to her community, in weakening by her fatal example the love of regularity! Is not her example capable of leading others into the same relaxation? Would it not have been better for this young person had she remained in the world, than to enter religion to scandalize her sisters, and dishonour the sanctity of her state?

What misfortune for a spouse of Jesus Christ, to find herself in this culpable habit of transgressing her rules! Nothing any longer makes any impression on her. In the days of her first fervour the slightest infraction frightened her; now, accustomed to transgress, she neither knows nor feels the magnitude of her evil. Regular observance is burthensome to her: she no longer listens to the voice of obedience: she resumes the liberty she sacrificed to God so generously: the insensibility of her soul conducts her to blindness of the understanding, hardness of heart, and eternal reprobation. Sad and deplorable state, from which she can only arise with great efforts, and by a stroke of extraordinary grace! Behold how far voluntary transgressions of rule lead.

Thirdly. We may violate the rule and constitutions through contempt; and this is a grievous fault; but, according to St. Thomas, as all that is contained in the rules and statutes of a religious order is not meant as a precept, but is merely inserted for the maintenance of regular discipline and good order; the violation, then, is only grievous when it implies a formal contempt, that is to say, a decided opposition to what the rule ordains.

St. Bernard, so well instructed in the duties of religious life, and which he practised with so much fervour, is not less decisive on this point. Contempt of authority, says he, renders a transgression, which of itself was only a light fault, worthy of reprobation and eternal death. Collet is of the same opinion; the violation of even the smallest rule, he says, is always a mortal sin, when it is accompanied with contempt. But to constitute a mortal sin, we must remember that the contempt must be formal, and fully deliberate.

SECOND PART.

THE RELIGIOUS LIFE CONSIDERED AS A LIFE OF UNION WITH GOD.

RELIGIOUS life is a life of union with God; that is, a recollected and interior life, a life of sanctity and perfection, of pious practices and good works, a life which places the soul in constant intercourse with heaven, and establishes the reign of God in the heart. Enlightened by the most holy ascetics, we will trace the path which conducts to this sublime life; and, first, we will treat of the interior life, and of the virtues on which it is founded. Second, of the practices of an interior life. Third, of the trials of an interior life. Fourth, of the dangers in an interior life. Fifth, of the sanctification of ordinary actions by an interior life. Sixth, of certain exterior works of charity, which some religious orders join to the interior.

CHAPTER I.

OF THE INTERIOR LIFE.

SECTION I.—*In what the Interior Life consists.*

THE religious soul separates herself from all terrestrial things; and why? To find God and be united to Him. She forms within herself a kind of solitude, where, alone with God, she converses with Him of eternal things, makes Him the only object of her love, of her thoughts and desires. This is what the holy Fathers call an Interior life.

The interior, says Father Guillore, may be called

the audience chamber of the soul and God. In the world reunions are given, first, to see and know each other; secondly, to transact business; thirdly, for the sake of amusement. Is it not this which takes place in the interior, the divine reunion of God and the soul? For is it not in this divine reunion they commence to know each other the better? and, in effect, it is there that the soul, recollected within herself, discovers the greatness and goodness of God, which in the exterior world had been veiled from her by thick mists; and God also seems, according to our manner of expression, to become there better acquainted with the soul, which unveils herself to His eyes by a single expression of what she is. It is there solely that the great business of salvation and sanctification is treated of, that God enlightens the soul, instructs her, discovers to her His designs and intentions, and makes her a participator of His secrets; it is there that the soul enters into this divine negotiation by the communication of her thoughts; it is there, as in a reunion, that God and the soul enjoy divine pleasures, and where the soul alone is called to be with God alone, because He wishes Himself alone to be the delight of the soul. How often and how frequently has not this God of love awaited you in the retreat of your interior, and alas! how often have you allowed Him to languish with delay.

According to Father Baudrand, there are four different steps which lead to the perfection of an interior life: the thought of God; the presence of God; union with God, and being lost in God.

The thought of God is good, holy, and salutary; we willingly think of what we love, but this thought is rather the remembrance than the presence of God, as when we think of an absent friend whose memory we recall with pleasure.

The presence of God expresses more than the remembrance. We no longer require to think of God, we are always with Him, as two friends who are ever in each other's society; it is a strong affection of the heart for God, which it never withdraws, because its love becomes habitual, and its will is never separated from that of its well-beloved.

Union with God implies still more than the presence of God; union signifies two persons in unity; it makes them appear but one; the soul is so united to God, there is such concord, such harmony, such conformity of views, sentiments, and desires, that it seems as if there was no longer but one person, one heart and soul.

To be lost in God. This is the height of perfection and happiness of a soul. In this state the soul is so despoiled of herself with reference to God, and God has so taken possession of her soul, that she seems to be no longer a distinct object, but to be, as it were, lost, absorbed in God, and to have passed into God. This is the state of which St. Paul speaks: "You are dead, and your life is hidden with Christ in God." This state would consummate the perfection of a soul before God, and would conduct her to an union with God, as intimate as could be contracted on earth.

An interior soul has God ever present, and she is always present with God; she seeks and finds Him in everything; all recalls Him to her. At one time she considers Him filling this vast universe with the immensity of His being, and there she adores His ineffable greatness; at another time she contemplates Him, elevated on the throne of His glory, and penetrated with respect, she keeps herself annihilated in His presence; more frequently does she represent Him to herself dwelling in her heart, establishing in it His empire, replenishing it with His graces, consolidating His reign, and domineering over all her passions.

The presence of God is twofold; one is acquired by our care and application. When with the assistance of grace we apply ourselves to watch over our interior, to repress the irregularity of the senses, to restrain our thoughts, our affections, our powers within ourselves, then there is insensibly formed within us a holy habit of the presence of God. The other is as infused; it is a pure gift of God, and a gratuitous operation of the Holy Spirit, which prevents a soul in attracting her to Him by silence and union.

It is the usual conduct of heaven, when a soul has exercised herself for some time in the presence of God, acquired by the assistance of grace and many efforts, to make her pass to the superior state of the passive and infused presence of God, which is a pure grace rather than a virtue.

When grace attracts a soul to this state, she should occupy herself with God in a spirit of simplicity and union, that is to say, without a great multiplicity of acts, but by a single look, a single adhesion. It is not necessary to seek God when we have found Him; any effort then would only serve to trouble and confuse the soul.

As to those souls whose employments occupy them exteriorly, distract or withdraw them from this sweet presence, it is necessary, in a spirit of submission and without inquietude, to recall from time to time the presence of God by amorous aspirations, and frequent elevations of the heart; in often throwing their looks towards the Divine Sun of Justice, they will receive His beneficent rays, which, like so many burning darts, will enkindle the sacred fire of divine love within their souls.

If we were habitually recollected within ourselves, and constantly faithful to grace, we should not require to use any effort to be in the presence of God; it would become habitual to us like recollection and fidelity; such is the opinion of the holy Fathers. We must not, they say, seek God far from us, since He is within us; we must not seek Him with any great effort or exertion, since we find Him without any trouble; we must not seek Him to enjoy Him, nor to feel sensibly His presence and His operations, since very often we cannot be sensible either of His presence or His operations. In a true sense, we must not ever seek Him, but persuade ourselves He has found us, that He is living and acting in and by us. In this sweet persuasion, let us think but of keeping ourselves united to Him, of detaching ourselves more and more from created things, of despoiling ourselves entirely of self to be more intimately united to God; let us be resigned in His hands, submissive to His orders, conformed to His will, abandoned to His providence, that by His presence, He may work in and with us according to His good pleasure, which can only be for our perfection and our happiness.

The interior life, as we see, supposes two things, without which it cannot exist, that is, the soul who seeks God, and God who communicates Himself to the soul. God assures us in Holy Scripture, that "His delight is to be with the children of men." He is always ready to meet our desires, but on certain conditions of which He exacts the accomplishment.

And, first, God requires that she who invites Him to take possession of her heart, has previously subdued the passions which tyrannise over her; for, says the Scripture, "God cannot dwell in a heart the slave of sin." God also demands from the soul which aspires to the interior life, certain fundamental virtues, which are the indispensable ornaments of the solitude into which she invites Him to converse with her. The principal among these virtues are humility, the love of God and our neighbour, conformity to the will of God, fidelity to grace, interior recollection, silence, &c.

SECTION II.—*Of the Controul which the Soul which aspires to an Interior Life, should have over her Passions.*

David was not allowed to raise a temple to the Lord, because he had not entirely subjected the enemies of his empire. This glory was reserved for his son Solomon. This great prince, having reduced to submission all the enemies of God and of His people, reared the edifice of which his father had formed the project, and dedicated it to God, who was pleased to take up His dwelling in it, to manifest there His glory, and there to display His wonderful mercies.

The religious soul which wishes to erect to God a temple in her heart, and to be united to Him in an interior life, must, beforehand, impose silence on her enemies, that is, her passions, and make them subject to her by a decisive victory; otherwise she cannot be admitted to the favour she solicits, for God will never dwell in the soul enslaved to passion.

Victory over the passions is the first step to arrive at the interior life. In our first work, "The Path of true and solid Virtue," we have treated of the means of obtaining this victory; we refer our readers to it.

SECTION III.—*Second Means of arriving at an Interior Life—Humility.*

Humility is one of the virtues most indispensable to arrive at an interior life; for God himself tells us, that He holds the proud in abomination; that He resists the proud and humbles them, whilst, on the contrary, He takes pleasure in exalting the humble and communicating Himself to them. The religious soul should then be well impressed with the importance and advantages of this virtue, in order to determine to practise it, if she wishes to become interior. We will try and aid her in this task, by placing before her the doctrine of the Saints.

All spiritual writers, says Bellecius, make the most magnificent eulogiums on humility. If you ask, says one of them, what holds the first rank in religion, and in the doctrine of Jesus Christ, I answer that it is humility; and the second rank is humility; the third is humility; for the true doctrine of Christian wisdom consists in profound humility. What can be said more excellent ? What can we allege more proper to inspire esteem for this virtue ? Ah, thus thought St. Augustine, this brilliant light of the African Church.

Humility is the foundation of faith; it is it which reduces every intelligence into servitude; which blinding our reason, and extinguishing our natural lights, brings them under the yoke of faith; so that, where there is not humility, there is not faith. As faith is the angular stone of religion, the basis of Christian discipline, and the principle of eternal salvation, it is evident that the price and excellence of humility are incomparable, since it is the foundation of faith.

Again, humility is the solid and durable foundation of all other virtues. In the same way as pride is the source of all sin, so humility is the root of every virtue; it is it which plants them in our hearts, which cultivates and preserves them; it is the mother, the nurse, the column, the anchor, the support and the bond of all virtues. She, on the contrary, who amasses virtue without humility, acts as if she threw dust before the wind; when humility begins to waver, all the virtues we have amassed fall to ruin. All our good works are void, if not seasoned with humility.

Still more, without humility the greatest virtues degenerate into vices, and cause the ruin of man; without it, the greatest austerity of life is detestable hypocrisy, the highest contemplation a shameful illusion, extreme poverty silly vanity. Without humility, the deserts of anchorites, the penances of confessors, the torments of martyrs, the zeal of Apostles, are but a vain sport which strikes the senses, and amuses the demons. But with humility, even crimes lose their capability of injuring, and become, by an admirable metamorphosis, the matter even of virtue; for she who humbles herself profoundly under the powerful hand of God, on account of the faults she has committed, obtains pardon and augments her merit; since, as St. Augustine says, humility is more agreeable to God in bad actions, than good works infected with pride.

In fine, without humility, even the graces of God are hurtful. As the wind, says St. Nilus, when it swells with a favourable breeze the sails of a ship, only hastens the shipwreck, if the vessel is thrown on sand banks hidden beneath the waves; in like manner an abundance of celestial graces and chosen gifts causes the ruin of a soul which nourishes in her heart secret pride. The illuminations of the Holy Spirit blind such a soul, instead of enlightening it; heavenly graces are more prejudicial than useful to her; the knowledge of divine things puffs her up, instead of making her better; the gifts of prayer, of prophecy, of tears, of tongues, of curing, are for her deadly poison. Hence, we may learn to esteem the excellence of humility.

Its utility teaches us to love it. Everything that is useful and profitable to us, easily obtains our love; now the first grace with which humility enriches us, is a perfect resemblance with Jesus Christ. As the state of abjection was that of our Divine Saviour on earth, so a soul established and satisfied in this state is in some manner another Jesus Christ, and his faithful portrait; her sentiments and affections are conformable to those of our Divine Redeemer, who highly esteemed and ardently loved contempt and opprobrium, who had no other desire during life but to be contemned and despised. Such a soul drinks from the same chalice with Jesus Christ the bitter wine of abjection; she is fed with the same bread of humiliation; like Him, she is clothed with the same robe of confusion; she is treated by the Eternal Father, as He was; in a word, she joyfully bears the ignominy of Jesus Christ, esteeming it a more precious treasure than the riches of the Egyptians.

And who can tell how advantageous it is to retrace in ourselves the resemblance of our Divine Saviour, to revest ourselves with His robes; to adorn ourselves with His colours, to have the same taste and inclination; to esteem or despise, to love or hate, to seek or fly the same thing that He did; to be conducted by the same spirit and animated by the same soul; to be, in fine, by this resemblance of manner and equality of condition, the joy of the heart of Jesus Christ, His crown and His delight. How then is it possible that we would not love humility, which associates our soul to Jesus Christ; which renders it like to Him, who is the well-beloved Son of the Eternal Father, in whom He takes complacency, in whom He is pleased, because He annihilated Himself even to take the form of a slave ?

The second advantage we derive from humility is profound peace of heart. It is in this peace, that the humble soul, superior to all vicissitudes, passes cloudless days; for the first source of those annoyances which disquiet the soul, is removed by humility, which in place of ambitioning honour and esteem, rather flies from them, and far from dreading contempt and humiliation, it desires them.

For what could trouble her who delights in contempt and injuries, who receives blows with a smile of peace, who joyfully offers the other cheek to the person who has struck her? Who could doubt but that such a soul had arrived at the portal of heaven, that she enjoys an anticipated happiness, comparable to the tranquillity of the elect. And as, according to St. John Climacus, it is humility which gives us this foretaste of beatitude, we may conclude of how great utility it is; the following are his words:—
"Every time you will hear or perceive that any one has acquired in a short time a profound peace, do not believe that he has walked in any other path than that of humility."

The third advantage that we derive from humility consists in this blessed state of abjection, being the most proper to make us acquire the most sublime sanctity. Is a soul in humiliation, then her companions shun her, they dislike her society, they regard her with feelings of scorn and contempt; and she being rejected by the world, shuns it in her turn; being despised by the world, she despises it: being thus left to herself, and being occupied with God alone in the recollection of her soul, in this sacred solitude, which is the nurse of sanctity, she preserves her heart pure and exempt from those stains which are contracted by such intercourse with creatures.

By this purity of heart, she is in a proximate disposition to obtain the love of God, which is the consummation of perfection. This is what St. John the Evangelist taught St. Mary Magdalene de Pazzi in an ecstacy, in which he said to her. " The soul which will be perfect in humility will easily possess divine love, but wanting humility she will require to use many other means to obtain it. You will never find a heart replenished with humility, which is not also full of this love, which unites the soul intimately to its God, and makes it, as it were, one with Him." Here, we may remark, that from this love of God which is acquired by humility, there buds forth, as from a fruitful stem, the fourth advantage with which humility enriches us, which is union with God. The heart being free from all ambition and desire of honour, God possesses it, without pride, His impious rival being able to dispute its possession; and thus it is His delight to come into this soul, to make with her His dwelling, to converse with her, and to be intimately united to her by the bonds of love.

Hence results this affectionate communication of heavenly treasures; for these being hidden in the humble heart from the worm of vainglory, God, in His infinite munificence, is pleased to concentrate there his choicest treasures, but principally the seven gifts of the Holy Ghost. Not to speak of those celestial delights with which he inundates such souls even in this life, behold how, in one instant, He penetrates them with so clear knowledge of the most profound mysteries, that the most exalted genius, after years of labour and application, could not attain the same knowledge; witness St. Teresa, and a host of others, with whom humility was the key which introduced them to a most sublime knowledge of the divine secrets. Jesus Christ Himself teaches us, that the Eternal Father reveals to those who are little in their own eyes, what He has hidden from the wise.

And as these souls faithfully refer to the Author of all good the glory which arises from their good works, and as they do not attribute to themselves honour which they do not think they merit, God usually makes use of them to accomplish the prodigies of His mercy, and to execute his most important designs. Souls truly humble may well exclaim, "Every good has come to me with the holy virtue of humility." To sum up all in a few words, God loves the humble soul, He consoles her. He abases Himself to her, He lavishes on her His most abundant graces. He reveals His secrets to the humble of heart. He invites and attracts her gently to Himself.

Is it then possible that we would not love a virtue, which leads us to a perfect resemblance of Jesus Christ; to true peace of soul; to sublime sanctity; to intimate union with God; to a communication of celestial treasures; in fine, which renders us proper subjects to advance the glory of God, and the salvation of our neighbour.

Section IV.—*Third Means to arrive at an Interior Life—the Love of God.*

The interior life consists in a strict union between the soul and God. There is no more sure means of arriving at this sublime life, than that which makes God necessarily incline to the soul, and at the same time elevates the soul to God and keeps it united to Him; love produces this double effect.

It makes God incline towards the soul. "He who

loves Me," says Jesus Christ, "keeps my commandments, and he will be loved by My Father, and We will come to him, and make with him our abode."

Love elevates the soul to God and holds it united to Him; in effect, the heart directs and forcibly urges the thoughts of the soul towards the loved object; it keeps them fixed, as it were chained to it. We are in a manner necessitated to think of what we love; experience has often taught this to those, who wishing to give themselves unreservedly to God in solitude, have undertaken to banish from their minds the thoughts of the objects to which in the world their hearts had been attached. Let them tell if they were ever able to command their thoughts without first triumphing over their affections. The soul, then, which aspires to the interior life cannot arrive at it by a more certain way than by enkindling in her heart the sacred fire of divine love. But how can she arrive at this? In considering frequently how God merits to be loved. He merits to be loved:—

First, on account of the love with which He has loved us. His love for us contains in an eminent degree the three qualities, which, according to the testimony of spiritual writers, distinguish true from false love. True love worketh great things; it willingly and liberally communicates all it possesses to the object loved, it is always present with it in an intimate manner. Such is, O religious soul! the love of God for you. In the first place it worketh great things for you. God has drawn you forth from nothing in preference to so many others. He has formed you to His image; He has given you the three faculties of the soul, the entire use of the senses, and of the members of your body; He has enriched you with many good dispositions. For love of you, He

G

daily preserves this vast universe; He multiplies animals for your use; for you He makes the trees grow and produce fruit; for you He covers the meadows with grass; for you He enriches the fields with harvest crops; He consolidates the earth under your footsteps; He enlightens you with the sun; He rejoices you with the stars; He nourishes you with food; He slakes your thirst with water; He warms you with fire; he refreshes you with the air; concurring incessantly in all your actions, He at each moment works in you.

Add to these benefits the great work of the Redemption of man, when He became not the Liberator of angels, but the Liberator of the race of Adam. Let us again add, the mission of the Holy Spirit to sanctify the world, and teach all truth, your adoption as a child of God, as heiress of heaven, the grace of baptism, the benefit of education, of your vocation to the true faith and to religious life. Yes, He who is powerful has done great things for you; for love worketh great things wherever it is.

Secondly, God has made you participator in His goods, and He has given Himself to you entirely, when He has given you the principal benefits which His omnipotent hand has created; temporal things for your use, angels to guard you, and grace that you may merit heaven for your recompense. He has given you Jesus Christ as a master, His life as a guide, His flesh for your food, and His blood for your drink; in fine, He has lavished on you all the riches of His love in the Holy Eucharist, in such a manner that He who is Omnipotent has nothing better to bestow.

Again, He has communicated to you the immense and priceless treasures contained in His promises, namely, the assistance of His preventing and cooperating grace; the gifts of faith, hope, habitual charity and sanctifying grace, that you may thus become participators in the divine nature; for love liberally gives itself with all its goods to the object loved. Since God has so loved the world, that He has given it His only Son, that He has not spared Him, but has delivered Him for us, it is certain that He could not withhold from us any other gift. Yes, assuredly, it is in this the charity of God for men has appeared.

Third, God shews you His love in being ever present with you by His essence, His power, and His Providence.

By His essence, according to the doctrine of the Apostle: It is in Him we have our being, life, and movement, being more encompassed, more penetrated, more replenished, by the Divinity than by the air we breathe.

By His power, for He lives, He increases, He feels, He sees, He thinks, He speaks, and acts in us, by His concurrence in our actions.

By His Providence, He bears you in his arms, He warms you, He protects you as His darling child, He removes from you every evil, provides for your good, and even makes temptation a cause of merit for you; in a word, God, to testify His love for you, is always intimately present or residing in your body and soul, as in His temple; for He who loves desires to be continually united to the object loved.

And, as reason itself teaches us that we must give love for love, it follows that you must do something great for God, that you should offer yourself to Him, with all that is yours; that you should be ever present and united to your Sovereign Master by interior recollection, by the fervour of prayer, and by the exercise of the presence of God.

God merits to be loved on account of the manner

in which he loves man. He loves you with an eternal love; this love is so ancient that imagination could not reach its source; for God no sooner began to love Himself than He loved you from eternity; He has cast on you from eternity those merciful regards which have drawn you from the abyss of nothing, preferably to so many others who would have served Him better. God has a right to say to you by the Prophet Jeremiah: " I have loved you with an eternal charity, I have created you in My goodness."

He has loved you with a gratuitous love, without any merit on your part, and without any advantage to Him; for as St. John says, " the charity of God has appeared in this, that we have not first loved Him;" that we have not preceded Him in charity to merit from Him a reciprocal love; but that He has been the first to love us, even when we were His enemies, and by nature children of wrath. He has voluntarily loved us, without being constrained or obliged to do so; without having any need of us; without any advantage or utility to Himself, since He is a God who does not regard our goods.

His eternal Omniscience, His knowledge of the future, could discover in us but nothingness and sin, which should rather irritate His anger than gain His love; and, nevertheless, this God who has need of no one, who is happy in Himself, has loved you,—you a sinful soul, without any merit on your part, and without any profit to Him. What do I say? He has foreseen the numerous and grievous faults you will commit, and nevertheless He has loved you.

He loves you with an infinite love; with this same love, considered in its nature, with which this immense Being loves Himself, with which He loves His Trinity, with which He loves Jesus Christ and His saints; for He loves thee, O my soul! with all the infinitude of His nature, so that there is not in His Divinity a perfection, nor in His Trinity a person, with which He does not love thee with the unlimited extent of His charity.

In fine, He loves you with the most tender love, carrying you on His shoulders as the good Shepherd carries His sheep, or bearing you in His arms, as the nurse does the little child, guarding you as the apple of His eye, counting even the hairs of your head, always thinking of you to do you good, as if you were alone in the world, and were the only object of His infinite love!

It is then just, O divine love! that I love you with a gratuitous love, not excited by the fear of punishment, nor the hope of recompense, but that I love you purely and gratuitously for your own sake. I should love you with an efficacious love, loving you not in words alone, but in deed and truth. I should love you with a constant love, exclaiming with the Doctor of nations—" Who shall separate me from the charity of Jesus Christ? Shall it be tribulation, or persecution, or the sword? For I am certain that neither death, nor life, nor angels, nor principalities, nor things present, nor things to come, nor any creature, shall ever separate me from the charity of God."

God merits to be loved on account of His infinite perfections. His amiability is so great, that if heaven were opened but for one instant, all the damned souls in hell, in place of that sovereign hatred they bear Him, would be forced by gentle violence to love Him with the most ardent love! His beauty is so ravishing, that the lost souls would willingly endure a thousand hells to contemplate it for one instant! His goodness is so full of charms, that if the damned could experience in hell but the least effect of it, their horrible prison would immediately be changed into paradise! Such is the transcendant excellence of His sanctity, that the pain which the slightest fault occasions Him far surpasses the joy arising from the heroic actions of all the saints together! His knowledge is so infinite, that He forgets nothing of the past, that He is ignorant of nothing of the present; that He foresees the future with as much exactitude, as if it were represented to Him in a mirror! His omnipotence is so astonishing, that His power equals His will. His age is eternity! His course immutability! His dwelling immensity! His size infinitude!

He is so rich, that His treasures are inexhaustible; so clear-sighted, that He disposes all with weight, measure, and number; so constant, that in Him there is no change or shadow of vicissitude; so strong, that with three fingers He supports this vast universe, that He weighs the mountains and puts the hills in His hands as in a balance; He is so exalted in His power, that no one is like unto Him.

In a word, He is more elevated than heaven, more profound than hell, more extended than earth, and more vast than the sea. All is naked and unveiled before His eyes. He holds in His hand the life of every living creature; no one can resist His anger; thousands and thousands of angels serve Him, and millions and millions of blessed spirits stand before Him.

But who can recount His works? Who penetrate His wonders? Who speak of His greatness? As He dwells in light inaccessible, is it not just to love with our whole strength Him, whose perfections are incomprehensible? Let us frequently meditate on these sublime truths; let them be the habitual subject of our thoughts and reflections; then, the fire of divine love will necessarily be enkindled in our hearts, and the affections of our hearts captivating our thoughts, will attach them to God, and we will have the interior spirit.

SECTION V.—*Fourth Means for arriving at the Interior Life—Conformity to the Will of God.*

To become interior it is not sufficient to love God, we must love the will of God, however it may be manifested in our regard, and conform ours to it. In effect, the interior life is the result of the union of our soul with God, a union which supposes an inclining of God towards us His creatures, and a tendency of our will, which inclines us towards Him, our Creator, our Legislator, or Guide, the Sovereign Dispenser of all things, who directs everything within and around us as He pleases. It is then evident, that if our will is opposed to His, resists it, or rebels against it, the harmony which existed between Him and us is destroyed; by this rupture we remove from Him, and He, wounded by our insubordination and our ingratitude, withdraws from us, and the interior life is no longer possible.

It is then absolutely necessary for those who aspire to the interior life to be well grounded in perfect conformity to the will of God. We shall now consider how excellent, how just, and advantageous this conformity is.

Excellence of Conformity to the Will of God.

The most astonishing prodigy of the universe, says Bellecius, the miracle, superior to all that we read of the omnipotence of God, is the union of the Divine Word with human nature, a union that we adore in the person of the Man-God, and which causes astonishment even to the celestial intelligences. A second prodigy is the union of a fruitful maternity with a stainless virginity, which we honour in the Mother of God. After these two miracles of the divine power, wisdom, and charity, there appears to me no deed more sublime, more agreeable to heaven, and more salutary to us, than the union of our will with the will of God.

This union is the most magnificent triumph that victorious grace could obtain over the human will, at the same time leaving it free; it is this virtue whose charms attract the Divine Spouse into our soul, as into a garden of delight; it is this virtue which makes of our heart a temple of sanctity, a sanctuary in which the Most Holy Trinity desires to make its dwelling, according to the promise of Jesus Christ—" We will come to him, and We will make our abode with him."

This conformity of will is, without contradiction, the most perfect and the most agreeable sacrifice that can be offered to God. By it, man immolates to the Divine Majesty what He has most dear and precious, for there is nothing which it costs man so much to despoil himself of as his own will. In rejecting riches, in despising honours, in quitting pleasures, man makes the sacrifice of his earthly goods, but here he offers himself; in everything else, whatever he sacrifices to his Creator, belongs already to Him by a double title; but here man, who is the free arbiter of his will, abandons it entirely to his God. This is the reason that the conformity of will with that of God is the most perfect worship that can be rendered to Him, it is the most excellent homage of our heart, and the most agreeable holocaust man can make of himself; for by it, we subject to God, the only good that our malice has the power to withhold from Him. By it we fully accomplish this commandment; "My son, give me thy heart." What an incontestible proof of the excellence of this virtue!

She who applies herself to the practice of this virtue, contracts with our divine Saviour a strict tie of affinity and spiritual relationship. He has Himself said, "He who does the will of my Father who is in heaven, he is my brother, my sister, and my mother." Now, what is there of greater excellence than to be looked on as the sister and mother of Jesus Christ, and even to be exalted to an intimacy still more strict? This is what we may also conclude from the same part of the Gospel, where some one having said to Jesus Christ, "Behold your Mother and your brethren who are without and wish to speak to you;" the Saviour answered, "Who is my mother, and who are my brethren?" Then extending His hands towards His disciples, He said, "Behold my mother, and behold my brethren;" preferring thus to carnal and natural relationship, this spiritual affinity founded on the accomplishment of the divine will. I say more, the soul which practises this conformity of will is as another Jesus Christ, she is fed with the same nourishment. He tells us, that His food is to do the will of Him that sent Him; she then who imitates Jesus Christ in this respect proves she is nourished with the same food. The only and essential business of Jesus Christ is to accomplish the will of God, His Father, since He has said, "It is written of me at the head of the book, that I will accomplish your will, O my Father!" The soul which entertains similar sentiments in her heart, perfectly represents Jesus Christ, she is truly another Jesus Christ.

I add, with St. Bernard, that such a disposition deifies us in some manner; for to wish what God wishes is to be already like to God; and not to be able to wish otherwise than as God wishes, is to be in a manner what God is. As two balls of wax, melted together, form but one, so man, by this conformity of will, is identified with God; thus the Spouse in the Canticles says, "My soul is melted as wax," which is ready to take any form. St. Laurence Justinian, thus comments on those words, "My soul is melted with the burning fire of charity, it is become ductile like metal, and is ready to receive every impression of the divine will." And what is this but to be deified? Let us add still more, this soul participates in two attributes which belong to God alone, His Impeccability, and His Infallibility. In doing the will of God, she obeys Infinite Wisdom, and she cannot be deceived; she also acts conformably to the rule of Infinite Sanctity, and she cannot sin; thus she becomes, as far as a creature can, "all that God is Himself."

This noble practice embraces every virtue; in it shines so brilliantly that faith, by which we believe nothing happens which is not the will of God. By it we prove our confidence by abandoning ourselves to the conduct of His amiable Providence; with it we practise patience, humility, obedience, penance, &c. It is the most secure of all devotions, not being subject, as others are, to the artifices and illusions of hell. We may now conclude how transcendingly excellent it is, since we can say nothing more sublime of any virtue.

How just is this Conformity to the Will of God.

Reason itself tells us that what is right redresses what is wrong, what is immutable in its nature and not subject to vice, corrects what is inconstant and vicious.

The will of God is right, immutable, and essentially holy; ours, on the contrary, is false, inconstant, and depraved: the will of God is infinitely wise and just; ours is but blindness and iniquity: in a word, the will of God is the first rule of morality, and the infallible measure of good; ours is erroneous and sinful. It is then just, concludes St. Augustine, that our will be corrected by the will of God, and that the will of God be not subjected to ours; for ours is defective, and His perfect. Let the rule of all true wisdom then subsist, and let what is false be rectified by this rule; justice demands this.

The will of God is a sovereign will, for all is submissive to it; it is becoming that every human will be also subject to it; and since the Divine Being is the Prime and Sovereign Being, every created being should necessarily be subject to Him, so, as the Divine will is the prime and sovereign will, every created will should necessarily conform to it.

The will of God is not less holy and just than the intelligence of this Sovereign Lord is infallible and wise; we blindly submit our faith to the veracity of His word, why then do we not also render faithful obedience to the sanctity and equity of His will and commandments. Is it not just that the son, the disciple, the servant, the vassal, submits his will promptly to that of his Father, his Master, his Lord, and his King? The former titles belong to man, the latter to God: can there be anything more reasonable, then, than that the human will be subject to the divine? We may hence infer how just is this conformity of will.

Advantages of Conformity to the Will of God.

Conformity to the will of God is most profitable to us, it procures for us even in this life two inestimable advantages, perfect sanctity and unmixed happiness. As to what regards sanctity, it is certain that our perfection consists in an exact accomplishment of the will of God, and that our sanctity will be proportioned to our conformity to this adorable will. First, because our lives will be holy in proportion as they are conformable to the will of God, which is the rule of all sanctity. Second, that we shall be so much the more holy as we shall bear a resemblance to Jesus Christ, who submitted so perfectly to the Will of His Heavenly Father. Third, that our perfection and sanctity consist in charity, which is to be found in the accomplishment of the will of God, according to the oracle of St. John, "He who knows My commandments and observes them, it is he who loves Me."

The second advantage that conformity to the will of God procures for us, is unmixed happiness here below. To be happy in this life we must be exempt from every evil. Now, she whose will is conformed to that of God, is sheltered from every evil; from moral evil, which is sin; from natural evils, which are all kinds of calamities.

Sin is in effect but the rebellion of our will against the will of God. But when a perfect concord reigns between the soul and God, there can be no revolt, and consequently no sin. As to temporal evils, they can only be regarded as such when they contradict our will; for when we embrace them joyfully, so far from being evils, they become the source of inestimable good, as St. Chrysostom assures us. "You have suffered some affliction," says he, "if you wish, it may be to you no affliction; return thanks to God for it, and the evil will become a great good." It is then evident, that if we wish what God wishes, we shall be free from all evil.

Besides this exemption from evil, to be perfectly happy, we must have all our desires gratified, and this is the blessed state of those who are content and satisfied with all God is pleased to ordain; what they desire is always accomplished, because they desire only the fulfilment of the will of God, which cannot fail having effect when it is absolute.

It is a maxim universally received amongst men, that he is happy to whom nothing happens contrary to his will; this is the privilege of every one who submits unreservedly to the good pleasure of God.

In fine, control over our desires is here below a source of true happiness; the faithful soul becomes, by this conformity of her will with God, mistress of all her affections; depending solely on the good will of God, it is immaterial to her whether she is elevated to high honour, or debased beneath all. She is not tempted by ambition, the elevation of others causes her no envy, nor does her own abjection bring her sorrow. As she is perfectly indifferent to all the goods of fortune, she does not fear to lose them, nor does she desire to enrich herself. She loves and detests only what is pleasing and displeasing to God; she reposes happily in the bosom of His Providence, to Whom she commits all her care. By this means she procures that interior spirit which is the recompense of all those who apply themselves to conform their will to that of God.

SECTION VI.—*Fidelity to Grace the fifth Means of arriving at the Interior Life.*

Fidelity to grace is a disposition absolutely necessary to arrive at an interior life; and it is so for two reasons; the first is, that without grace the soul can do nothing; if it does not correspond with grace, it renders useless, deprives itself of it, and consequently cannot become interior. The second reason is, that the interior spirit, which is, as we have already said, a kind of commerce or habitual union of the soul with God, can only exist by the aid of a perfect harmony between the soul and God, which prevents it with grace and solicits it to good: a harmony that the least resistance of the soul can interrupt and annihilate. All spiritualists have strongly inculcated the necessity of fidelity to grace.

"Our principal attention in the interior life," says Baudrand, "ought to be fidelity to grace, attention to discover the ways and movements of the Spirit of God in our souls, and perfect docility to this Divine Spirit; our perfection depends thereon." We may perform different exercises of virtue, different practices of piety, of zeal, of charity, of mortification, and of penance; all that is holy, all that is great, all that is worthy of God; but there is a path still more secure and more exalted; it is to follow the movements of the Holy Spirit and of grace. Let us suppose that two persons consecrated themselves at the same time to God; one is entirely devoted to good works and exterior practices; the other is occupied in following the lights of the Holy Ghost and the inspirations of grace; the latter will advance more in this way in one day, than the former in entire years by other practices.

Very few persons arrive at the full accomplishment of the designs of God over them, because few have the generosity to correspond faithfully to the voice of grace. The Holy Ghost sometimes waits for them to become docile to His voice; He invites them; He solicits them; He presses them; but if they abuse the time and the grace that He offers, He withdraws, and leaves them in a certain obscurity and ignorance with regard to their interior, in which they live with great danger of their perfection, and sometimes even of their salvation.

Nevertheless, such is frequently our conduct and our misfortune; we spend whole years, and sometimes a long life, in disputing with grace the dominion of our hearts, and in balancing if we will give ourselves wholly to God; we cannot resolve to make the entire sacrifice; we reserve to ourselves certain affections, views, designs, hopes, and desires of which we do not wish to despoil ourselves, in order to be perfectly dependent on grace and on the Spirit of God; these are so many chains with which the enemy holds us fast, and prevents our advancing in the path of perfection. How happy should we be, I may add, how holy should we be, if, by prompt and generous fidelity, we should renounce, once and for ever, these useless amusements, these vain satisfactions, to abandon ourselves unreservedly to the empire of grace which invites us, to the spirit of God which presses us!

How astonishing and how sad it is sometimes to see souls, whom God calls to an interior life, where, in recollection, in prayer, and in the exercises of piety, they could acquire immense treasures for heaven, enjoy ineffable delight, and drink at its source the purest water of grace! How astonishing it is to see those souls, to whom God presents the delights of heaven, amused and arrested in their upward progress by unworthy and contemptible objects, seeking their satisfaction in natural attachments, in frivolous occupations, and in vain conversations, which hinder them from knowing and possessing the real goods which grace has prepared for them who, by a generous renunciation, leave all to give themselves to God, and to correspond to the designs of His Providence over them.

And need we be astonished if such souls, notwithstanding the graces they receive, still lead a life quite natural, if they are flattered when praised, if they are sensitive when blamed, if they have resentments and whims, if they love their ease and convenience, &c. Their deliberate infidelity to grace, their continual resistance to its voice, obstruct its salutary impressions and its divine effects.

This habitual state of opposition and of resistance should make them tremble and fear lest this grace which is neglected, scorned, and despised for so long a time, may at last be withdrawn, and that they may be abandoned to their infidelity. What misfortune for those souls, if God punished them in so terrible a manner, and thus revenged Himself for His outraged grace.

There is, however, for them a secure and consolatory means of return. When a soul has long lived in this state of tepidity and languor, there is one means to arise from it, which is to practise purity of heart, to shun every deliberate fault, to be perfectly docile to the inspirations of the Holy Ghost, and to assume a new and determined resolution of being more faithful.

Let us henceforward apply ourselves without relaxation to this holy exercise, with a determined will of refusing nothing to God; by this means we shall soon be released from the bond which holds us captive; grace will return to us when we return to it; the Holy Ghost will speak again to the heart, and we shall see ourselves once more inundated with His precious gifts, when we shall have resolved to give to them a faithful correspondence.

Let us receive each inspiration as a divine word which comes to us from heaven. But, what do I say? As a drop of the blood of Jesus Christ shed on us.

Let us regard as the greatest misfortune a single voluntary infidelity to grace; it is capable of long retarding the soul in the interior life.

Let us, particularly, ask of God to make us expiate in this world our infidelities to grace, in order that we may not carry the remorse and guilt of them into the next world.

Then harmony will be re-established between our soul and God, then the source of grace will again be opened to us, and aided by this assistance, we may aspire in an efficacious manner to the interior life.

SECTION VII.—*Fraternal Charity the Sixth Means of arriving at the Interior Life.*

The Nature and Importance of Fraternal Charity.

The powerful motives we have alleged to prove how necessary the love of God is to arrive at the interior life, equally demonstrate the necessity of fraternal charity in attaining this sublime end. In effect, these two branches of charity have the same nature, the same essence, the same end, and are but one and the same thing; their obligation is imposed on us in an equally pressing manner, under the same penalty, and by the same precept; consequently, it is as impossible for a soul to practise the interior life without fraternal charity, as without the love of God. Let us study profoundly the nature of this virtue, its importance and its characteristics.

Theologians say that fraternal charity is a virtue by which we love our neighbour for God. Mankind in general is the object of this virtue, therefore we should not confine our charity to the few persons with whom we may be connected, either by the ties of blood or of affection; it should extend to all our fellow-creatures without exception, according to this general precept of our Saviour, "I command you to love one another."

The motive of this virtue is the love of God. It is not because the creature is amiable in herself, or because she has first loved us, or because she is benevolent towards us, that we are to love her; these are carnal and terrestrial motives; the motive of our charity must be more exalted, it must be supernatural. It is the love we have for God that should make us love our neighbour; we should love her because God loves her, and commands us to love her.

The principle of this virtue is the Holy Ghost, who enkindles in our hearts the fire of divine love. Consequently fraternal charity cannot have its source in that carnal and blind propensity of the heart which carries us to love our fellow-creature in a sensible manner; its principle is elevated above nature and comes from on high; it is a gift of the Holy Ghost, which we should earnestly beg, and which we may hope to obtain through the mercy of God.

We may here remark that the love of God, as well as the gifts of the Holy Ghost, which are in us the principle of fraternal charity, do not necessarily act upon our hearts, so as to affect us, or induce us to love our neighbour with a sensitive or demonstrative affection, as some timorous souls falsely imagine, who are afflicted and dejected when they do not experience any sensible love for their neighbour, but on the contrary feel for them a natural repugnance. It is on the soul and the will that the gifts of the Holy Spirit and the love of God act; and peculiarly divine action urges us to love our neighbour in a spiritual and supernatural manner; so that true fraternal charity is a spiritual love, the seat of which is particularly in the will.

Fraternal charity is not simply a counsel; Jesus Christ has made of it a formal precept;—a precept which he calls the greatest, the most important of all after the love of God; and in order clearly to prove its importance, He makes it the subject of His dying testament. Before immolating Himself on Calvary for the salvation of the human race, He solemnly convenes His disciples to dictate to them His last wishes, and to give them His parting instructions: He begins, according to His custom, by giving them an example; He humbles Himself even to wash the feet of His disciples; He makes the beloved disciple, who is seated near Him at table, recline on His sacred breast; He feeds them with His Body and Blood after instituting the Holy Eucharist; then raising His Voice, He says in accents of the tenderest charity, "Little children, yet a little while I am with you. ....Before leaving you, a new commandment I give unto you: That you love one another, as I have loved you. By this shall all men know that you are my disciples, if you have love one for another." Shortly after, He seals as it were this precept by a last example, in giving His life for us.

The Apostles, the depositories of this precept, of this sacred testament, have published it throughout the earth, according to the order they had received.

"I recommend you," says St. Peter, in his first Epistle, " to have before all things a constant mutual charity among yourselves." And St. John, "In this we have known the charity of God, because He hath laid down His life for us; and we ought to lay down our lives for the brethren. He that saith he loveth God and hateth his brother, hath not the truth in him."

St. Paul, filled with the spirit of these precepts, declares, that he wished himself to be an anathema from Christ for his brethren, and he adds, "If I speak with the tongues of men and of angels, and have not charity, I am become as sounding brass, or a tinkling cymbal. And if I should have prophecy, and should know all mysteries and all knowledge, and if I should have all faith, so that I could remove mountains, and have not charity, I am nothing. And if I should distribute all my goods to feed the poor, and if I should deliver my body to be burned, and have not charity, it profiteth me nothing." "We form together but one and the same body in Jesus Christ," continues St. Paul, "we who participate in the same heavenly bread, and who are all members one of another; let us then be united by the bonds of the most sincere charity, bearing each other's burthens."

Fraternal charity is prescribed to all Christians; it is ordained by a commandment the most clear, the most decisive, and the most solemn that was ever given; but this commandment obliges in a particular manner persons consecrated to God in religious life. In effect, it is the charity of God which has drawn and united them to Him by ties so strict. Now, the love of God being inseparably connected with the love of our neighbour, or rather being but one and the same thing with it, the religious should be drawn to her neighbour in the same proportion as she is attracted to God; and even as the Apostle said, that he who says he loves God, and does not love his brethren, has not the truth in him; so we may say that she who boasts of loving Jesus Christ, who takes the title of His spouse, and nevertheless is not drawn to her neighbour by a generous and sincere charity, injures truth. According to the oracle of our divine Saviour, it is by the mutual charity which unites them, that we should recognise His true disciples; so it is equally by mutual charity we are to recognise His true spouses, since in forming, according to the expression of Holy Scripture, but one and the same body in Jesus Christ, they are truly the members of each other, and they should love and cherish one another.

But what is the nature and extent of that charity which ought to unite the different members of a community?

The masters of the spiritual life compare this charity, in its nature and effects, to the union and correspondence which, according to the remark of St. Paul, exists between the different members of the human body. Behold, says Rodriguez, quoting St. Basil and St. Augustine, how these different members serve and help one another: the eyes direct the feet, the hands defend the head, and all jointly endeavour to succour and help the weakest part, as experience sufficiently teaches us, when we have received a wound or any other hurt. In the distribution that is made of nourishment, each member only receives what is necessary for it, and leaves the remainder for the other members. Besides, there is such a sympathy between them, that the stomach, for example, cannot be out of order, but also the head suffers and feels for it. All the members interest themselves one for another; the pain of one communicates itself to all the rest, and it is no sooner cured than all the others are eased and comforted. St. Augustine explains this in an admirable manner: it happens, he says, that the foot treads upon a thorn; what is more remote from the eyes than the feet? It is indeed, by situation, very far off, but it is very near by the mutual correspondence of all the members; as soon, then, as the foot has been pricked by the thorn, the eyes begin to look for it; the body stoops to find it, the tongue asks where it is, and the hands try to pull it out. Yet the eyes, the hands, the body, the head, and the tongue are all well, and even the foot is hurt only in one place; but all the members interest themselves for each other. Behold, how we ought to conduct ourselves towards our brethren; we ought to have as great care of them as we have of ourselves; we must rejoice as much at their good fortune as at our own, and feel as much for their misfortunes and sufferings as we do for our own afflictions.

That which is still to be considered in the comparison of St. Paul, continues the same author, is, on one side, the diversity of members, suitableness, qualities and different functions; and, on the other, their strict union, mutual correspondence, and the satisfaction which each one takes in the employment destined for it, not at all envying the higher employments of those that are more elevated.

'Tis thus we ought to act. Each ought to be content with the employment he is in, without envying those who are more elevated. Moreover, as in the body a superior member despises not the inferior, but, on the contrary, esteems, conserves, and helps it as much as possible; so those who exercise the chief employment in religion, ought not to contemn those who are below them: they ought, on the contrary, esteem, assist them carefully in their wants, and consider them as members absolutely necessary. For the eye cannot say to the hand, I want not your help; the head cannot say to the feet, you are not necessary; for the members that appear to us the most contemptible and the weakest, are in effect those of which we have the most need.

Observe, for example, how necessary our feet are, and to what distress we should be reduced if we were deprived of them! God has ordained things thus in His infinite wisdom, says St. Augustine, to the end that there may be no disunion in the body. It is the same in the body of a monastery; some are the head, some the eyes, others the hands and the feet; and the head cannot say that it wants not the hands, nor the eyes that they stand not in need of the feet. On the contrary, it seems that each one is particularly the person we stand most in need of in religion; and without doubt, the Providence of God would have things arranged in this manner, that there might be no opposition of sentiments amongst religious, and that we might always live in a strict union of mind and a perfect charity of heart.

St. Paul thus gives the characteristics of charity: " Charity is patient, is kind; charity envieth not, dealeth not perversely, is not puffed up; is not ambitious, seeketh not her own, is not provoked to anger, thinketh no evil; rejoiceth not in iniquity, but rejoiceth with the truth; beareth all things, believeth all things, hopeth all things, endureth all things." In a few words we may explain these characteristics assigned to charity, or rather let us listen to the Abbe Tronson.

"*Charity is patient.*" It supports without murmuring or complaining the imperfections and failings of the neighbour.

"*It is kind.*" It never gives utterance to harsh and cutting words, and although it knows that the persons to whom it speaks have strength and virtue, and would not be easily offended, nevertheless it behaves towards them with respect and circumspection. We never hear it speak coldly, nor reprehend with bitterness, nor command with haughtiness.

"*It envieth not.*" Far from envying the happiness of its neighbour, or from being afflicted at her success, it wishes her as much good as herself, and rejoices as much at the good fortune and preferment of her friend as at her own.

"*It dealeth not perversely.*" It knows not feigning, dissimulation, or flattery; it is not light, inconstant, or rash.

"*It is not puffed up with pride.*" It makes every one have more esteem for her neighbour than for herself; it is deferential to all.

"*It is not ambitious.*" It has so little ambition that there is nothing, however vile, abject, or humiliating, that it will not joyfully embrace for the love of the neighbour.

"*It seeketh not her own.*" All its happiness consists in the advantage of her neighbour, and it is far removed from any self-seeking.

"*It is not provoked to anger.*" It always preserves sentiments of tenderness and benevolence for every one, no matter what reasons it may have for displeasure.

"*It thinketh no evil.*" It does not think evil even when it has reason to do so, and very far from regarding as an injury any affront it may have received, and seeking to be revenged for it, it dissimulates, it excuses, it pardons, it forgets.

"*It rejoiceth not in iniquity,*" in the careless life and faults of its neighbour; but it makes its joy consist in seeing all advance in the paths of justice, by the practice of virtue.

"*It beareth all things*," and its constancy in serving its neighbour is so great, that neither sufferings nor temptations can shake them.

"*It believeth all things.*" It believeth all the good that can be believed of the neighbour, and without any difficulty it pays deference to the opinion of all.

"*It hopeth all.*" It never despairs of the conversion of any one; and as it never loses the good opinion it has of the neighbour, it always hopes that she will be faithful to God, and will obtain from Him new graces.

"*It endureth all.*" It endures with courage the burthen of every office, it is indefatigable in its employments, and never yields under the weight of the duties which are imposed on her.

Section VIII.—*Of private Friendships, how opposed they are to Fraternal Charity.*

In the preceding section we have observed, in speaking of fraternal charity, that its motive is neither the natural qualities of our neighbour, nor the affection that she bears us, nor the kindness which she testifies for us, but the love of God alone. Nor has it its origin in that blind and carnal propensity of the heart, which urges us to testify sensible affection to our fellow-creatures, but its source is in those gifts with which the Holy Ghost replenishes our hearts. Going still farther, we must warn spiritual persons against this natural and blind inclination of the human heart, whose tendency is ever to substitute terrestrial and corrupted sympathies for those pure and sublime motives that religion proposes to us, and to lead us into a path so much the more dangerous, as in following it we believe we accomplish an imperative duty.

There is nothing more common in religious communities, above all among persons of a sensitive disposition, than this natural inclination to form particular friendships with certain persons whose exterior, or whose qualities of mind and heart, or a similitude of character attract; and according to the maxims of spiritual writers, nothing is more opposed to true charity, nothing is more fatal to those who are enslaved to it, and to the monasteries of which they are members. On this subject we will quote the pious and learned Fenelon.

"We commonly believe," says he, "that there is nothing more inoceht than to form a strict friendship with persons possessed of some merits, in whom we discover qualities suitable to our taste. It is a necessity of life, say we, to have some confidential person to whom we can open our hearts, and from whom we may seek consolation; none but stoics can dispense with the pleasure of a virtuous and solid friendship. And these very things, which are so fraught with danger in the different states of secular life, are much more to be feared in religious communities; when souls are called to religious life, they should regard those friendships in quite a different light from what they would have done had they remained free in the world. Behold the reasons:—

"1. We have sacrificed ourselves to obedience and to subordination, therefore, we belong no longer to self. If we can neither dispose of our time nor of our labour, we ought still less dispose of our attachments, since those attachments, if prolonged, would eventually engross both time and application of mind. When you contract intimacies of which your superioress disapproves, you disobey, you assume sensibly a particular spirit, quite contrary to the general spirit of the convent. In your eagerness to advance the interests of the person you love, you commit many faults which you would be ashamed to commit on your own account. Superiors, then, have reason to distrust your moderation, your discretion, your detachment, and your other virtues.

"These particular attachments render you indocile to the views of your superiors, above all when they wish to give you some occupation which will partially remove you from the society of the person to whom you are attached. This is sufficient to embitter you against your superioress, to make your obedience compulsory, and cause you to seek pretexts to elude it. You break silence; you have a great many secrets to tell; you are delighted to steal a few moments to converse, contrary to the rule. One quarter of an hour, in which the heart thus freely gives vent to its feelings, does more injury to the soul, and withdraws farther from obedience, than any other conversations possible could.

"Superiors, seeing the evil, try to remedy it, and all the charitable remedies they employ are considered by you as so many acts of distrust and cruelty. You may say, 'What do I do? Why am I thus reproached?' I esteem such a sister for her merit; however, I do not flatter her; we love each other in God. My superioress wishes to deprive me of the only consolation which I have. With what severity would I not be treated if I did anything contrary to the rules, since for so innocent a thing I am treated with such unrelenting harshness.'

"Superiors are conscious of the evil, and can hardly explain it. They perceive that this indiscreet friendship will insensibly empoison the heart; and in detail they do not know how to ward off the contagion. The sister at first is a little heated, then irritated, and finally revolts and wanders from obedience. The most holy beginnings may end thus unhappily.

"2. These sisters do a great injury to the others; their example is most pernicious. Each one believes herself permitted to form private friendships, which lead farther than they had anticipated. This excites a kind of emulation and opposition of sentiments amongst those who have different attachments. Hence arise those cabals and intrigues which overturn the most regular communities. Besides, it very frequently happens that jealousy springs up between two persons, when they are attached to the same person. Each fears that the other may be preferred to herself. Hence what folly! What loss of time! What disgust for the exercises of an interior life! What fatal abandonment to vanity! What extinction of the spirit of humility and fervor! What trouble and what scandal in these indiscreet attachments!

"Nevertheless, it must be confessed, that communities are very much exposed to this danger, for these friendships are most contagious. From the moment one sister takes this liberty, it is like forbidden fruit which she makes others eat, after having first tasted of it herself. And others do not wish to be deprived of the consolation and support which this sister enjoys, who wishes to love and to be an object of love.

"3. Those sisters do an irreparable injury to the sister whom they love too much. They cause her to enter into herself with complacency, and think of herself in the most flattering phases of self-love. They draw down on her many mortifications on the part of superiors; she afflicts them, and they, in their turn afflict her. They see themselves obliged to distrust her, to suspect her even sometimes of things which she has not done, to watch her every movement, not to believe what she says, to restrain her in many little things which wound her to the heart.

"You who are attached to her, you participate with her in her crosses and your own; between you is formed a dangerous intercourse, for both having your breasts embittered, you convey to each other your bad feelings; you murmur against superiors; you strengthen yourselves by vain pretexts against the simplicity of obedience. Behold a fatal consequence of private feelings!

"One single friendship of this kind is enough to disturb general union: a person loved by another often excites the jealousy and criticism of an entire community. This person is hated, she is contradicted in everything; no one can endure her because her ordinary deportment is haughty and disdainful, or at least, it is cold and indifferent towards those whom she does not like. When we act on the principle of a universal charity, we are universally loved, and we edify every one; when, on the contrary, we are influenced by particular friendships, we wound universal charity by the indifference we testify for some.

"4. In fine this conduct is most hurtful to the person herself. Is this that self-renunciation inculcated by the precept of Jesus Christ? Is this to die to all? Is this to forget self and walk after Jesus Christ? In place of being crucified with Him, we seek alleviation; we allow ourselves to be intoxicated with a foolish attachment; we lose recollection; we no longer relish prayer; we are always eager, restless, fearful, mysterious, and distrustful. The heart is full of what we love, that is the creature, not God. We make of this creature an idol, and we wish to be her idol; it is a perpetual amusement for us.

"Do not say, 'In this friendship I will keep within bounds.' If you presume thus, you are incapable of restraint. How will you restrain yourself in a descent so rapid, since you could not do so before you got into it? Do not flatter yourself then; that tender and affectionate disposition which will not allow you to be without attachment, will not admit of any moderation in those which you form. At first they will appear to you necessary and moderate, but soon you will discover how requisite it is to know how to govern your heart, and to arrest it precisely where you please.

"I conclude by saying, that if you have no particular attachment, you cannot watch too vigilantly over your heart, nor guard it with too much precaution, in order never to let it expand in vain affections, which are always most sad in their consequences. Do not love so much any particular person, but love more all those God commands you to love. Oh! what peace and happiness would you enjoy, if the love of a God so good and powerful would take from you the desire of amusing yourself with the love of creatures who are always imperfect and incapable of satiating the heart.

"But if you are already infected with this disease; if the infatuation of carnal affection occupies you, at least try and cure yourself by degrees; open your eyes; the creature you love is not without defects Has she never given you any occasion of suffering? Turn your affections towards the Sovereign Goodness, from whom you have never received but kindness. Open your heart to the love of order and obedience; relish the pleasure of charity, which embraces every one, and causes no jealousy. Love the work of God, which is the peace and union of the house to which He has called you; if you are under any obligation to a certain sister, acknowledge it gratefully, but not at the expense of hours of silence and regular duties. Love her in God, and for God.

Retrench those indiscreet and murmuring conferences, those vain joys, those frequent breaches of silence; let your friendship be grave, simple, and edifying in everything. Love God, His work, your community, and your salvation, more than the sister of whom there is question."

SECTION IX.—*Of Antipathies—their Source, Dangers, and Remedies.*

Fraternal charity, in order to be preserved in all its purity and integrity, requires not only to be guarded against natural sympathies, which give birth to private friendships, its rivals, but still more against antipathies or aversions, which tend to suppress it in the heart, and to plant in its stead division, discord, and hatred.

We may attribute antipathies to several different sources, of which the principal and most usual are the diversity of tastes, natural defects, imperfections and faults of the neighbour, jealousy, and wounded self-love.

First, diversity of taste. Nothing amongst men is more varied than taste. There exists as many different inclinations as society is composed of members; what is most agreeable to one person, affords but partial pleasure to another, is an object of indifference to a third, and may excite the repugnance or aversion of another. Hence the popular adage, "Every one to his taste." This variety of inclination with regard to things, is not less real in respect to persons; a little reflection will suffice to convince us of this. Now, this diversity and variety of taste is the first source of antipathies, and the first obstacle to that universal charity which should reign in a community; for, if we follow our inclinations, we are drawn towards some and withdrawn from others, we will be kind towards the former, and cold or distant to the latter: in either case charity will be violated.

The second cause of antipathies is natural defects. What variety do we not observe in the gifts of the Creator, in respect to the qualities of body, mind, and heart? These gifts are combined in each in a very different manner, and on account of the great diversity of taste, produce not on all an equal effect; we may safely say, that in general the less the Creator has been lavish to certain persons, and as it were, the more they have been disgraced by nature, the more food do they present for the antipathy of their equals; for man naturally experiences repugnance for whatever is defective.

The third source of antipathies are the spiritual imperfections and defects of our neighbour, unfortunately a most fertile source in man, since so long as he will sojourn in this world, he will be ever subject to them. This principle of antipathy exercises its influence above all on virtuous persons, because having a greater horror of evil, wherever they perceive it, they are led to hate the persons infected with it, and to withdraw from them.

The fourth source of antipathy is jealousy. The love of self, the desire of appearing, of being exalted, of domineering, which is so natural to man, makes us feel a secret sadness in seeing another more esteemed, treated more confidentially, or placed in a more exalted office than we occupy; hence, coldness and aversion arise in the heart for the person whom we regard as a rival; we can hardly look on her with a calm glance, speak to her with confidence, or preserve in our intercourse with her this cordiality, sympathy, and courtesy, which true charity suggests; we have only antipathy for her.

Another source of antipathy is wounded self-love. A sister, perhaps inadvertently, may have wounded us by a sharp word, by haughtiness of manner, or by an unkind refusal; then exasperated feelings cause an irruption in our hearts, extinguish in them every sentiment of benevolence and of charity, and give birth to antipathy.

Who does not see what bitter fruit these fatal and numerous buds may produce in a community, if they are allowed to develope. Father Marin says, "If the religious who is infected with antipathy is of the number of those who live in relaxation, who have no care for their souls, who easily yield to their natural inclination, and the bent of their passions, it will often make her break forth in invectives against the object of her aversion, and the greater her antipathy is, the more frequent and considerable will be these invectives. Owing to her vicious disposition, everything will displease, disgust, and alienate her from the religious against whom she is thus prejudiced; and as she can scarcely restrain herself in her regard, she will find fault with all she does; her words, manners, and even her virtues will disgust her; a kind act or affectionate offer to oblige her will but excite her indignation, and she will only return incivility for the kindness she does her. Thus the more she nourishes her antipathy, the more fatal will it be to her; it resembles an executioner that torments, and a poison that will cause the death of her soul; she will be a brand of discord and confusion in her convent."

But if the religious who feels in herself this bad disposition, be virtuous and attentive to the care of her perfection, and if sincerely desirous of pleasing Jesus Christ, she is grieved to be subject to this temptation; truly we cannot dissimulate how dangerous an enemy it is, against which she should watch incessantly, as it is perpetually close to her, and may injure her very considerably. Let her take care not to be dejected; with the assistance of grace she will be victorious; she can do all in Him who strengthens her, and Who will not permit her to be tempted beyond her strength. If this temptation lead her to great evils, it may also be a subject of merit if she resists it, and what the devil intended should destroy charity in her heart, may serve to make her practise very meritorious acts of virtue. If the religious who is afflicted with these temptations asks us what she is to do, what means she is to make use of to overcome them, we will reply with Father Marin:—

1. She should never let a single word or gesture escape which may denote her antipathy, and when she speaks, or hears others speak of the person against whom she feels it, she must be extremely attentive lest something which savours of this passion may glide into the discourse.

2. Never deliberately indulge any thought which may increase or satisfy your aversion, and if any come into your mind excite in yourself a horror for it, rather cast yourself in spirit at the feet of this religious, interiorly begging her pardon for your want of charity in her regard.

3. If you happen to hear her spoken ill of, or blamed, do not indulge a secret joy, but suppress it as much as you can, and excuse her in your own mind, and to others.

4. Endeavour to form sentiments of meekness in your heart when you think of or meet her.

5. Regulate your exterior conduct so well, that she may not perceive your antipathy. Always speak to her with great gentleness, never complain to others of what displeases you in her, nor let it appear that you can with difficulty bear with her.

6. Try to oblige her on every occasion, and be more attentive to please and gratify her than you would a friend.

7. Surmount your antipathy so far as sometimes to give her exterior marks of particular friendship, and to do so with less difficulty, represent to yourself that it is to Jesus Christ you testify your love, since it is for Him you do it.

8. Do not avoid meeting her, nor occasions of giving her pleasure, or of being with her, or of discoursing with her, at recreation or elsewhere.

9. If you are put into any office with her, do not refuse it, and accept her for a companion, as if Jesus Christ Himself recommended her to you. As you will then be more frequently with her, you will require more than ever to moderate your imperfect feeling, but if you happen to let it appear on any occasion, do not fail to repair it immediately, as well to prevent her from being sad, as to punish in yourself your want of charity, and also to check your aversion. In fine, pray much, pray with profound humility, with entreaty and perseverance, especially at the Meditation and at Holy Communion, to be delivered from this temptation, for it is principally by prayer that this demon is subdued.

SECTION X.—*Of Rash Judgment—How opposed it is to Charity.*

Rash judgment is that by which we hold as certain, and assert that our neighbour is guilty of a fault, of which we are not infallibly sure. There is no fault more usual among persons in whom the spirit of charity is not solidly established. The object of this judgment may be either actions evidently bad in themselves, or those which are susceptible either of a good or bad interpretation, or mere suspicion.

1. Actions evidently bad. We may be guilty of rash judgment relative to such acts, principally in three ways. First, if remembering a fault into which a person has previously fallen, we judge that she is still under the guilt of this fault, or in the habit of it, it is rash judgment; because this fault may have been in her but the effect of fragility, and she may have atoned for it. Secondly, if seeing a sister commit a fault, or even many faults, we conclude that her life is tepid, that she is incorrigible, we are guilty of rash judgment; for these faults may be in her the effect of the violence of a passion under which she groans, and which she combats courageously; it may be, she has done penance for her faults, and by the ardour and fervour of her contrition has obtained pardon from God; charity should lead us to believe this, to pray for her, and to diffide in ourselves; for it is written, " Let him who stands take care lest he fall." If we were tempted so violently, we might not escape without committing more grievous faults. Thirdly, we commit rash judgment, when, beholding some small faults which escape a sister, we conclude that she commits much greater, to which she was formerly subject; because as Bossuet say, although these persons have not become angels, we are not to infer that they are demons, nor that passions domineer over them, because they are not completely overcome.

Rash judgment may have for object, actions susceptible of a good or bad interpretation. A person naturally curious, confident in her own opinion, precipitate in her judgment, is struck by some of these acts of which the nature and principle are doubtful, and admit of a double interpretation; her curiosity and precipitation lead her to suspect evil, and as she never wishes to be deceived, her suspicion is soon changed into a certainty, she pronounces, she judges, and calls conviction what is at best but a conjecture. This is rash jugment.

3. Simple suspicion may be the subject of rash judgment. A sister naturally suspicious will pronounce that her companion, for whom she has no sympathy, and who perhaps occupies an office to which she aspires, is ambitious, jealous, guilty of duplicity, &c. This is rash judgment in a serious matter and without foundation.

What now is the source of these rash judgments? Spiritual writers assign several; the first is pride, which is the root of every sin, and particularly of this. It is clear that she who is guilty of this fault exalts herself above her sisters, cites them to her tribunal, and pronounces on them with the authority of a judge, an act which could only be inspired by presumption and pride. St. Bonaventure remarks that those who believe they excel most in spirituality, are generally more tempted than others to judge their neighbour, and to censure her conduct, because, imagining themselves possessed of greater gifts of God, in place of being more humble on that account, they become more haughty, they regard others with contempt, and censure their conduct.

A second principle of rash judgments, according to St. Thomas, is the innate corruption of the heart, by which, judging the inclinations of others by our own, we easily suppose in others what we feel in ourselves. "*A fool,*" says Ecclesiastes, "*believes all he meets to be fools, as a robber thinks all the world thieves.*" As when we look through a coloured glass, all things appear of the colour of the glass, thus a person with a corrupted heart judges every one by herself; she interprets all for the worst, because she views things through a false medium; and as she has such or such views in what she does, and governs herself by such or such maxims, so she believes that all others govern themselves by the same maxim and principles.

A third source of rash judgment which St. Thomas gives is envy, jealousy, and aversion; for as we believe easily what is pleasing to us, the bad disposition in which we are with regard to our sister, makes us find something defective in all that comes from her, and thus we interpret her actions for the worst.

It seems that it suffices, in order to make the religious understand the grievousness of this fault, to point out its poisoned sources; thus we will add but a few words more to make it be perfectly comprehended. According to theologians and masters of spiritual life, rash judgment is always accompanied with contempt, and it essentially wounds justice.

Rodriguez says, that the great evil of this vice is, that by it we injure the reputation of our sister in our own hearts, and by degrees we despise her within ourselves; in acting thus we do her a serious injury. This fault may be more or less serious, in proportion to the matter upon which we frame our judgments; and as the motives upon which we form them is strong or weak. In order to see in a more clear light the magnitude of this fault, consider how great a sin it would be if you would destroy the reputation of your sister in the mind of another, and by staining her character you would lessen the esteem and affection the other had for her. You injure her not less, when without cause, and without sufficient proof, you conceive a false opinion of her; for it is as necessary for her to preserve her reputation with you as with any one else. Each one may easily judge by herself what prejudice she does thereby to her sister; would you not be offended if any one entertained a bad opinion of you, without having on your part given occasion for her doing so? You offend your sister in the same manner in thinking disadvantageously of her without any legitimate foundation. Judge of another by yourself; and let charity and justice make use of no other rule than this to measure your charity towards your neighbour.

Holy Scripture forbids rash judgment in the most rigorous manner. "Judge not, and you shall not be judged, condemn not, and you shall not be condemned."

We must, however, be guarded against confounding rash judgments with unkind thoughts about our sister, which sometimes attack the most charitable and timorous souls; judgments, to be rash, must have advertence, reflection, and a determined will; otherwise they are but thoughts of surprise, that must be rejected with contempt, and replaced by some charitable thoughts. When we perceive anything really evil or wrong in another, we must attribute it to fragility, and reflect that perhaps were we situated as this person is, we would commit more serious faults, and we must interpret everything in the most favourable light.

Superioresses charged with the government of convents, to maintain them in discipline, to repress any disorders which might glide in, to warn and correct inferiors, not only can, but even ought to examine their conduct, and wisely suspect evil, in order to repress and prevent it; for they are the sentinels of the Lord, obliged to perpetual vigilance, and their eyes ought to be continually open to all that passes.

Still they must only act from a principle of order and charity, they must be on their guard against pride or a spirit of antipathy, and they must always suspend their judgment until they can rest it on a real and solid foundation.

What we say here is equally applicable, first to mistresses of novices; secondly, to mistresses of class, in communities where there are pupils; and thirdly, to all those who are charged with any surveillance relative to those persons whose care or direction is confided to them.

SECTION XI.—*On Silence, which is the Safeguard of the Interior Life.*

Victorious over herself and her passions, solidly established in Christian humility, enriched with the precious gifts of charity, submissive in all to the good pleasure of the will of God, docile to all the movements of grace, the religious soul may safely aspire to the sweet communications of the interior life. God fulfilling His promise has granted her His love; He is come to her, He has made His abode with her, and now He is ready "to speak to her heart." In order to grant her this favour, He exacts but one condition, which is, that she renounces all useless intercourse with creatures, and that in solitude, silence, and recollection, she lends an attentive ear to His voice. "I will lead her into solitude, and there, I will speak to her heart." Thus, all ascetical writers recommend silence to the religious soul, they style it the guardian of an interior life.

Let us listen to their doctrine with regard to the importance and the advantages of this practice, in order to increase the love of it in our hearts. "Whoever does not sin by the tongue is a perfect man."

This oracle of St. James is the foundation of the rule of silence established in religious orders.

St. Jerome assures us, that amongst the ancient fathers of the desert, who kept silence so exactly, there were some who had not spoken for seven years. Spiritual writers rest much on this authority, to demonstrate the excellence and necessity of silence.

Père Marin says, there are three kinds of silence, that of the tongue, mind, and heart; the first, without the two latter, makes a religious silent, but does not suffice to render her interior; to attain this end, she must practise solitude and silence of the mind by the retrenching of vain and superfluous thoughts, and of the heart by renouncing all vain affections.

We break silence not alone by speaking, but also by all unnecessary or loud noise. We should carefully avoid making noise in the places and at the time ordained by the rule of silence. If a sister walk too smartly in a dormitory, if she close the door too quickly, if in her cell she move the chair or table with so much noise as to be heard in the dormitory or next cell, she by all this breaks silence, which is established as much to preserve the tranquillity and recollection of the sisters, as to prevent sins of the tongue.

In every community there are certain hours of the day, specified in the rule, during which silence is to be more strictly observed, because these hours are destined in a particular manner for prayer and recollection. During this time, called the time of the great silence, we ought positively refrain from saying anything that might be deferred to another time. It is a very pious practice, established in regular communities, to employ signs, rather than speak at the time marked by the rule for silence, when there is a necessity of making something known to a sister which could not be deferred without inconvenience.

During the other hours of the day which elapse between this time and that of recreation, silence should also be observed, but in a manner less rigorous; we can then say what is necessary, taking care, however, to do so in a low tone of voice, in order not to disturb recollection.

No practice is more important or more edifying than the faithful observance of the rule of silence in a community. When silence is faithfully observed, each one thinks but of the end for which she left the world and entered religion. To grieve over past faults, to efface them by the tears and austerities of penance; to wage war against the passions, to uproot them, or at least, to bring them into subjection; to form the soul to the sublime virtues of Christianity, to humility, patience, meekness, charity, and the love of God; to lament over her exile and sigh for her heavenly country,—such is the great occupation which serves as food for the mind and heart of the religious. Order, peace, harmony, and union reign everywhere. Entering such a convent, we inhale an odour of sanctity which ravishes, enchants, and forces us in some manner to exclaim with Holy Scripture: "The Lord is truly here! This is the house of God, and the gate of Heaven!"

But when silence is not observed in a convent, dissipation, idleness, the spirit of the world, reports, criticisms, complaints, murmurs, division, and hatred are introduced and propagated most rapidly by the liberty of conversations; we forget the end we have proposed to ourselves in leaving the world; the love of piety vanishes; we fall into relaxation and disgust; we lose our time, and cause others to do the same. One disorder leads to another, and very soon religious discipline is completely overturned; the spirit of piety is extinguished, order and peace disappear; and this establishment, formerly so edifying, now presents no aspect but that of a profane dwelling.

When silence is rigorously observed in a community, we may justly say that piety is honored there, and that fervour reigns; but when it is not observed, and when dissipation has usurped the place of recollection, we have but too many motives to fear that piety and fervour are exiled from this convent. We may make the same observation relative to each religious in particular; if she be faithful to silence, generally speaking, she will be found virtuous and fervent; on the contrary, if she continually allow herself to be dissipated by useless conversations, she has neither piety nor fervour.

Those who devote themselves to spirituality, and converse ordinarily with God, become deaf and dumb for the things of the world, and neither wish to speak of them, nor to hear them spoken of; because they only wish to converse about what they love, any other conversation inspires them with weariness. We experience this sometimes ourselves, when God has replenished us with His grace, and that we are penetrated with devotion. Are we then anxious to speak to any one? Do we turn our eyes from side to side? Do we yield to the impulses of curiosity? Rather, might a person not say, that we were deprived of the use of our senses? And whence comes this? It is because we are occupied in the depth of our soul, conversing with God, and in this state we do not dream of seeking distractions exteriorly.

On the contrary, when we love to speak it is because there is no fervour within, and that we are occupied with nothing spiritual; it is that we seek our consolation in creatures; that we are glad to relieve our hearts of the many thoughts which oppress them; that we take pleasure in speaking of the things we love, or of those we fear. We cannot live without some satisfaction, and when we have not any interiorly with God, we seek it exteriorly from creatures. The reason why in religion so much account is made of the violation of silence, and that it is so severely punished, is, that the fault, though small in itself, is the sure work of a soul little advanced in virtue; and the religious, in accustoming herself to it, shows that she has no love for spirituality, that she has not yet begun to relish God, since she knows not how to converse with Him. When there is no lock to a box, we immediately conclude it contains nothing precious; so when silence does not guard the lips of a religious, we may suspect she has but little virtue.

Let us not fancy that a life of recollection and silence has anything sad or sorrowful in it; it is quite the reverse; for the pious soul it is a life of consolation and sweetness. This life of retreat, in which the soul freely mortifies her tongue and ears, in which she neither wishes to speak nor hear of anything unnecessary, in which, for the love of God she becomes deaf, dumb, and blind, is neither sad nor wearisome; it is infinitely sweet and agreeable, it is so much the more so, as the conversation and society of God, to which it elevates the soul, has a thousand times more attractions than that of men.

The greatest saints, says the author of the Imitation, avoided the company of men as much as they could, and chose to live in secret with God. Retrench useless discourses; shut your ears to the vain noise of the world; leave vain things to vain people. Shut thy door upon thee, and call to thee Jesus thy beloved; stay with Him in thy cell, for thou shalt not find so great peace anywhere else.

In the silence of creatures, says another author, God speaks to the heart; and His word is so marvellous, so sweet and so ravishing, that the soul wishes to hear but Him, until the day when the veils being withrawn she will contemplate Him face to face.

CHAPTER II.

THE PRACTICES OF AN INTERIOR LIFE.

Section I.—*Of Mental Prayer.*

We commonly define prayer to be an elevation of the mind and heart towards God, to render Him our homage, to expose to Him our wants, and to attract on us His blessings. But let us hear what the masters of the spiritual life say on this matter.

Prayer, says Père Nouet, is the work of God and man; of man, who exalts himself to God; of God, who attracts man, who elevates, sustains and unites him to Himself; for as God is the end of prayer, He is also its principle, without whose influence man could not ascend so high; if left to himself, he could not even form a good thought. We will first see what the creature, on her part, does in this holy exercise, then we will see what God contributes to it.

We may say that everything in the creature should unite in order to make prayer well. Her mouth: "I have raised my voice to cry unto the Lord, and He has heard me." Her hands: "I have sought God in the day of my affliction; I have stretched out my hands towards Him, and I have not been deceived." Her eyes: "I have raised my eyes towards Thou, O Lord! who dwelleth in the heavens." However, properly speaking, it is but the soul that prays; for, it is it alone which elevates itself above all that is created, to be united to God as to its end; the body remains in the different postures of respect and devotion that the heart makes it take. The soul alone ascends to God; and for this effect it employs all its powers, memory, understanding, will, and imagination.

The memory works first, and furnishes the understanding with the matter of its discourse and contemplation. The understanding acts conjointly with the imagination, and makes use of what is presented to it, either to know objects, or to form a salutary judgment, or to deduce solid consequences, or, in fine, to attach itself by a simple glance to the centre of its repose. The will follows the understanding, and produces different affections of love and hatred, of grief and joy, of fear and hope, and similar movements which arise from the diversity of the objects which the understanding proposes to it, and which are sometimes stronger, sometimes weaker and more slow, according to the application and disposition of the mind.

The two principal powers which concur in prayer are the understanding and the will, on the good use of which depend all the fruit and success of our communication with God; they have an equal share in this holy exercise, because consideration, which is the work of the understanding, is but a means to excite the affections of the will; and in prayer we pass from affections, which are interior acts of virtue, to the execution of exterior acts, and to the practice of good works. Thus when I consider, in the presence of God, the malignity of vice, I ought not to confine myself to this knowledge, but to conceive a hatred for it in order to shun and avoid it. In the same way, if I consider and represent to myself the perishable goods of this world, it is to despise them; if I meditate on the beauty of virtue, it is to embrace it; if I study the life of Jesus Christ, it is to imitate it; if I contemplate the perfections of God, it is to love Him.

Prayer then is the work of the mind and heart, which are its two principal springs, springs that St. Bernard compares to the two wings of the seraphim, which cannot be separated. It is true, says he, that knowledge elevates the soul, but that alone does not suffice. She who wishes to fly with only one wing, falls as quickly as she ascends; and the more elevated she is, the more dangerous is her fall; for she is doubly culpable who knows what is right, but does not do it. We have now seen what the creature does in prayer, let us consider what God contributes to it.

Although God has given to the creature two powers to raise herself to Him by the way of knowledge and love, it is true that they are both too weak in themselves to raise the soul, if they be not fortified and sustained by the supernatural assistance of the Holy Ghost. The understanding requires light, and the will heat, says Père Alvarez de Paz; we will see how God enlightens the one and inflames the other.

The understanding St. Bernard compares to the eye, which sees nothing without light; but there are two sorts of lights; those which are natural, as the light of reason which increases with age, and that of science and experience, which we acquire by our own reflections and by our industry. The other lights are supernatural, as those of faith, and the gifts of understanding, wisdom, counsel, and knowledge, which come from on high, from the Father of lights.

The first alone do not suffice to make prayer; whether because the truths and mysteries that we consider are above nature, and that human wisdom could not instruct us in them, or because the affections that are elicited in prayer are acts of infused virtues, which at least suppose the lights of faith, without which we could not produce them. It was for this reason that David, who was truly a man of prayer, so repeatedly begs of God to enlighten his understanding, that he may consider the wonders of His law and learn His holy will. "Give me understanding, and I will enter into the secrets of your law." Entreaties such as this, often reiterated, make us see how thoroughly persuaded the Royal Prophet was of the necessity of the divine assistance in order to pray.

But if the divine light is necessary to enlighten the understanding in the exercise of prayer, the fire of the Holy Spirit is still more required to inflame the will, because it is more difficult to love humility, patience, mortification, evangelical poverty, &c., and to form strong resolutions about them, than simply to conceive fine ideas of virtues.

Prayer is then a sublime commerce between God and man; in it the creature raises her understanding, her will, and all her faculties towards God; and God enlightens the understanding by His celestial lights, and inflames her will by charity. It is an exercise of the mind which elevates itself to God, and which mounts, as on a chariot of light and flames, to the throne of His grandeur; the creature cannot go to God without ascending, nor can God come to the creature without descending, because He is infinitely elevated above her. This alone should prove to us the excellence of prayer, which elevates man above all creatures, equals him to the angels, and in some manner makes him like to God Himself. Every time we pray, says St. Chrysostom, we avoid the alliance we have with animals, we are associated to the society of angels; prayer is an angelic action, and to pray is a duty common to us with the angels.

We hold the mid place between corporal creatures and spiritual creatures, we participate in both these extremes, of which one is beneath and the other above us. To eat, drink, sleep, these are the gross actions which are common to us with the brute creation, who are beneath us; when we perform these actions we assimilate ourselves to them in their baseness; but, to aspire after heaven, to reflect on the misery of self, to know the beauty of virtue, to hate vice, to praise and bless the Divine Majesty, to walk in His presence, these are spiritual actions, proper to the angels who are exalted above us; when we perform them we elevate ourselves to the condition of the blessed spirits, and we become their equals.

St. Gregory of Nyssa calls prayer an equal honor with the angels, and St. John Climacus styles it the occupation of the angels, the employment of the Seraphim, the world of those blessed spirits whose life is an uninterrupted contemplation of the Divine Essence.

SECTION II.—*Prayer is the first and most important Exercise of the Religious Life.*

A soul is touched by grace, she renounces all perishable goods, honors, and frivolous pleasures; she withdraws from the tumult of the world, and seeks a retreat in the solitude of the cloister. And why? What end does she propose to herself? Ah, she has understood the truth of this oracle of our Saviour, "One thing alone is necessary." She wishes to be occupied with this one thing alone; she thinks exclusively of her salvation, of eternity, and treats of it familiarly with God alone. And where is she thus occupied? In meditation, in prayer; for to meditate, to pray, is to be occupied with her salvation, with eternity; it is to treat of it with God. In the retreat into which she is retired, in some sort buried, prayer ought to be her first, her principal, I will say almost her only occupation, all other employments should be subservient to it; in devoting herself to them she ought never to lose sight of it, which is the only end of all her labours and sacrifices; like the saints she should make it her study, day and night, or, at least, she should consecrate, with the greatest fervour, to this holy exercise the time appointed by the rule. To spend in tepidity these precious moments would be to forget her pious designs; to abandon this holy exercise would be to look back and to be guilty of apostacy.

Prayer is the nourishment of the soul, and the only means of arriving at a spiritual life. Prayer, says Fenelon, is like the stomach, just as from it we derive the flesh, blood, and strength for the limbs, hands, arms, and feet, so, in prayer, love vivifies the vital spirit of the soul, it gives that patience, meekness, humility, charity, disinterestedness, sincerity, and, in fact, all virtues, inasmuch as we require them to repair our daily strength. If you apply merely to virtues exteriorly, you form but a constrained outline, but a superficial plan, but a heap of legal and judaical works, but an inanimate body, it is a whitened sepulchre; the exterior is a decoration of marble where all the virtues are in bas-relief, but within there are but dead bones; the interior is without life, all is skeleton, all is dried up, for want of the unction of the Holy Ghost. We cannot expect to plant love in the heart by a multitude of exterior practices, performed scrupulously; on the contrary, the interior principle of love cultivated by prayer at certain hours, and maintained by the familiar presence of God during the day, diffuses nourishment from the centre to the exterior members, and makes the soul exercise with simplicity, on each occasion, the virtue suitable to the moment.

Rodriguez confirms this truth, and adds, that prayer is the support and sustenance of every virtue.

Prayer, says he, is to the soul what natural heat is to the body. And as without heat it is impossible that food should do a person any good, or even that she should be able to live, so by means of heat she converts it into good juice and nourishment, which dispenses itself throughout the whole body to furnish each part with sufficient strength to perform its functions. In like manner our spiritual life cannot subsist without prayer, for it is prayer that gives us strength to fulfil all the obligations of our profession, and to profit, as we should do, of even the most troublesome events; it is this that makes us easily bear all injuries and hardships, and makes them become easy and supportable, so that there is nothing can happen to a soul of which it will not make its profit and advantage. In fine, if we make good use of prayer we shall find therein a remedy for all our faults, and an assured help and means to maintain ourselves in the vigor and purity of religion. For if, perhaps, you have not been faithful in the observance of your rules, if you have given yourself too much liberty in anything, or, in fine, if you feel some passions which were before in a manner asleep that begin to awake anew in you, have recourse presently to prayer, and, by the grace of God, you will find in it a speedy and efficacious remedy for all things. But if you should fall into remissness and tepidity during your prayer it is still to prayer that you must have recourse; for it is this that will restore you that first state of fervor in which you were before. For prayer has proper remedies for all evils, and even for those faults that are committed in it. It is a very appropriate comparison to say, that prayer is to the soul and to the spiritual life, what the hand is to the body. The hand serves for an instrument and help to the whole body in general, and to itself in particular; it labors for nourishment, clothing, and all the other necessities of the body; it also labors for itself. If the hand be wounded it is the hand that dresses it; if the hand be soiled it is the hand that washes it, and if the hand be cold it is the hand that warms it again; in fine, the hand does everything for the human body. It is the same of prayer with regard to the soul, it is it that provides for all its wants, and remedies all its evils.

SECTION III.—*Mental Prayer is an Exercise easy and natural to the Creature.*

It is not unusual to find persons who persuade themselves that there is nothing more difficult, nothing which exacts more application and greater efforts than meditation, and that to apply successfully to it you must torture mind and heart; they regard it as the fruit and recompense of long and painful labors, and they imagine that it can only be the portion of those who are consummated in sanctity. This is an error; for meditation is an exercise which is natural to the soul, it is an exercise to which those who have only taken the first steps in a spiritual life can apply, as well as those who have attained sanctity.

To meditate, according to the general acceptation of the word, is to think, to reflect, to wish, to love.

We continually produce these acts, and, consequently, meditate incessantly on some subject; thus, he who cultivates the earth meditates on his land and on the means of obtaining an abundant harvest, which he loves as a good, which he desires, and which he wishes to obtain; the artisan meditates on his art, and on the manner of becoming perfect in it, that he may conciliate the esteem and confidence of those to whom his industry may be useful; the merchant meditates on commerce, and is continually engaged in new speculations; the physician meditates on the art of curing; the warrior on the art of gaining battles; the lawyer on the law; in a word, there is no one who does not meditate, either in a manner more or less serious, on the things of earth, and who does not know how to converse of them with his equals.

Now, she who aspires to Christian perfection has only to change the object; in place of the creature, of earth, of perishable goods, she has only to substitute the Creator, heaven, and imperishable goods, and to make them the subject of her thoughts, her reflections, her love and her desires; in place of conversing with the creature of terrestrial things, she has only to converse with the Creator of eternal things, and behold she has arrived at this end which appeared to her so difficult to attain, meditation taken in its real acceptation.

It is a great error, says Père Guilloré, to think that meditation is only intended for learned and talented persons; all are called to meditate, the ignorant even more than the learned, because God communicates himself more easily to the simple and lowly.

To meditate, it suffices to be well penetrated with our wants and miseries, and to think as seriously of our salvation as of our temporal affairs.

Souls advanced in virtue will do well to follow the attractions of grace, and to abandon themselves to the movements of the Holy Spirit in their meditations; those who are less advanced may read a subject of meditation, may stop at what touches them most, may take up or leave aside the book, as they are more or less distracted; as to those who are only novices in this exercise, we propose to them the following method, recommended by Bellicius:—

All do not sufficiently possess the science of meditation, or rather they are not always disposed to make it. This is why St. Ignatius, who desires to render this exercise useful at all times and to all the faithful, proposes three methods of prayer suited to the dispositions and capacity of those who are only beginners in this holy exercise.

The first method is less a prayer than a spiritual exercise, in which we reflect in a manner more practical than speculative, upon the commandments of God or of His Church, upon the seven capital sins, upon the three powers of the soul, and the five senses of the body. Going over the commandments, one after another, we should reflect upon them, and take notice how we have observed or violated them. In the same manner the capital sins, we may reflect how much and how often we yielded to them; we may consider with respect to the powers of the soul and the senses of the body, how far we have abused them. It will be sufficient to remain on each of these points as long as it would require to say a *Pater noster*.

In the commandments we consider:—First, the commandment in itself; how good it is, how just and holy. Second, how advantageous is the observance of it. Third, how we have hitherto observed it. With regard to sins, we examine what malice each one in particular contains, and with how much reason it is forbidden. Second, how fatal sin is in its effects. Passing in review the powers of the soul and the senses of the body, we may reflect:—First, how noble each one is, and how advantageous to us. Second, for what end we have received them. Third, what use we have made of them. To conclude this exercise, we ought to testify our gratitude to God, to form a good resolution, and beg the grace to accomplish it.

This manner of making prayer differs from examen, in this, that in prayer we must not descend to a minute research of our particular sins, since our intention is not then so much to examine our conscience, as to seek to know what is commanded or forbidden, in order afterwards to make a general reflection on ourselves. We are only to stop a short time at those commandments we transgress rarely or ever, and to insist more upon those we are on which in the habit of infringing more frequently.

The second manner of prayer consists in stopping at the words and sense of a psalm or of some verse of Scripture, or some prayer, as the Lord's prayer, the Angelical Salutation, in order to discover the spiritual signification, continuing to meditate on each phrase or expression as long as we find sufficient matter to nourish the soul.

This last manner of prayer differs from the former:—First, with regard to the matter; in the preceding the subject is generally such things as are commanded or forbidden; in this, on the contrary, we meditate on some prayer, some pious maxim, or some of the truths of faith. Secondly, with respect to the end; for the first method is not limited to a single speculation, but it passes to the practice, since it tends, according to our wants, to the reformation of our conduct. The second method has a speculative end; we propose to ourselves the spiritual signification of what we meditate. If a few expressions of the prayer on which we meditate furnish an abundance of reflections, accompanied by an interior unction, we must remain there, but without being anxious to pass further, and after the time of meditation has elapsed, it suffices to recite the remainder of the prayer.

The third manner of making prayer is the same as the second, but that we insist less on the same reflection, and that we allow between each word but the interval of a respiration. Thus, we should only remain a short instant at each word of our prayer, in place of meditating on it as long as we discover some signification or pious sentiment in it.

This third method only differs from the second in being a shorter manner of meditation, and even as short as possible on the sense contained in the words, and is the test of the prayer, whilst the second manner supposes a more prolonged meditation on the sense of the words. To conclude, the first manner of prayer belongs to the examen; the third is more simple, it is properly neither a meditation nor an examen: it may be useful to accustom a person to contract the habit of making vocal prayer with attention and suitable devotion.

SECTION IV.—*An abridged Method for making Mental Prayer.*

There are in Prayer three parts: the Preparation; the Substance of the Prayer; and the Conclusion.

First Part of Prayer—The Preparation.

The preparation contains three acts. First, we must place ourselves in the presence of God by an act of lively faith, firmly believing that God is everywhere present, that He is in the place where we are, and even in our hearts; which should make us adore Him, and hold ourselves in respect before His Divine Majesty.

Second. We should acknowledge ourselves unworthy of appearing before God, on account of our sins, beg His pardon by an act of sincere contrition, unite ourselves to Jesus Christ to appear more worthily before His Father, and to pray in His Name.

Third. We should acknowledge that of ourselves we are incapable of making prayer, and beg the light of the Holy Ghost to make it well.

Second Part—The Substance of Prayer.

The body of prayer is divided into three points. In the first point, we are to consider the subject of prayer in God or in the person of our Lord, paying particular attention to what He has said, done, or thought on this subject, we are then to render Him our homages of adoration, praise, love, and thanksgiving, to which we may occasionally add acts of admiration, joy, and compassion.

In the second point, we are to consider, with regard to the subject we have selected, what we are to do or avoid for our sanctification, and to excite ourselves to this by the most pressing motives. Afterwards we are to reflect on ourselves, to discover if heretofore we have been faithful; if we find we have failed we are to humble ourselves and make an act of contrition; then earnestly beg of God, through the intercession of the most Holy Virgin and the Saints, the grace of fidelity in future.

In the third point, we ought, in order to cooperate with the grace we have asked of God, form good resolutions conformable to the subject and to our present necessities. These resolutions should be not alone general, but also particular, and suited to our present wants; they should be efficacious, and lead us to adopt the means to overcome every obstacle. Our resolutions must be accompanied with great distrust in self, and great confidence in God.

The Third Part of Prayer—The Conclusion.

The conclusion of prayer has also three parts. First. To thank God for the grace we received in prayer. Second. To ask pardon for the faults we have committed in it. Third. To beseech Him to bless our resolutions, our entire being, our life and death.

We must then form the spiritual bouquet, which is nothing more than to select some of the good thoughts or holy affections, which have touched us particularly, in order to call them to mind from time to time during the day. We may then conclude by placing our resolutions and the fruit of our prayer under the protection of the Blessed Virgin, and recite for this intention the *Sub tuum præsidium*.

This method of prayer may be reduced to a few words, in which it is all comprised.

I. *Preparation.*—1st. Presence of God. 2nd. Act of Contrition. 3rd. Invocation of the Holy Ghost.

II. *Body of Prayer.*—1st. Considerations. 2nd. Affections and supplications. 3rd. Reflection on the past, examen of the present, and resolutions for the future.

III. *Conclusion.*—1st. Acts of Thanksgiving. 2nd. Of Repentance. 3rd. Prayer to our Lord, the Blessed Virgin, and Saints. 4th. Selection of a pious affection.

SECTION V.—*Some Hints taken from spiritual Writers in order to make Mental Prayer profitable.*

First. To consider attentively what will strongly excite the will, for, as Rodriguez says, " If we are not well penetrated with the importance of virtue, and the spiritual good we may derive from it, if we are not well persuaded of the necessity we have of acquiring it, we cannot ask for it with the requisite fervour and earnestness; and it is ordinarily from this defect that arise that tepidity and inactivity in which so many persons pass the hour of prayer. On the other hand, we must be on our guard not to spend the whole time in reasoning and reflecting, we ought only do so as long as is necessary to excite the heart and move the will.

Second. To make the will act in unbosoming our heart in the heart of God, in adoring Him, in testifying to Him our confidence and love, in asking Him with a filial confidence the spiritual good we require and in begging Him to cure the infirmities we have discovered in our souls; this is the most important part of prayer, and here we must long remain.

Third. When a sweet calm seizes the soul and fixes its powers in a kind of immobility, we must not interrupt this holy repose by our own action. ‘God asks nothing more of those He places in this disposition, than attention to the inspirations of the Holy Spirit. Père Surin says that many fail in this point, because fearing sloth, they use many movements, which, casting the soul into trouble, prevent them from enjoying God and receiving the operation of His grace.

We do not mean to exclude that action which does not trouble the repose into which God leads the soul, but only that which is incompatible with the tranquillity of this repose. When then the soul perceives that her action and efforts embarrass in place of assisting her, she should cease them, and only act as much as is necessary to co-operate with grace. This co-operation very frequently consists in a peaceful enjoyment of God, and those persons are very much deceived who look on this disposition as idleness.

Fourth. We should never go to prayer, says Père Guilloré, with a mind flying for enjoyment; this is a motive too sensual and interested; we should go to it to please God without seeking our own satisfaction. A truly upright soul never seeks herself in prayer, her only desire is that God may be glorified by her annihilation. It may even happen that the less sweetness she experiences in prayer, and the more she feels God has deprived her of His consolations, the more she rejoices, because she feels that this substraction of graces causes them to return to their true source which is God.

Fifth. This same Father considers, that when grace does not otherwise attract the soul, it is a very profitable manner of prayer to accustom ourselves to make it in form of examen; that is to make serious reflections on ourselves and the movements of our hearts, to see how we act and how we should act; presenting ourselves thus before God as our Judge. He will be more favourable to us when the time of judging comes. Several souls for want of acting thus remain in a deplorable ignorance of themselves, and with passions as strong and active after years of prayer, as they were in the beginning.

Sixth, never adhere scrupulously to the subjects you have prepared, nor to any particular method, but allow yourself to be guided by the attractions of grace, according as you will feel them in your soul. If you act otherwise, you resist the Holy Ghost and confide in your own resources. Obey, then, the sweetness of His operations, and although they do not appear to your mind as distinct and well arranged as are the points of your meditation, do not for that reason imagine you lose your time. They speak to the soul in an efficacious manner, and produce in it other effects; besides, there is no greater glory for the soul than to know how to follow the attraction of God. You must not then be the slave of your points and methods in prayer, but follow with great liberty all the impressions of the Holy Spirit.

It may often occur that all the preparations you have made will make no impression on your heart, and that grace will not affect you particularly; have always in reserve some subjects conformable to the state of your soul, which may serve as a refuge in the time of desolation; you will do so partly to console yourself in your trial, and in order that you may not lose your time. Without this precaution, you will incur the danger of passing your prayer in great pain, and very uselessly.

Seventh. However, if all these subjects of reserve and refuge make no more impression on your soul than those you had prepared, I give you the following advice, in order to derive at least some profit from your prayer :—Not knowing what to do in the midst of your aridity, never fail to place your soul in one of the four positions I am going to indicate, or in all four successively as you may require. Those four positions are of adoration, annihilation, silence, abandonment. This occupation, besides being most fruitful, will be not less useful to you than worthy of God.

Give to your soul interiorly a position of the most

profound adoration; and in order to sustain yourself in this position, look on God as the author of your being, to whom you render this tribute and this homage, humbly acknowledging that He alone is, and that He alone merits to be, and that everything in existence is but a small emanation flowing from Him as from its source.

Annihilate yourself profoundly, seek your own nothingness in the depth of your being, remain there lost to your own eyes; and to vivify this posture, contemplate the greatness of God, before whom all is as nothing, and before whom you willingly confess your annihilation, saying as it were, Oh! how great is God! what a poor and contemptible nothing I am!

Again, hold yourself interiorly in a profound silence; do not permit your heart nor the powers of your soul to be disturbed by any operation. Act thus from a deep conviction of the exalted majesty of God in whose presence you are. What can a worm of the earth say in presence of so great a Being? You may think that you can have no language more worthy of God than a respectful silence, as much on account of your own baseness, as of the exalted majesty of the Being before whom you are.

In fine, abandon yourself freely to God, and to all the trials to which He may please subject you. Do this from the consideration of the great and supreme dominion of God, to whom all creatures should be blindly submissive, and from whom they should be ready to receive annihilation when it may please Him and as it may please Him.

These are the four positions which I would wish you to render familiar to yourself in the time of prayer, and with which all will go on well, no matter in what disposition you may be, either from disgust for the subjects prepared, or from a subtraction of sensible favors.

SECTION VI.—*Of Distractions in Prayer.*

There is nothing more common than to meet persons sad, afflicted, and even discouraged, on account of the distractions they experience during the precious time they devote to prayer. We will first examine what are the ordinary sources of these deplorable wanderings of the mind, then we will give some consolation and advice to those who experience them.

Distractions may arise from three principal sources; from negligence, from the malice of the demon, and from the natural weakness of the creature.

First, from negligence. When, during entire days, we allow ourselves to be voluntarily dissipated by a multiplicity of unprofitable occupations and thoughts, neither watching our heart nor our senses, it is useless to inquire whence arise our distractions in prayer, and the pain we feel in applying to it; for it is certain, that the images of those objects which have made an impression on the mind and heart, will not fail to disturb and besiege us during the time we wish to consecrate to this holy exercise; they are the punishment of our negligence and infidelity.

Second, from the malice of the demon. As this cruel enemy, says St. Basil, sees that prayer is the means by which God replenishes us with all sorts of blessings, he tries by all means to withdraw us from this exercise, in raising up a thousand obstacles, in order that, being deprived of this assistance, he may more easily find access into our souls. He does the same against us as Holophernes did against the city of Bethulia, when, in order to facilitate the taking of it, he destroyed the aqueduct with which the city was supplied with water; prayer is the aqueduct or channel through which our soul receives the waters of grace, and the devil uses his utmost endeavours to break it, and render it useless. St. John Climacus says that when, at the sound of the bell, the faithful and religious assemble visibly to praise and bless God, our enemies assemble invisibly to tempt us and divert us from this holy exercise.

The devil, says the Abbot Uilus, suffers patiently other good works, as fasting, taking the discipline, wearing the hair cloth; but he cannot suffer us to be a moment in prayer, without using every endeavour to disturb and distract us. Hence it is, that when we apply to this holy exercise, a thousand distractions pour in upon us, and we are usually more tempted than at any other time; bad thoughts come in crowds, as if we were there only to be tempted; then the devil presents to our minds strange and fantastical images which he seems to have reserved for this time. St. Thomas and many other spiritual writers say, that it is on account of this persecution, set on foot by the spirit of darkness against those who pray, that the Church, directed by the Holy Ghost, ordains that we should commence all canonical hours with this verse: "O God incline to mine aid, O Lord make haste to help me." Words by which we implore the assistance of God against the temptations and snares of the enemy.

Third. From the natural weakness of the creature, for sin has rendered man so weak and miserable, and our imagination chiefly partakes so much of the corruption of our nature, that we cannot be a moment in prayer without having our mind continually carried away by the material things which strike our senses.

When our distractions arise from dissipation, from negligence during the day in guarding our hearts and senses, they are wilful in their source, and are imputable to us; but when they proceed from the malice of the devil, or from our own natural weakness, and that we regret them, humble ourselves for them and combat them, they will not be imputed to us; on the contrary, they are meritorious, for each act of humility that we will practise on these occasions, each effort that we will make to recall our thoughts, and to banish the distractions that importune us, is an act of fidelity of which God is a witness; it is a decided preference that we give Him over the exterior objects which seek to rob Him of our thoughts and affections; it is a victory we obtain over our enemies, a victory already inscribed in heaven.

God, in this case, is not offended with our distractions, He has compassion on us, even as " a father has pity on his children, so has He compassion on those who fear Him, because He knows of what slime He has formed us." He knows our infirmity and weakness. As a father, who has an idiot son, is touched with compassion when in the midst of his discourse he breaks forth into a thousand incoherent expressions, in the same way our heavenly Father has pity on us, when, conversing with Him, He perceives that from our natural weakness, or the temptations of the enemy, our mind wanders in vain and ridiculous thoughts. Our prayer is not less meritorious in His sight, on the contrary, what we suffer in prayer for love of Him makes it more meritorious and agreeable to Him than if we had been inundated with sensible consolations. And as the nourishment, taken by an invalid, fails not to strengthen and fortify her, although she may take it with pain and disgust, and cannot perceive the benefit she derives from it, so, in the same way, prayer fails not to nourish the soul, and to give it new strength to serve God, although we find but difficulties and aridities in the time we devote to it, and we feel as if we received no benefit from it.

It is then a great error to leave off prayer on account of the thoughts and temptations with which we are importuned. However, we must take care not to fall into tepidity and relaxation under pretexts of natural weakness, and allow our mind and imagination to rove uncontrolled from object to object. We must, like Abraham, take care to chase away the birds of prey that descend on the sacrifice, that is to say, we must apply ourselves to banish all thoughts which may trouble our prayer; provided we do all in our power, we need not be troubled.

SECTION VII.—*Of the Void and Insensibility we sometimes experience in Prayer.*

Père Guilloré says, there is nothing more usual, in the spiritual life, than these trials in prayer; nevertheless, there is no point almost turned to less account, and which is less understood. With this learned Father we will consider:—1st. The criminal cause of these trials. 2nd. Their sanctifying cause. 3rd. Their excellence. 4th. The conduct we should pursue when we experience them.

First. Of the criminal cause of the void and insensibility we feel in prayer. We must not be astonished to hear so many persons complain of being quite destitute of good thoughts in prayer: they come to this holy exercise without any preparation, and they find in it what they have brought to it, a barren and fruitless soil; thus is their negligence punished. Others do not fail preparing the subject of their meditation; but they wish that when they present themselves in prayer with this subject that all should succeed according to their desires; they expect to arrive at the wished-for end without labour or trouble. Yet God demands that besides preparing the subject, we add application of the mind and considerations. The void of their souls is the punishment of their tepidity and laziness. In fine, there are other souls who neither fail in preparation or application, but whose levity of mind does not permit them to rest on any particular subject; they rove about from point to point without finding anything to rest on or replenish them. Their aridity is the punishment of their inconstancy.

As to insensibility, it proceeds frequently: First. From the immortification of the senses, to which we deny none of those satisfactions and pleasures which they demand. Secondly. From the culpable affections which we allow to enter our hearts, which divide, enslave, and corrupt them, and render them insensible to heavenly consolations. We may be exempt from the preceding defects, but perhaps we may bring to prayer too ardent a desire of enjoying God. He refuses Himself to those who wish to taste Him with sensual ardor. Besides, the natural efforts we make to arrive at this end embarrass and harden the soul, rather than attract consolation.

To remedy the criminal cause of this aridity in prayer, it is necessary to prepare carefully the subject of meditation; to apply to it with zeal and perseverance, to mortify assiduously the senses, to keep the heart free from all terrestrial affections, to be guarded against desiring too ardently spiritual consolations.

Second. The sanctifying cause of aridity in prayer. It may occur that the soul the most faithful, and the most attentive in avoiding the preceding faults, experiences this same aridity which weighs so justly on the unfaithful soul. This conduct of God towards the faithful is one of mercy and tenderness; by it He purifies her and raises her to high perfection. By this void and aridity, He punishes and destroys in her that unbounded thirst, which she brings to prayer, for spiritual things; He crushes in her that immoderate desire of knowing, understanding, and penetrating into the things of God, and the sublime paths of prayer; He veils Himself from her sight, and leaves her in extreme poverty; by this means He tempers her ardor, and teaches her to seek Him more peacefully, with more uprightness and perseverance. God leaves this soul in aridity to punish her and to moderate the avidity with which she desires and relishes spiritual consolations. He teaches her to seek Him and not His gifts; to seek Him in darkness as well as in light; in sadness as in joy; by the painful way of the Cross, and even in the bitterness of Calvary, as well as by the sweet and pleasant road of Thabor. He wishes to accustom her to seek her sanctification and perfection, not joys and spiritual consolations.

Third. Excellence of the aridity which the faithful soul feels in prayer. Many allow themselves to be dejected and discouraged, when during prayer they feel this void and aridity; they imagine God has left and abandoned them, and that it would be better for them to give up the exercise of prayer. This is a most dangerous error.

When God operates in the soul by a general subtraction of all His favours, it is because he wishes to substitute Himself in their stead; it is He Himself who desires to replenish the great void, for it is certain that God is in all His plenitude in a soul, whence everything created is banished. Emptiness and nothing, are they not well replaced by the substitution of a God, and is it reasonable for the soul to be disquieted?

This aridity establishes the soul in the most perfect purity, the most complete disengagement, and conducts her to the consummation of happiness, which is intimate union with God. In fine, this aridity and annihilation in prayer eminently includes the exercise of every virtue. Patience is practised, for assuredly there is much to suffer where there is nothing to relish. The fidelity of the soul shines forth, in not for one moment abandoning prayer, nor the most respectful attitude it can assume, although it may be abandoned as a vile wretch. Faith is there conspicuous, because in this nothingness and deep void, you see that God regards you and operates in your soul marvels of grace. In a word the high esteem you have of God appears prominently, for you seek Him, though at the loss of everything imaginable.

Fourth, what line of conduct we are to pursue when we experience this dryness in prayer. The soul having first used all reasonable care to retrench the culpable causes of this dryness and insensibility, being besides convinced how useful and excellent this state is, ought, as far as possible, be occupied only with one subject. If she cannot do so, she ought to enter peacefully into herself, and repose there as God wishes it. Her impotence will clearly demonstrate to her that God desires her to be in this state. She should be faithful and firm in not quitting the sanctuary of her own interior, and in not leaving off prayer through *ennui* or disgust. She must excite herself to love her spiritual poverty, remaining divested of all before God, as a modest and timid pauper in the presence of a rich man; she says not a word, but exposes her misery, and tries to excite His compassion.

We will conclude this subject by a few words from the wise and learned Fénelon: "When," says he, "you are in consolation and fervour, count then as nothing the good works which flow from this source; when, on the other hand, you feel dryness, darkness, poverty, and almost an interior impotence, remain a little under the hand of God in a state of naked faith; acknowledge your misery, turn towards your Omnipotent Lover, and never distrust His assistance. Ah! how delightful it is to be despoiled of that sensible support which flatters self-love, and to be constrained to acknowledge the truth of these words of the Holy Ghost—'Nothing living will be justified before me.'

"Advance always in the name of God, although it may seem to you you have not strength to put one foot before the other. It is so much the better that human courage fails you; abandonment to God will strengthen you in your weakness. St. Paul exclaims, 'When I am weak, I am strong.' And when he asks to be delivered from his weakness, God replies to him, 'Virtue is perfected in infirmity.' Allow yourself, then, to be perfected by the experience of your imperfection, and by humble recourse to Him who is the strength of the weak."

SECTION VIII.—*Of Different Kinds of Prayer.*

There are, says Rodriguez, two kinds of prayer; one common and easy, the other extraordinary and sublime, and which is formed in us by the Holy Ghost.

Common prayer or meditation is that of which we have spoken, and for which we have given some rules, and in which the three powers of the soul, the memory, understanding, and will, act alternately. St. Teresa, in speaking of this kind of prayer, compares those who practise it to a gardener, who with much trouble draws water from a well to irrigate his garden and make the flowers grow. The garden, according to her idea, is the heart, the flowers are virtues, the well is meditation, and the water we draw is light and grace. It is by means of the memory, understanding, and will that we draw the water.

This prayer is the surest and least subject to error; and Rodriguez urges the soul to remain faithful to it until God comes and says to her as to the guest in the Gospel: "Friend, ascend higher;" and why? Because the second sort of prayer, extraordinary prayer, is a particular gift of God—a gift which He bestows on whom He pleases, and as He pleases, and to which we could not pretend without much pride and rashness.

St. Bernard, writing on these words of the Canticles, "Our bed is all covered with flowers," says, " your bed, which is your heart, is still sullied; it is still infected with the corrupted odour of the vices and bad habits you have brought from the world; and, notwithstanding, you have the boldness to invite the Spouse to come and repose there. You presume to raise yourself to contemplation and to the most sublime exercises of union with God, as if you had acquired the highest degree of Christian perfection. Think beforehand of purifying the bed of your heart with your tears—' Every night I will wash my bed, and water my couch with my tears '—adorn it with the flowers of virtue, and then you may, with the spouse, invite the Beloved to come and repose in it.

"Be occupied with embracing His feet, in humble repentance for your faults; in embracing His hands, in offering Him all the good you do, and in trying to receive from Him the grace of solid and true virtues; but as to the kiss of the mouth, as to this union so sublime and so perfect, wait, wait until it pleases God to elevate you to it."

An ancient religious, distinguished for piety and well versed in spirituality, remained twenty years in the exercises of the purgative life; and we, hardly have we commenced than we grow weary immediately, and wish to pass to the exercises of the love of God. The foundations must be deep and solid on which we pretend to raise so high an edifice.

What is peculiar to this exercise of the purgative way is, that besides the many advantages and benefits we derive from it, there is no more specific remedy nor better preservative to hinder us from falling into sin; she who is continually occupied in detesting sin, who, at every moment conceives a holy confusion for those she commits, who maintains herself in an abiding sorrow for having offended God, is far removed from offending Him anew. The saints, on the contrary, observe that the fall of several, who appeared very much devoted to a spiritual life and to contemplation, may be attributed to this want of self-reflection. By dint of applying themselves to the more sublime states which pleased them, they have completely laid aside the knowledge of themselves, and the consideration of their sins. The confidence they had in their own strength accustoming them not to be so much on their guard as they should have been, they have fallen into the most lamentable disorders. This is the reason that we must ever be occupied in prayer, in lamenting our faults, and this must be our exercise until our Lord stretching out His hand, says to us, " Friend, ascend higher."

But as it sometimes pleases God to call souls to sublime and extraordinary prayer, in a few words we will give an idea of it.

Holy Writ teaches us in the following words what this prayer is:—" If the Lord wishes, He will replenish her with the spirit of intelligence. Words of wisdom will come from her mouth as rain, and in her prayer she will bless the Lord." If God wishes, during your prayer, He will send a ray of His light from heaven, which, like a bright flash, will strike the eyes of your understanding; then, in a moment, you will fully comprehend what before was hidden and obscure, and the Scripture calls this the spirit of intelligence. When it pleases God to raise the soul to this state, she is never weary of contemplating Him, and without using any reasoning or experiencing any *ennui*, she keeps her sight ever upon Him. Then the soul being replenished and transported, establishes a divine conversation with God, and ravished in delight, speaks to Him, heart to heart.

Thus, in this second kind of prayer, the soul, according to St. Teresa, can no longer be compared to the gardener who with much difficulty carries the water necessary to fertilize his garden; but to him, who, with crossed arms, sees the rain fall from heaven and water his garden, without having anything to do but to allow it to fall, or at most to give it an incli-

L

nation towards the roots of his trees, to render them more fruitful.

Those who are called to this kind of prayer should above all be on their guard against vain-complacency, self-love and pride, otherwise they would be exposed to serious danger, for God takes delight in exalting the humble, whilst he abandons and humbles the proud.

St. Bernard, St. Teresa, and several other saints and doctors, distinguish in extraordinary prayer many degrees. We will confine ourselves to what we have said, without following them in their extraordinary paths, the limits we have prescribed to ourselves not permitting it.

CHAPTER III.

OF THE DIVINE OFFICE.

SECTION I.—*Definition and Origin of the Divine Office.*

PRAYER which supposes a feeling conviction of our wants, and a perfect confidence in Him who can relieve them, is so essential to religion, that Collet says, we may regard as false religious, those to whom the spirit of prayer is foreign. The great Legislator of the Chosen Nation, founded on the model of the just who preceded him, knew well the value of this holy exercise. He made use of it even against God Himself, and by it more than once he appeased His anger, which was ready to burst forth. David was only an accomplished prince because he knew how to offer to the Most High vows worthy of Him. The sacred fire which burned in his heart during his meditation, even yet inflames with its light and heat those who study his canticles. Prayer, to which he returned seven times daily, was not enough for his ardour; he rose again at midnight to publish the greatness of his Master, and he did so but to render Him attentive to his wants and lamentations. Solomon walked in the footsteps of his father; the days in which he humbled himself in prayer were those of his glory; and it was only because, when near the term of his career, he had the misfortune to abandon this exercise, that his salvation has become a problem as fearful as it is impossible to resolve. Daniel prayed three times a-day; Esdras four times. And who can doubt but that those prayers, of which the Sacred Text has preserved the remembrance, were not multiplied to infinity.

The Son of God, who was to form a nation of adorers in spirit and truth, taught His followers, by His example and His words, the great art of prayer. Their fall, at a time when they flattered themselves as being possessed of an unshrinking fidelity, was for them a touching lesson of the necessity all Christians are under, of joining prayer to vigilance; they did not delay making use of it. It was by unanimous and interrupted prayer that they disposed themselves to receive the Holy Ghost, and they taught others what they themselves had learned from their Divine Master. The precious memorials which now remain to us of them, almost all terminate in love, and in the prayer which obtained it. This fertile seed budded and produced the hundred-fold amongst the first faithful; and when the fury of tyrants prevented their having temples, they knew how to form them on the sea and land, in deserts and plains, and even in the prisons in which Nero and Domitian enchained them.

Their prayer, like their faith, was announced throughout the universe; friends, enemies, all concurred in publishing it. Tertullian, in his Apology, celebrated those of their assemblies which preceded the aurora of morning. Celsus, the philosopher, made a crime of their prayer; Pliny the younger informed the emperors of it.

But although the life of the primitive Christians was a continual prayer, yet, nevertheless, there were times more especially devoted to it; St. Basil, St. Jerome, St. Ambrose allude to the seven hours now called canonical. Cassian, after having said that the monks of Egypt and Thebais, except on Sundays, were assembled but at eve and night to chaunt together the praises of God, observes that for this great and glorious occupation the monks of the monasteries of the East, of Palestine, and Mesopotamia, assembled six times daily. Virgins consecrated to the Lord had the same pious custom; mention is made of it in several places in the writings of St. Jerome. Nothing can be more impressive than what he wrote to Seto; he wishes that he place near his daughter, a mere child, a wise and virtuous person, who, by her example, would teach her to rise at night to recite psalms, to chaunt hymns in the morning, and at the hours of Terce, Sext, and None, to keep herself like a warrior of Jesus Christ; in fine, to crown the day in offering, by the light of a lamp, the evening sacrifice.

This multitude of prayers has long subsisted in the Church, and it still subsists with all it has painful for nature; I mean the length of the offices and the obligation of devoting a part of the night to them. A Council of Tours, held toward the end of the sixth century, ordains that vespers and matins should never contain less than twelve psalms, and that during

Lent, matins should consist of thirty psalms. The Anthems were in proportion, and both were followed by a great number of prayers. With regard to the night office, it is said in many churches at the same hour in which it is usually said the eve of Christmas. The murder of two canons, who were assassinated as they went to matins, caused it to be discontinued at Rome and Chartres, and now it is principally confined to religious communities.

When things changed in the thirteenth century, in the Pope's chapel they began to abridge the office, the length of which took a considerable time from other duties which could not be deferred. This office, mutilated in all its parts, was thence called Breviary, or Abridged Office.

From these preliminary observations it ensues:— First. That the office, considered in itself and its substance, is of the highest antiquity, and that it is from the synagogue it has passed into the Church. Second. That chanting the praises of God was, for the just of the Old and New Law, an occupation as consoling as it was painful in many respects. Third. That having before us a host of witnesses, who have preceded us, in a path which was as difficult then as it is easy now, we are inexcusable if we do not recite it as we ought.

As to what regards the names that have been given to public prayer in different times there are several much in use; at first, it was commonly designed by the name of Divine Office, that is to say, a matter of obligation and of duty that must be fulfilled with regard to God. It has also been called by the name of Ecclesiastical Office, because it is recited in the name of the Church, and by the name of Canonical Office on account of its being recited conformably to the rules prescribed by the holy canons, and at the hours of the day and night which correspond to them.

In fine, it has received the name of Breviary, either because it is but an abbreviation of what was formerly recited, or, because it is an abridgment of whatever is most touching and instructive in the Scriptures, in the Holy Fathers, in the sighs and supplications of the saints of the Old and New Testament.

SECTION II.—*Of the Recitation of the Office.*

When the constitutions of an order, approved by competent authority, ordain the recitation of the divine office, the religious are bound, under pain of mortal sin, to recite it, unless they are legitimately dispensed. It should be recited in choir; if not at least, in private. The foundation of this obligation does not depend on the vows of religion, nor on the rules of each order, but on an ancient custom which has the force of a law, and which is considered such by the Church and all Catholic doctors.

This obligation concerns neither novices nor postulants, who, under pain of sin, are not strictly obliged to religious duties until after their profession. It is the same of lay-sisters, even professed, who are not taken into convents for choir duties, but for exterior and manual works; they are under no obligation on this point, unless the rule prescribes a certain number of *Paters* and *Aves*, or the *Rosary*, as is usual in most religious orders, but even to these prayers they are not bound as to other points of rule.

The obligation of reciting the office in choir concerns all religious, except lay-sisters; it is above all strict for those who have to direct it. Although novices are not strictly obliged to the office in choir, when they recite it by themselves, according to the rule, they satisfy the obligation of the community, provided they are not less than three.

Religious, who, for legitimate causes, do not assist in choir, commit no sin, and they fulfil their obligation by reciting the office in private; but if they absent themselves from choir, without legitimate cause, they commit a fault more or less grievous, according to the circumstances; their fault is grievous when accompanied with scandal, or when their presence is necessary.

If a religious could not read sufficiently well to follow the choir, she may satisfy the obligation by reciting the office of the lay-sisters, until, according to the judgment of the bishop, confessor, or superioress, she is able to recite the office in a becoming manner. Clement VII. granted this permission to the religious of St. Clare; Innocent IV. extended it to all those who were directed by the Friars Minors; and since, this permission has been granted to the religious of every order, who can make use of it, when from a reasonable motive they cannot recite the canonical hours; as, for example, when they are agitated by scruples, when the mind is fatigued from over exertion. This is the opinion of theologians, founded on the Bull of Innocent IV.

Religious can change nothing of the office. In reciting the *Confiteor* they cannot say, " *Tibi Mater vobis Sorores*," but as it written in the Breviary, *et tibi Pater, et vobis fratres*. Such is the decision of the Sacred Congregation of Rites.

From what causes may religious be dispensed from reciting the office? These causes may be reduced to three; impossibility, serious difficulty, and legitimate dispensation.

1. Impossibility. It is a universally admitted

maxim, that no one is obliged to do what is impossible. She, then, would be dispensed from the office who had no Breviary, because she had lost her own, and could not procure another. If she wilfully deprived herself of it, either in destroying it or otherwise, she would sin grievously, and the omission of the office would be imputable to her; however, if she repented sincerely of her fault, she would not commit an additional sin by omitting the office until she procured another Breviary.

A person deprived of sight would be dispensed from the office, also a paralytic who could not articulate.

2. Serious difficulty or moral impossibility. All theologians admit this maxim—"Positive laws do not oblige when their accomplishment meet so great an obstacle." Hence we may conclude, first, that she is exempt from the obligation of the office, who is suffering from fever, severe headach, &c.; second, she who would have a just fear that the recitation of the office would injure her health; third, she who is convalescent is at least dispensed from it for some days, until she recover her usual strength. Any doubt with regard to her delicacy should be referred to the physician or any prudent person; fourth, she who, in time of persecution, would have reason to fear that the recitation of the office might lead to her discovery, and cause her to be delivered up to the persecutors; fifth, she who during the entire of the day would be devoted to works of charity, which could not be omitted without considerable damage to her neighbour.

3. Legitimate dispensation. The obligation of the office is neither imposed on religious by the natural or divine law, but by the laws of the Church. The Sovereign Pontiff can validly dispense with it, even

without any cause. Bishops and their Vicars-general have in France the same power; however, they can only grant the dispensation for legitimate causes and for a limited time.

A religious who cannot recite the canonical hours herself, is not bound to have them recited by another, because the obligation is personal; nor is she strictly obliged to recite equivalent prayers, because this compensation is not ordained by any ecclesiastical law; however, pious religious usually do so. Collet, Navarre, and others recommend this practice. (In this case, what should be recited is the office of the lay-sisters.)

The canonical hours should be recited in the order in which we find them in the Breviary; that is, we must say matins before lauds, and lauds before prime, &c. Nevertheless, the inversion of this order is not a grievous sin, unless it be accompanied with contempt. When there is a reasonable motive for changing the prescribed order, there is no sin; thus, she who would not have said her morning hours when the time for reciting vespers in choir arrived, can follow the office, and afterwards resume the hours she had omitted.

From midnight to the same hour the following night, we can satisfy for the office of the day; but from a custom which existed, even in the time of St. Thomas, we can, when the sun is midway between noon and setting, recite matins and lauds for the following day. It is, however, more perfect to recite each of the hours at the time indicated; for example, matins in the middle of the night, lauds at dawn, prime at sunrise, terce at nine o'clock, sext at noon, none at three, vespers at sunset, complin at twilight, as Benedict XIV. declares. In communities, religious should conform to the hours specified by the rule.

During Lent, it is customary to recite vespers before dinner. The end of this custom is to recall the ancient discipline of the Church, when the faithful did not break their fast until after sunset, when they had recited vespers.

When there is a reasonable motive, we may anticipate or defer the office; however, it is more perfect to anticipate than to defer; because, as Hugh of St. Victor observes, to pray before the hour appointed is prudence; to pray after it, is negligence. The Fathers of the Society of Jesus and the Friars Minors, obtained an indult, by which they are empowered to recite in the morning all the hours to complin inclusively, either when they are travelling or are very much engaged.

Each religious is strictly obliged to recite the office appointed for the day, and cannot recite any other in its place. However, if through inadvertence she recited another, she would not be obliged to recite what she omitted; because the Church is not an exacting mother, and would not impose such a burthen: it suffices to say of the office omitted whatever was peculiar to it.

The *Pater*, *Ave*, and *Credo*, at the beginning and end of the office, constitute an integral part of it; but not the *Aperi*, *Sacrosanctæ*, *Salve*, &c., which are merely of devotion. For the integrity of the office, the words must be articulated; it will not suffice merely to read the Breviary with the eyes, or to pronounce the words with the teeth; acting thus would not satisfy the obligation. In reciting the office, religious should be penetrated with respect and reverence in the presence of the Almighty, and in order to acquit themselves well of this holy exercise, they should carefully observe what is prescribed in the choir ritual. In reciting the psalms, the mind should be fed with holy consideration, so that our thoughts and affections may be in union with our words.

The Office of the Blessed Virgin, like the Divine or Canonical Office, consists of seven parts, which are composed of psalms, hymns, lessons, chapters, and prayers. In the psalms we call to mind and praise the sovereign majesty of God. The lessons and chapters are intended for our instruction. The prayers are forms of petition and supplications. However, in the psalms and hymns, petitions and instructions are frequently introduced, because our necessity for both is so constant in this valley of tears. In heaven alone we can hope to offer to the Lord a tribute of pure praise, since there alone we shall no longer need light to remove our ignorance, or the medium of prayer to provide for our necessities.

CHAPTER IV.

OF THE EXAMEN OF CONSCIENCE.

ONE of the most important exercises of an interior life, is the examen of conscience. Thus, according to Rodriguez, the saints constantly recommend the practice of it to the faithful. St. Basil, one of the first who gave rules to nuns, orders them to devote some time to it every evening. St. Augustine mentions it in his rule; St. Anthony took great trouble in forming his disciples to it. St. Bernard, St. Bonaventure, Cassian, and generally all the founders of religious orders, wish that their followers devote daily some time to it.

As merchants, who keep a daily account of their profits and losses, and who finding they have experienced any loss, immediately set about repairing it, so should we each day examine our profits and losses in the traffic of salvation, fearing our losses might accumulate and lead to our utter ruin.

There are two kinds of examen, the general and particular; the general examen is made on all the faults we have committed during the day; it is called general, because it embraces all. The particular examen is made on one point only, and for that reason is called particular. We will only speak here of the latter, and the rules given for it may be applied to the general examen.

The particular examen is made three times daily, morning, noon, and night. In the morning, by way of foresight, we may produce the four following acts: Oblation of the day, repentance for past faults, renewed resolutions regarding the passion we wish to overcome, supplication to God for the grace necessary to keep this resolution; this may all occupy but a moment. At noon, we take an account of our conduct during the morning, and at night, of our conduct during the afternoon. The examen made at these times contains six acts. First, thanksgiving for benefits received. Second, prayer to the Holy Ghost. Third, examen of faults. Fourth, contrition. Fifth, renewed resolutions of amendment. Sixth, supplication for necessary grace. We may also impose some penance on ourselves.

We should devote a quarter of an hour to the examen; the one-third of the time is sufficient to discover faults and for the preceding acts; the most important parts of the examen are, to excite in our hearts deep sorrow and regret for our faults and negligences, and to make a firm resolution to correct them; to these points we must devote the longer time, for on them depend all the efficacy and virtue of the examen. One of the chief reasons why very many profit so little by their examens is, that they are occupied almost exclusively in discovering how often they have failed in their duty; and when they have finished this, the time of examen being almost ended, they pass very superficially over the rest. And thus, no time remains to repent of their faults, to ask God pardon for them, to make a purpose of correcting them for that afternoon or the next morning, or to beg grace to be more successful. Thence it happens that the next day they commit as many faults as the preceding; because, having done nothing but call to mind the number, they sought not the means of avoiding them; namely, to conceive a sincere regret for them, to make a firm resolution not to fall again, and to beg God for grace to do so. Without these precautions, we can never hope to improve; for future amendment depends so greatly upon regret for the past, that the one is in proportion to the other: it is plain that the more we detest anything, the greater care shall we take to avoid it.

The particular examen, continues Rodriguez, should be confined to one subject. Reason teaches us we have more power over one vice, than over all together. The sense which is divided between several objects, has less power over each separately; and we can conquer enemies one by one that we would find impossible to vanquish in a body.

We need not fear, says Cassian, that in giving all our attention to master one defect or passion, we shall neglect the others; first, because the exertion we make to overcome this defect will inspire us with a horror of every other. Secondly, because the care we take in our examens to root out this defect, will gradually cut the root of every other.

Even when making the examen of one single defect,

it is advisable to divide the matter into several points or degrees. If, for example, our design is to overcome pride or to acquire humility, we must not propose to ourselves in general, to yield to pride in nothing, to be humble in everything, because this examen being more extended than if we made it on three or four different points, we would infallibly make little progress. It is better to divide the subject, for our enemies being thus taken separately, it will be easier to overcome them.

If the subject of our particular examen be humility, we may thus divide it. First. Not to say anything that might draw praise upon us. Second. Not to take pleasure in being praised, or in hearing others speak well of us. Third. To do nothing to attract the esteem of creatures. Fourth. Neither to excuse our faults, inwardly or outwardly. Fifth. To banish all thoughts of pride and vainglory. Sixth. To prefer every one to self, both in theory and in practice. Seventh. To receive from the hand of God every occasion of humiliation. Eighth. To produce interior and exterior acts of humility. In the same manner, we may divide any other subject that we take for our particular examen, confining ourselves, however, to one point at a time.

We must not too lightly change the subject of our examen, chosing sometimes one defect, and sometimes another; this would be to go over old ground and weary ourselves uselessly without advancing; we must remain at one point until we conquer, and then pass onwards to the rest. One of the reasons why some persons derive so little profit from their examens, is, that they do nothing but by caprice. After having applied themselves for eight or ten days, or at most for a month, to a particular virtue, they soon grow weary, and without having acquired it, they pass on to another virtue, which they abandon in a similar way; then they apply to a third, in which their success is as doubtful as in the former.

If a person undertook to convey a large stone to the summit of a high mountain, and when he had got it a certain distance allowed it to fall back again; and did the same thing every day, it is certain, no matter what trouble he took, he would never be able to bring it to the appointed place. It is the same with those who, after having embraced a subject for their examen, leave it, abandon it, before attaining the goal, adopt another, then another; they give themselves a deal of trouble, and will never attain the proposed end. The business of perfection is not an affair to be undertaken by starts; it is the business of a long life of perseverance; it must be taken to heart; violence is necessary to bear away the kingdom of heaven.

But for what length of time should we continue our examen on the same subject? The surest way is to consult a wise director, who is aware of our wants and the violence of our passions. On some matters it suffices to make the examen for a short time; on others we may continue for a year, or even for several years. In order to change the subject it is not necessary to wait until we have overcome the passion, and have no more combats to sustain; this is the happy lot rather of angels than of men. It is enough, if the passion we have proposed to overcome has grown less troublesome, and is surmounted with less difficulty than before. We may pass then on to another subject.

Let us now consider what subject we are to select for our examen. St. Bonaventure and St. Ignatius say, that the devil acts against us like a general who wishes to gain possession of a city. The general makes use of every means to discover the weak parts of the place, in order to direct his batteries against it; knowing, that if he becomes master of this part, he will easily conquer the rest: thus the devil tries to discover our weak point, that he may more easily gain possession of our hearts. We must therefore examine what part of our soul is the weakest and the least capable of resisting the attacks of the enemy; this point we must surround with ramparts of defence, by taking it for the subject of our particular examen. The principal point to which we are to attend is, our predominant passion, which is the source of our faults.

However, if we have any exterior defects which offend and scandalise our neighbour, we must commence by retrenching them; though we should have interior defects far more considerable. For example, if a religious speaks too much, or too hastily, or too sharply to her sisters, or lets herself be carried so far, as to say what may affect their reputation, &c., she must commence by attacking this defect; because reason and charity require, that she should destroy everything that is disagreeable to her sisters: at the same time she must beware of remaining too long at the exterior, and neglecting the interior.

It is advisable to renew our resolutions every time we make the particular examen. And, to consult for our weakness, it is well to make our resolutions for the space of time between one examen and another. St. Chrysostom, St. Ephrem, and St. Bernard recommend this practice as most efficacious. We are only to propose to ourselves one thing at a time, and that for a short space; for a few hours only. For if we should undertake many things, or one thing for a long time together; if we should resolve to keep silence for a whole year together, to keep a guard on our eyes during our entire life, the bare thought of such protracted restraint would cause us to be discouraged; we would despair of persevering so long. But when we think that it is but for the morning, we look upon it as a trifle, and there is no one who is not able to overcome herself so far as to keep a guard on her eyes and tongue for so short a space. In the afternoon, we make the same resolution till night; God will take care to provide for the next day; and how do we know if we shall live to see it? Suppose we do, it will be but another day; and in rising in the morning we shall feel no regret for having spent the preceding day in a holy manner, nor shall we feel what we had imposed on ourselves to be a restraint: on the contrary, it will assist us in persevering in the same method until we arrive at the desired end.

CHAPTER V.

OF SPIRITUAL READING.

THERE is nothing more useful to the soul which aspires to perfection than spiritual reading. St. Athanasius was so persuaded of it, that, in an instruction which he addressed to religious, he says:—"You will never find any one, attached to the service of God, who has not been devoted to this reading; we can neither embrace nor abandon it without profit or loss."

St. Jerome shows us the esteem in which he held it, when writing to Eustochia, he said to her: "Let sleep surprise you in your reading, and let your weary eyes close only on the holy letters of the Scripture." The founders of Orders, resting on the authority and experience of the Saints, have so much recommended the utility and importance of this exercise, that they have ordered it to be practised by all their religious. Thumbert says that St. Benedict was not satisfied with prescribing a time daily to be devoted to it; but he orders besides, that at the hour appointed for spiritual reading, two of the more ancient religious should visit the monastery to see if any dispensed themselves from it, or caused others to do so. He ordained that the religious guilty of this fault should, for the first and second time, be gently admonished; but if they should again relapse, a severe punishment was to be inflicted, to serve as a warning to others.

St. Augustine compares the Holy Scriptures to letters which we receive from our home. Let us then read them with such eagerness as a person would, who had received a letter from his country, from which he had been long exiled; let us read them, to see what news they bring us from heaven, our true home; to see what they tell us of our fathers, brothers, and friends, who have preceded us; to discover what they relate of that country to which we are travelling.

St. Gregory says that the Holy Scriptures (and this may be applied to all pious books) resemble a mirror, which we place before the eyes of our soul, to see our interior reflected in it; by which we may discover what good or bad qualities we possess, and how far we are advanced on the road of perfection. Sometimes they reveal to us the admirable actions of the Saints, in order to excite us to imitate them; and that the view of their victories and triumphs may sustain our courage in temptations and sufferings; or again, they speak to us of the Saints' falls, that we may know on the one hand what we are to imitate, and on the other hand, may learn what we are to shun and avoid. Now they represent to us a Job, whose virtue increases in the midst of temptation; now, again,

David, yielding to the first assault. The constancy of the one serves to fortify us in the rudest trials, and the frailty of the other teaches us to have an humble fear when surrounded by prosperity and the consolations of grace; never to presume on ourselves, and to walk with all possible vigilance.

The Saints, when comparing spiritual reading to the preaching of the word of God, say that, if it has not the force and energy of the latter, in some respects it has many advantages over it. First; it is not as easy always to have a preacher as a good book. Secondly; what a preacher says passes quickly, and does not produce all its effect: whereas we may return several times to what we have read, examine it, weigh it, and remain at it as long as is necessary to impress it on the soul. Thirdly; in a good book, we find a faithful counseller: for, as a great philosopher said with truth, " what no one would dare tell us, a book tells us without disguise." It reproves and exhorts all persons with equal liberty. Besides, by devoting our time to reading, we enter into conversation with the great Saints and Doctors of the Church: we can sometimes converse with one, sometimes with another, and listen to them, as if they were really present, and we heard them speak. Good books are most deservedly styled a public and inexhaustible treasure; there is no one who cannot at any moment derive from them immense goods and infinite riches.

But in what manner and in what spirit are we to give ourselves to spiritual reading? To derive profit from this exercise, we ought to perform it, not hastily, as if we read something simply for our diversion, but without hurry, and with great application of mind. Stormy rain does not penetrate the earth, or fertilize it: it is only gentle, continuous rain which produces this effect. So, that spiritual reading may penetrate the heart, it must be done with calmness and attention. It is even recommended, says St. Bernard, that when we find any passage peculiarly touching, we should pause on it to make some reflections, and to excite our will, as we do in prayer. However, in spiritual reading we are not to give so much time to these reflections, as in meditation, in which we are to dive deeply into them; but we must, at least, make some useful reflections on what we read: this is the advice of the saints, who say we should, in this, imitate birds, who, when drinking, frequently leave off, and each time raise the bill to heaven.

St. Bernard counsels those who apply to spiritual reading, not to seek so much to know the things of God as to relish them; for the simple knowledge of the mind is dry and barren, if it does not inflame the will and excite in it that fervour which is the fruit and end of spiritual reading. This precaution is of great importance; for there is a great difference between reading to acquire knowledge, and reading to advance in virtue; between reading for others, and reading for ourselves; the one is a pure study, and the other is spiritual food.

The saints recommend us not to read much at a time, lest a long lecture should weary and tire out our mind, instead of fortifying it; and this counsel, which is very good for all persons, is most particularly necessary for those who imagine that all their sanctity consists in reading or rather devouring a great many books.

St. Bernard advises us to take care to engrave in our memory some passage from what we read daily, in order to digest it better, by revolving it in the mind; and this must be something also that agrees with the good purposes and resolutions you have made before, and that may be proper to strengthen them, and hinder your mind from distracting or dissipating itself upon other thoughts.

What I have said shows us clearly, that those are very much deceived, who when they have read a book, never read it a second time, how good soever they find it to be. A good book ought not to be read over only once; therefore, take it again into your hands: the second reading will touch and move you more than the first, and the third more than the second, and you will always feel new pleasure and satisfaction in it, as those experience who read with a desire of reaping fruit from what they read

CHAPTER VI.

OF THE HOLY SACRIFICE OF THE MASS.

FIRST, says Rodriguez, we must recognize as certain, that holy Mass is the representation of the passion and death of Jesus Christ, who has willed, by this means, to renew the memory of His love and sufferings, to excite us to love and serve Him with more ardour. The holy Mass is the continuation of the sacrifice of the Cross, and has the same virtue and value. Though the priest alone utters words, and offers the Holy Sacrifice, yet all who assist at it offer it conjointly with him. But, how are we to assist at it? The best method is to unite ourselves with the intention of the priest; following him in all he does; as being assembled in the church not only to hear Mass, but also to offer with the priest the adorable body and blood of our Lord Jesus Christ. Thus, that the assistants may dispose themselves to it, like the celebrant, with all the preparation the Church demands, he is ordered to pronounce in a distinct and rather raised tone, all that regards this preparation, that both priest and people may offer this holy sacrifice with all possible reverence and devotion.

First Part of the Mass.

*To reduce this method to practice more easily, we must observe that the Mass is divided into three principal parts. The first, which includes all that is said from the Introit to the Offertory, is only intended to prepare the faithful to offer worthily the Holy Sacrifice. This end is particularly attained beforehand by the recitation of the psalm *Judica me* and of the *Confiteor*, which the priest says before ascending the altar, and by the frequent repetition of the *Kyrie eleison*. This prayer not only signifies the miserable state in which we were before the coming of Jesus Christ, but also teaches us that in every petition we make to God, we should found our hope on His mercy alone. We then recite the *Gloria in excelsis Deo*, to glorify God for the Incarnation of His only Son, and to render Him thanks for so great a benefit; then follow the Orations or Collects.

Observe, that the priest says not *Oro*, I pray, but *Oremus*, let us pray; because in fact all the assistants ought to pray with him, and he prays in the name of all. In order that this prayer may be made with more fervour, the priest, turned towards the people, invokes previously the assistance of the Holy Ghost by these words, *Dominus vobiscum*, The Lord be with you; and the people answer, *Et cum spiritu tuo*, And with thy spirit.

The Epistle signifies the teaching of the Old Testament and that of St. John Baptist, which were the preparation for the Gospel. The Gradual, which is said after the Epistle, indicates the penance which the people did at the preaching of the Baptist; and the Alleluia, that follows the Gradual, marks the joy of the soul when by penance she has obtained pardon of her sins.

The Gospel signifies the doctrine taught by Jesus Christ; the priest, before reading it, makes the sign of the cross on the book, because it is Christ crucified whom he is to preach; he then traces the sign of the cross on his forehead, on his mouth, and on his breast, which the people likewise do, and which is as a public declaration on the part of all Christians to carry Jesus Christ in their hearts, and a solemn promise to confess Him by word before the whole world, and to die in this confession.

We hear the Gospel standing, to show the readiness with which we should be prepared to submit to it and to defend it. The Creed is then said. It contains the principal mysteries of our faith, the fruit we are to draw from the Gospel.

Second Part of the Mass.

The second part of the Mass includes all which is said from the Offertory to the *Pater noster*. This is the principal part of the Mass, because now the consecration takes place, and the priest offers the sacrifice of propitiation to the Eternal Father. Being about to offer the sacrifice, the priest, in a spirit of deep reverence, says the prayers in a low tone of voice, so that the assistants cannot hear him. This he does in imitation of Jesus Christ, who, a short time before His passion, withdrew into the city of Ephrem, near the desert, and did not show Himself in public for a long time. When on the point of offering the sacrifice to God, the priest washes his hands, to indicate with what purity we should approach this adorable sacrifice. Afterwards he turns to the people, recommending the assistants to pray with him, that the sacrifice may be agreeable to the Divine Majesty; and after having said a few prayers in a low tone, he again interrupts his silence by the Preface, which he says aloud, and which is the immediate preparation for the sacrifice. In it he exhorts the people to raise their hearts to God, to thank Him for having descended from heaven to assume human nature and redeem us by His blood. He glorifies Him by these words, *Sanctus, Sanctus, Sanctus, Dominus, Deus Sabaoth;* words which, according to the prophet Isaias and St. John, the blessed repeat incessantly around His throne; and by these others, *Hosanna in excelsis, Benedictus qui venit in nomine Domini;* marks of joy and acclamation, used by the people when Jesus Christ entered triumphantly the city of Jerusalem. The Canon is then commenced, in which the priest begs of the Eternal Father, through the merits of His only-begotten Son, to accept the sacrifice which he offers for the Church in general, for the Pope, for the Bishop, and for the king. He then prays for all whom he includes in the first Memento for the living, and having offered the sacrifice for their intention, he also offers it particularly for all present.

It is a most useful practice to assist at Mass; those who assist at it have a greater share in the gifts of God than others. The Abbot Rupert says, to assist at Mass is to assist at the obsequies of Jesus Christ; but to render ourselves worthy of the graces God grants to those who assist devoutly at it, we must be present in the same spirit in which the Blessed Virgin, St. John, the Magdalen, and the good thief, assisted at the death of Jesus Christ.

The Consecration next follows, in which the sacrifice essentially consists. It is then offered for all those of whom mention was made in the Memento. As we observed before, Mass is offered for all those who are present; hence, the most devotional method we could recommend would be to follow the priest as much as possible; so that when the priest makes the Memento for the living, we should do so, imploring the mercy of God for all those who are sojourning in this land of exile; and when he makes the Memento for the deceased, we may very profitably unite our supplications with his in behalf of the poor suffering souls.

St. Francis Borgia made use of the following method:—After having considered this sacrifice as a representation of that which Jesus Christ offered on the cross, and as being effectively the same, at the Memento he applied himself to contemplate the five wounds of our Saviour. Contemplating the wound of the right Hand, he recommended to God the Pope, cardinals, bishops, pastors, and all the clergy; at the wound of the left Hand, he recommended the king, all religious orders, particularly the Society of Jesus; at the wound of the right Foot, he prayed for his parents, friends, and benefactors; at the wound of the left Foot, for all the faithful in general. The wound in the Side he reserved for himself; begging of God to pardon his sins, and imploring at the same time the graces and favours of which he stood in need. He used the same method in the Memento for the dead, offering the Holy Sacrifice, first, for the souls for whose intention he celebrated; secondly, for the souls of his parents; thirdly for those of the deceased religious of the Society; then for the souls of his friends and benefactors, and for those who had recommended themselves to his prayers; and finally for the souls of the most destitute, or who suffered most, or for those who were nearest their deliverance, or for whom it was a great charity to pray. Each person can follow this method, or some similar one.

We must offer this sacrifice principally for three ends: First, in thanksgiving to God for the benefits we have received, general and particular. Secondly, in satisfaction and expiation for our sins. Thirdly, to obtain the graces necessary to work out our salvation. It is advisable daily at Mass to offer ourselves in sacrifice with Jesus Christ to the Eternal Father for these same intentions, sacrificing to Him without reserve all that we have, and are; for although of themselves our actions are of little value, yet, when united to the merits and passion of Jesus Christ, and tinged with His precious Blood, they become of great price, and most pleasing to God.

Third Part of the Mass.

The third part of the Mass extends from the *Pater noster* to the end. It includes the priest's communion, and the prayers which he recites in thanksgiving for the inestimable grace he has received. It is true we may not be disposed to communicate daily at Mass, but, at least, we should do so spiritually; it is a most holy and useful devotion to communicate spiritually when the priest really communicates under the two kinds.

Spiritual communion consists in having an ardent desire to receive this adorable Sacrament. The Council of Trent remarks on this subject, that the desire of communicating, in order to become a spiritual communion, must proceed from a lively faith, animated by a sincere charity; that is to say, she who has this desire must be in the grace of God, in order to be able to unite herself spiritually to Jesus Christ, and enjoy the fruit that this communion produces. She, who is in mortal sin, not only cannot communicate spiritually, but even the desire of communicating in that state would be a sin.* If, indeed, she only formed this desire conditionally, and in case she were free from mortal sin, this desire would be without doubt good and laudable; still it would not be a spiritual communion, because we can only communicate spiritually in a state of grace; in that state we communicate spiritually every time we have an ardent desire of doing so.

It may even happen that she who only communicates spiritually may receive more abundant graces than she who communicates really; because, although it is true that sacramental communion is in itself of greater price and advantage than spiritual communion, because in quality of sacrament it confers grace by a virtue peculiar to itself, which spiritual communion does not; still it is, nevertheless, true that our desire of communicating may be so ardent, and accompanied with so much reverence and humility, that we may thus receive more abundant graces than another who would communicate actually, but with less perfect dispositions. Spiritual communion has this advantage, that we can renew it as often as we please. Sacramental communion can be received at most but once a day, whilst spiritual communion may be made several times daily. It is the pious custom of many persons to communicate spiritually, not only daily at Mass, but every time they visit the Blessed Sacrament.

* The author must be understood to mean, that the desire to communicate without a corresponding desire to renounce mortal sin would be sinful, inasmuch as it would involve a desire to communicate in mortal sin.

CHAPTER VII.

OF VISITING THE BLESSED SACRAMENT.

BOURDALOUE says this is a solid devotion, because Jesus Christ Himself is the object; not Jesus Christ in figure, in representation, in imagination, in memory, but Jesus Christ really and substantially present: present in person as God and Man, in a word, such as He is in the highest heavens at the right hand of the Father. So that in the visits we make to the Blessed Sacrament, it is really Jesus Christ we visit; it is before Him we bow down, it is with Him we converse. He is there to receive us, to hear us, to answer us. He is there, surrounded by an infinite multitude of heavenly spirits, who never leave His presence; and we are, as it were, in the midst of this blessed company, with whom we unite in offering our homage and incense to this God hidden under those slight appearances.

If we heard of any place in which He manifested Himself to the outward sense, and unveiled, we imagine we should be all eagerness and ardour to see Him, that we should even undertake the longest journeys to do so; we should regard this as an act of virtue, and fancy we could not better testify to Him our zeal and attachment. Now, He would not anywhere be more really present than He is in His temple; and without being obliged to seek Him in a distant country, we have Him dwelling with us. We do not see Him, it is true; but we have faith, which supplies the defect of the senses; and what we know by faith is much more certain than what we behold with our corporal eyes.

Whence comes it, then, that Christians, even religious, have so much indifference for a Sacrament which is Jesus Christ Himself, and are so tepid in paying the homage and adoration they owe to it? There are times in the day in which we present ourselves, like others, before this Divine Sacrament; but, if we ceased to flatter ourselves, should we not be obliged to acknowledge that we would retrench them very much, were they not times prescribed by obedience, of which we cannot dispose at our pleasure? Independent of these times, times when obligation, not sincere piety calls us, how often do we go of ourselves to the feet of Jesus Christ, to manifest to Him our hearts' affections, and keep Him company in the solitude to which He reduces Himself for love of us? Is it not true, that hardly have we been a few moments with Him than we begin to grow weary? Instead of love, gratitude, reverence so attaching us to Him, that we must use violence to withdraw, on the contrary, we are under the necessity of using violence to remain with Him, as long as regular observance requires.

What is still more strange is, that while we abandon, or neglect, the Sacrament of Jesus Christ, we make it an inviolable practice to visit certain oratories in honour of the Saints. If we failed in this point we should reproach ourselves with it as with a piece of unfaithfulness, and never be satisfied until we had repaired the omission. To honour the Saints is, indeed, a pious and laudable devotion; but, after all, our first duty regards the Holy of Holies, and every other should yield to that. David desired nothing so ardently as to enter the temple of the Lord, and he would have esteemed himself happy never to have left it. Daniel, far from Judea, and a captive in Babylon, thrice each day opened the windows of his room, on the side which looked towards Jerusalem, and, kneeling down, addressed his prayer to the God of Israel as if he had been in His temple.

The primitive Christians wished to have the Blessed Sacrament always with them. There have been Saints who have spent their entire lives in presence of it. And in how many societies and communities is not perpetual adoration established? Or to adopt an illustration afforded us by the courts of princes, how many of the courtiers never, if they can help it, lose sight of their royal master? Now, the first Master, the first Superior of every community is Jesus Christ. How is it, then, we go to Him so seldom, when we have only a few steps to take, and He is so near us?

To visit the Blessed Sacrament is a devotion the most conformable to the views and intentions of Jesus Christ. The great secret of human policy, for those who approach the kings of the earth, and are employed in their service, is to study their inclinations and to conform to them. These it is often difficult to know: but we require no long research to become acquainted with the inclinations of the Son of God, the King of kings, the Mediator of men; they are sufficiently declared in the Holy Scriptures, and He has made us fully understand that His greatest delight is to be with the children of men and to converse with them. It is the increated Wisdom who informs us of this; and this wisdom of the Father, is it not Jesus Christ? He does not say, it is His glory to converse with us; but His delight. His glory is manifest in a thousand other things; but He would show us that His desire and pleasure are to have us near Him, not so much to glorify Him, as to treat familiarly with Him.

Thus, when He announced to His apostles that He was about to leave them and return to His Father, He promised that He would not leave them orphans in this world; and, that although He would deprive them of His visible presence, He would, nevertheless, be with them until the end of time.

This did He promise to us in their persons, and this He accomplishes daily in the sacrament of our altars. He repeats to us incessantly in His Tabernacle what He said then to His disciples, "Behold Me with you, not for a day or a year, but until the consummation of the world. I have returned to the abode of My eternal beatitude; I have ascended to My heavenly country: but do not believe you have lost Me; My sacrament is the supplement of My ascension. As you cannot sustain yourselves without Me, so I cannot live without you." Thus spoke this divine Saviour, or such, at least, is the sense of His words.

Now, in order that He may remain with us, we must abide in Him: for if we are not desirous to go to Him and to abide with Him, He will not abide in us; and thus we shall reverse all the designs of His love.

We may hence conclude that we can do nothing more agreeable to Jesus Christ than to visit Him frequently in His Holy Sacrament. He calls us, He invites us; and with the same eagerness with which He attracts us, should we not respond to His loving invitations? With a steadfastness like to that with which He awaits us, should we not as far as possible remain near Him? But because the different occupations of life and the various employments committed to our charge often withdraw us from His sanctuary, and do not allow us to remain there as long as our devotion would suggest, what will the soul do, that is solidly virtuous, and truly devoted to her heavenly Spouse? Animated with a holy desire of pleasing Him, she will economise her time, that she may be able regularly to visit Him. In the morning, she will go to adore and offer Him the first fruits of the day, or the entire day in advance. In the middle of the day she will return to His Divine Presence to recollect herself, and to recover from the dissipation into which her exterior duties may have cast her. In the evening she will come to beg His blessing before taking her repose; to acknowledge at His feet the faults she may have committed; to implore His grace and the succour of His omnipotent hand against her invisible enemies and the dangers to which she may be exposed during sleep. These visits do not consist in long prayers, but in affectionate sentiments, in which each may indulge more or less as time may permit, or piety suggest.

We cannot show greater contempt for this Sacrament of Jesus Christ than to neglect It; nor can we offend more sensibly this God of love than by being regardless of His entreaties and invitations. Again to borrow a comparison from princes and the great ones of the world, the sanctuary of Jesus Christ is like the palace in which He holds His court. Now, when the court of a prince is deserted, it is a slight which he must feel bitterly, because it indicates in how little esteem his subjects hold him. And certainly our Divine Saviour, so unworthily treated and so justly irritated by similar neglect, may well make to us the same reproach He made to His Apostles in the garden of Olives, when they slept while He prayed: " Couldst thou not watch one hour with Me?" They could allege nothing in their justification; and what pretext can we use in palliation of our negligence? He is but too much abandoned by the world: and who is to supply for this universal neglect, if not Religious, whom He has specially chosen to maintain with Him an intimate and undivided intercourse?

To visit the Blessed Sacrament is a devotion useful to ourselves and to our spiritual advancement. One of the most usual courtesies of the world is the interchange of visits; and what are the greater part of these visits? What fruit do we derive from them? In the first place, they cause a great loss of time; and however innocent they may be, they are, at least, very useless. Often, from the importunity of persons, or from their disagreeable conversations, they are very annoying and inconvenient. In these visits peace of mind is frequently lost, and the conscience wounded by detracting speeches; in a word, these visits are nearly always dangerous and hurtful, by the dissipation they cause and by the variety of objects they present to the mind. But it is not so in the visits we make to Jesus Christ; these are holy visits, visits full of consolation and divine unction. The soul finds in them numberless advantages, and reaps from them inestimable fruit.

They are all holy visits, whether we regard the end we have in view, or the motive which animates us, or the virtues we practise; especially lively faith, firm confidence, ardent charity, profound humility, perfect submission, sincere contrition: for these are the sentiments we should chiefly occupy ourselves with.

They are salutary visits, since they bring us to the very Source of all grace; for as the plenitude of the Divinity resides corporeally in Jesus Christ, so it is in the Sacrament of His body and blood that all graces are contained; herein He lavishes them most abundantly. The same miracles He formerly wrought in Judea, with regard to the maladies of the body, He now operates in His tabernacle in behalf of the soul; He enlightens the blind, He strengthens the weak, He cures the sick, He raises the dead.

They are consolatory visits. It is only those who are in a state to experience this, that can know it and speak of it. The life of man is but misery and affliction of spirit; and, notwithstanding the many advantages of the religious profession, in religion as elsewhere there are pains and trials. But how happy is the afflicted soul who knows where to find the remedy for her ills, and who seeks her consolation in Jesus Christ! Sometimes it requires but a visit to the Blessed Sacrament to change completely the disposition of the heart, and cause a sweet peace and repose to succeed trouble and agitation. We went to it sad and languishing, and we leave it full of strength, courage, and joy. How does all this happen? It is a secret reserved to the knowledge of God. It is enough for us to know that this often occurs. Let us be satisfied with the experience of so many holy souls who daily render testimony to it. Let us imitate them, and what they have felt we may experience also.

CHAPTER VIII.

OF CONFESSION.

It is the opinion of all the Saints, that frequent confession is the most powerful means of overcoming our passions, and arriving at the interior life; but as abuse is to be dreaded even in the best things, we must be guarded against it in this likewise. Pious persons require to be greatly guarded against the abuse of frequent confession; even more, perhaps, than great sinners. For the latter, when faith is revived in them, feel fully the importance of the sacrament of penance; they seek every means of securing the fruit of the sacrament, as being the only means left to them by which they can heal the wounds of their souls. But religious persons, not having their conscience charged with grievous faults, are less impressed with the importance of this sacrament, the application of which is not absolutely necessary for them; and for this reason, they are very much exposed to approach it without the requisite preparation and dispositions.

The sacrament of penance is an act of great importance for all those who receive it; for if we do not approach it with the necessary dispositions, not only are we deprived of the graces attached to it, but we are exposed to the risk of profaning it. Three things are particularly requisite in order to receive worthily this sacrament: careful examination, true contrition, sincere and humble confession.

1. Careful examen of conscience. We will insist little on this point. We address persons consecrated to God, who examine themselves several times daily, and who, on that account, require to make but a short examen when they approach the holy tribunal. Without doubt, they should attach importance to the discovery of their faults; but, prepared as they are by their daily examen, some minutes well employed will suffice to enable them to confess their faults exactly.

2. To approach worthily the sacrament of penance, we must have true contrition. God has only promised and only grants pardon to contrite and humble hearts: this is the doctrine of Holy Writ, of the Fathers, and of the Universal Church. Reason itself clearly demonstrates that God, although so good, cannot pardon us if we preserve affection for sin, His most cruel enemy. It is to be feared that persons consecrated to God, exempt from grievous faults, approaching

often the sacrament of penance, are exposed to receive it without this indispensable contrition; because naturally we are less struck with light faults, and are less carried to repentance for them. They should, then, be very careful on this point, and excite themselves to true sorrow each time they present themselves at the holy tribunal. They should employ the greater part of the time allotted for preparation, in lamenting the faults they have committed, and in forming resolutions to avoid them in future. Lest sorrow for these faults should not be lively, we should excite ourselves to contrition by the remembrance of past sins, which we may add in a general way to our accusation.

3. To approach worthily the sacrament of penance, we must make an humble and sincere confession of the sins we have committed.

First, sincere, because God knows the depths of our conscience, and promises pardon to those only who sincerely return to Him. The priest in the sacred tribunal fulfils the double office of physician and judge, an office which he cannot discharge if we do not make known to him the true state of our soul.

Secondly, the confession must be humble. 1st. In the interior sentiments which accompany the avowal of our sins, God will only pardon the humbled heart; He rejects the proud and haughty. 2nd. Humble in the tone of voice and in the expressions we make use of in our confession: a tone of arrogance, of indifference, or of levity, haughty or jesting expressions, would form a strange contrast with the attitude of a person who on bended knees solicited pardon. 3rd. Humble in the avowal of the faults committed, not casting blame on others. Some, but thank God the number is small, in this point labour under a deplorable illusion; their confession is a lengthened justification of their own conduct, and a bitter censure of the conduct of their neighbour. Such conduct in confession, which should be limited to the simple and candid confession of faults, far from appeasing the anger of God provokes His indignation and vengeance. 4. Humble, and therefore free from that kind of sensitiveness which would lead the penitent to be troubled, agitated, and even irritated, when the confessor would make her feel the malice and greatness of her faults. 5. Humble, and therefore exempt from any sallies of temper, any lively and misplaced repartees, accompanying the answers to such questions as may be addressed to her, to show more clearly the grievousness of the faults committed. Exempt, moreover, from that spirit of contention inspired by pride, which would lead the penitent to enter into argument with the confessor to prove to him he should absolve her, when his conscience declares the contrary. She who confesses with a truly contrite and humble heart is ready to give all required explanation; she always fears not to be sufficiently known, and believes herself more unworthy of absolution than he who receives her confession can himself believe.

The confession should be simple; that is to say: First, we should avoid every story, narrative, and discourse, foreign to the faults confessed. Secondly, we should strip the faults of the causes, circumstances, and consequences, which do not change their nature or increase their malice. All theologians are agreed, says St. Francis de Sales, that we need not tell all the preparatives and accompaniments of our sins. One who says, "I have killed a person," need not say, "I drew my sword upon him. I caused great affliction to his relatives. I disturbed the entire street in which I killed him." All this is sufficiently understood without mentioning it; it suffices to say, "I killed a man through anger, revenge," &c., and then leave judgment to the confessor. A person who had burned a house, does not require to give an exact account of all that was within; it will be sufficient to say whether or not there were people within, &c. Third, we must avoid vague formulas, as having failed in the love of God, in fervour, recollection, mortification, &c. If we have anything to reproach ourselves with on these matters, we must mention it precisely, and the number of times we think we have failed. This is the opinion of St. Francis de Sales, and of many other saints, theologians, and masters of the spiritual life.

CHAPTER IX.

OF FREQUENT COMMUNION.

No more powerful means exists to conquer ourselves, and attain to the interior life, than frequent communion. St. Augustin says, that Jesus Christ has proposed it to us as a remedy for all the evils of our souls; and St. Ignatius the martyr calls it an antidote which preserves us from eternal death.

As the adorable flesh of Jesus Christ is the flesh of God, by the frequent reception of it you will be perfectly disengaged from all the affections which attach you to earth, and you will be exalted and united to your Heavenly Spouse. As the adorable flesh of Jesus Christ is virginal flesh, it will purify the thoughts of your mind, the desires of your heart, the disordered appetites of the body, and will impose a restraint on rising passions.

The more frequently we communicate, the more abundant graces do we receive; we acquire new strength, we become more vigilant in watching over our heart, regulating its movements, sanctifying its desires, and rooting out of it all that breathes not of God.

But let us examine what are the dispositions required for frequent communion. It is not necessary to speak of the dispositions of the body, with which every one is acquainted, nor of the first and most indispensable disposition of the soul, which consists in being in a state of grace, exempt from mortal sin. All are fully aware of the necessity of this, even for annual communion. At present, we will merely consider the dispositions of the soul with regard to those venial faults and imperfections to which pious persons are liable.

It is certain that it is not necessary to be perfect, nor even to be exempt from light faults, to be admitted to frequent communion. Let us listen to St. Francis de Sales, whose doctrine is in accordance with the Church: "If you are asked," says he, "why you communicate so frequently, you may reply that there are two classes of persons who require frequent communion; the perfect and the imperfect. The perfect, that they may persevere in perfection, and the imperfect, that they may become perfect; the strong, that they may not become weak, and the weak that they may become strong; the sick, that they may be cured, and the healthy, that they may not become sick."

Father De Grenada speaks in like manner: "Our misery," he remarks, "should not withdraw us from this Sacrament; it is for the poor this treasure has been left; it is for the sick and infirm this remedy has been given. Thus, no matter what may be our imperfections, nothing should withdraw us from the Sacrament, if we desire sincerely our cure."

"I sin daily," says St. Ambrose; "I ought then

daily to have recourse to the remedy." And St. Augustin: " Each day some weakness surprises you; each day, then, avail yourself of the antidote which is presented to you."

Let us now try and thoroughly penetrate the doctrine of these holy men on this important point; and, in order to do so, we may distinguish two classes of weak and imperfect souls.

The one, sighing over their weaknesses and imperfections, desire sincerely to arise from them, and labour with more or less courage and success.

The others, on the contrary, crouch in their imperfect state, without being in any trouble to leave it. They fall into a multitude of small faults, without ever dreaming of adopting the means of correcting them. Provided they preserve themselves from grievous faults, which might alarm their conscience, they fancy they do quite enough; they are not determined to make the sacrifice of their inclinations, their conveniences, or of their many earthly and sensual inclinations, which are altogether opposed to Christian and religious perfection: they are even affectionately attached to them.

The advice and the decisions we have adduced, relative to frequent communion, are evidently addressed to the former. They are poor, weak, and infirm, as says St. Francis de Sales; but they desire to leave this deplorable state, and they make many efforts to do so. Let them then approach frequently the holy table; they will there find an abundant treasure to supply all their need, an efficacious remedy for their infirmities, an admirable nourishment which will render them strong and vigorous; they will find there every means of assisting them to attain the end to which they aspire.

Those who crouch down in their imperfection, and

are at no pains to arise from it, who fall each day deliberately into faults more or less serious, without labouring to amend them, and to which they are affectionately attached, as their conduct proves:— to them, unless they change their disposition, frequent communion cannot be granted; because, not desiring their cure, and not labouring to co-operate with grace, they would evidently abuse the treasure, the remedy, and nourishment placed at their disposal, and far from being useful to them, it would be most hurtful.

It is a manifest error (says an advocate of frequent communion with Benedict XIV.) to grant frequent communion to those who approach the holy table with affection to venial sins, which they do not labour to avoid; and further, to those who are in the habit of deliberately committing venial sins, without any desire of amendment, it should not be granted more than once a week; and it may be often useful to deny it to them for a time, in order to inspire them with horror for their faults, and reverence for the Sacrament.

The reception of the Holy Eucharist should be rare for those who are in a state of imperfection, if this state be such as to impede the fruit of communion; for frequent communion, when fruitless, is dangerous.

"I think," says St. Francis de Sales, "that frequent communion is the surest means of attaining perfection; but we must approach it with a sincere desire of removing from our heart everything displeasing to Him whom we invite to be our guest." And elsewhere he says: "You have done right in obeying your confessor, whether he has denied you the consolation of frequent communion in order to prove you, or because you were not sufficiently careful to correct your faults; and I believe he has acted so for both reasons, and that you should persevere in this penance as long as he pleases. If you thus obey humbly, one communion will be more beneficial to you than two or three made under other circumstances."

We should therefore restrict the number of communions to weak and imperfect souls, who are not labouring at their self-amendment.

It may be useful to observe: First, that these principles are applicable to persons who live in community as well as to those engaged in the world; and they should be even more rigorously applied to religious. For, being obliged by their profession to aspire to perfection, if they voluntarily remain in the habit of venial sin, they fail habitually in an imperative duty, and are consequently more culpable than worldlings. What sometimes deludes persons living in community, is the article of the rules which determines the number of weekly communions.

Secondly, that the article of the rules or constitutions, which appoints two, three, or four communions to be made in the week, is not an imperative article, as are those which prescribe silence, punctuality, prayer, examen, lecture, &c. It is a point simply permissive and conditional; the meaning of it is, that the sisters who, by the rules of the Church, will be judged worthy of frequent communion, may be admitted, two, three, or four times weekly, to partake of this great benefit, as may be ordained; and that the desire of the holy founder was, that each one should strive to become worthy of approaching this heavenly banquet.

Thirdly, that the confessor is the judge to whom alone it appertains to pronounce on the expediency of more or less frequent communion: for he alone knows the secrets of the heart. Each sister should in this point be guided by his decisions.

Fourthly, that when the confessor, for adequate reasons, has deemed it suitable to diminish the number of communions for any particular person, she cannot, either in virtue of any rule which allows a greater number, or in virtue of any permission obtained otherwise, go beyond the permission which she received in the sacred tribunal.

Superioresses of communities can, in certain circumstances, grant additional communions to those subjects, in whose regard the confessor has not diminished the number appointed by the rule. They can also, in punishment of some exterior fault, limit the number of communions, or even withhold all granted by the confessor.

CHAPTER X.

OF SPIRITUAL DIRECTION, ITS NECESSITY AND ADVANTAGES.

CASSIAN assures us, that the first practice the ancient fathers recommended to those who wished to consecrate themselves to God, was to discover to their superior their temptations, vexing thoughts, and all which passed in their inmost souls. These holy men regarded this practice as the basis and foundation of the spiritual edifice. Saint Antony, Saint John Climacus, Saint Basil, Saint Jerome, Saint Ambrose, and Saint Bernard, recommend it in the most pressing terms Saint Ignatius, resting on their authority and example, prescribed it to the religious of the Society of

Jesus. "After having," said he, "examined the matter before God, it seemed to us most necessary that the religious should be perfectly known to their superiors;" and he immediately assigns the following [reasons: That the superior is obliged by his office; First, to assist the religious in the cure of their spiritual maladies. Secondly, to form them to virtue, and the practices of a perfect life. Thirdly, to distribute to each the employments suitable to them. All this he cannot do efficaciously, if subjects do not let him know the state of their souls, freely and sincerely. How can he apply a remedy to their spiritual infirmities, if he knows neither their principle, nature, nor grievousness? How can he form them to religious virtues, if they do not render him an account of their success, or of the obstacles they encounter? How can he place each in the post suitable to him, and entrust to him the employment for which he is fit, if he knows neither his capacity, his character, nor the degree of virtue to which he has arrived; if he does not know what may be useful or dangerous to his spiritual advancement, or even to his salvation?

Nothing is more advantageous to those who aspire to perfection, than spiritual direction; in it they discover the most abundant consolation. "A faithful friend," says the Wise Man, "is a remedy against all the evils of life." Saint Augustine says, "Nothing is comparable to a friend, who can console us in our afflictions, counsel us in our doubts, rejoice with us in our prosperity, and relieve us in our necessities." "Whoever has found such a person," says the Wise Man, "has found a treasure, and all the gold and silver in the world cannot be compared to the value of his fidelity." Now this friend we find in our superior; the superior is to us a father, a master, a physician, a brother, a mother; a mother who loves us with more tenderness than ordinary mothers love their children; who makes it a special business to watch over our interests, and is ever ready to hear our griefs and to relieve them.

In spiritual direction we find a sovereign remedy against temptation; for the demon can no longer deceive us by his frauds and deceits, as he too often succeeds in deceiving those inexperienced persons who insist on guiding themselves in the difficult path of salvation.

But how should inferiors manifest their souls to their superioress? " They should," says Père Lafiteau, "discover to her the depths of their soul, that is to say, they should not conceal from her the good or bad inclinations they possess, the passions which move them, or their most prevalent temptations: so their rule prescribes. They should discover to her their aversions and their inclinations, their fears and their desires, their consolations and their disgusts, their firmness and their inconstancy in good, their progress and their slowness in virtue; they should even add to these defects their faults and failings in regular observance; in a word, they should confide to her everything, even the rovings of their imagination, the sallies of their temper, and the dissipation of their senses; this is what is meant by discovering to the superioress the very nooks and corners of the heart, as the rule ordains."

How far should this manifestation of the inmost soul in spiritual direction extend? We are not obliged, in virtue of the rule, continues the author just quoted, to manifest our sins, at least those which are grievous, nor to mention their acts, their kinds, circumstances, or number. In manifestation of conscience the rule does not exact such an avowal.

If ever the founder of a religious order had at heart the practice of so holy a rule, we may say it was Saint Ignatius. "Let all," says he, "make themselves thoroughly known to their superiors, and keep nothing hidden or secret from them." Nevertheless, what says Rodriguez, a man so versed in theology, and so perfected in the ways of God, when he explains this important article of the constitutions of his holy founder? He teaches us that we must distinguish with great care what is sinful from what is not so. On the one hand, he declares that in virtue of that point of the rule, inferiors should, in manifestation of conscience, discover to their superior all their imperfections and infirmities, unveiling to him their defects and bad inclinations, and telling him their faults. But on the other hand, with regard to grievous faults, he pronounces with the firmest assurance that it is not the intention of the holy founder that they tell their sins out of confession. He even adds that superiors ought not to interrogate any one out of confession on things which it would be difficult to mention; subjects of this kind should be reserved for the sacred tribunal.

It is in the sense of this decision that we must understand what is said in the constitutions of several Orders, that the novice, in taking the habit, should make to her superioress an abridgment of the history of her life, both good and bad, manifesting her temptations and interior pains, opening her heart, and unfolding its secrets. This, we see, does not mean that the novice is obliged to tell her superioress the sins of her past life. So, the constitutions add that this manifestation should be made summarily and briefly, and as far as will be necessary to enable the superioress to guide her. Therefore, such manifestation is not a confession in which the novice, who is to take the habit, or the sister who has taken it, is obliged, as in the tribunal of penance, to specify the sins she has committed; it is but a summary, or review, to enable the superioress to guide her in the way of perfection.

CHAPTER XI.

OF THE CHAPTER OF FAULTS.

By chapter of faults, are meant meetings which take place from time to time in convents, in which all the members assemble, choir sisters, lay sisters, novices, and even postulants. These meetings are for the purpose of fraternal correction, the practice of humility, the maintenance of order and regularity.

First, fraternal correction. Each sister comes in turn to the feet of the superioress, to make before the whole community the avowal of the exterior faults she has committed during the week; and it is for this reason that this exercise is named chapter of faults, that is, chapter in which we acknowledge our faults.

The superioress addresses to each one some remonstrance on the faults she mentions; she places before her those she had not perceived, or of which self-love prevented her from accusing herself, and imposes on her a penance, in satisfaction, and as a remedy.

Secondly, the chapter of faults is most efficacious in increasing humility. This virtue being the basis and foundation of every other, those who aspire to religious perfection should strive to be thoroughly grounded in it. Practice alone makes perfect.

Rodriguez observes that it is an acknowledged maxim among philosophers that the perfection of any virtue consists in producing acts of it promptly and with great facility. One who has acquired any art or science knows how to reduce it to practice with wonderful ease. A good lute-player has no need of any preparation to execute what he knows; his art has become so easy to him, that even when thinking of something else, he plays his instrument remarkably well. It is the same with those who have acquired the habit of virtue; they practise it without any trouble. Do you wish then to know if you have acquired the habit of humility? Examine if you perform acts of it easily and joyfully. But how are we to arrive at this? By frequent practice. Now it is in this holy practice of humility that religious are exercised in the chapter of faults. They exercise themselves in humility, by publicly declaring their faults and imperfections; their superioress exercises them in it, by accustoming them, after the example of Jesus Christ and the Saints, to receive reprimands, humiliations, and penances, without allowing any complaint or murmur to escape them.

In order to enter into the views of our holy founders, and to profit by these chapters, it is indispensably necessary to nourish in our souls certain dispositions, not only while we assist at them, but also before and afterwards.

A good religious, before presenting herself at chapter, should: First, recall the obligation she contracted on the day of her profession, of tending constantly towards perfection, of which humility is the foundation. Secondly, she should be convinced that it is impossible to become perfect without knowing our defects and correcting them. Thirdly, she ought to excite in herself a sincere desire of knowing her faults and correcting them; and with this design in view she should present herself at chapter: proposing, after the example of Jesus Christ, who for her was humbled to the death of the cross, to humble herself; and like her Divine Model, to offer to the Eternal Father all the reproaches and humiliations, merited or unmerited, that she may receive.

During chapter, she should continue in the dispositions we have mentioned, without paying any attention to the faults of which the other sisters accuse themselves, or to the admonitions and penances they receive. Secondly, she should make an humble and sincere avowal of her faults, receiving with reverence and humility the reprimands and reproaches which are addressed to her, without examining by what means the superioress has come to the knowledge of the faults she lays to her charge, or whether she treats her with more or less severity than the other sisters. Thirdly, she ought to excite in her heart sincere gratitude towards her superioress; looking on her as an instrument of which God makes use, in His infinite goodness, to assist her to correct her defects, and arrive at perfection.

"It would be receiving correction very badly," says Père Marin, "to form suspicions, and endeavour by inquiries to discover who has informed the superioress, that you may bear her any ill-will, and reproach her for it. You who act in this manner know very little of the value of correction, either with regard to the glory of God, or for the good of the convent, and the sanctification of your soul. Ah! how far would you be from any such feelings, if you had the spirit of the saints. If another has committed the same fault as you, without anything being said to her, while you are reproached for it, and perhaps with a great deal of severity, what then? If, indeed, you listen to self-love, it will tell you that others are spared, and many things passed over in them; nothing is said to them, because they are more in favour than you; that you, on the contrary, are treated with rigour, that the superioress is prejudiced against you, and that it is precisely on this account she magnifies your smallest faults. This excites you to murmuring, jealousy, resentment, mistrust, and indocility. If, on the other hand, you hearken to grace, it will make you receive the correction as a favour the superioress grants you preferably to others; as a proof of the good opinion she has of you, since she presumes you have sufficient virtue to receive correction with humility, and to profit by it; as a proof that she loves you, and that she is zealous for your advancement in religious perfection, since she does not spare your defects, in order that you may perceive and correct them. If, when reproved for a fault, you try and discover who informed the superioress of it, you not only abuse correction, but you give the devil an advantage over you. What matters it to you who has acquainted the superioress with it? You ought only to think of the fault you have committed, and endeavour to correct it; it was only with this intention, and through a spirit of charity, that you were reprimanded. If, then, instead of receiving it in the same spirit, you form a thousand suspicions to discover who has disclosed your fault to the superioress, you change into poison a most salutary remedy for your soul; you make that serve for its ruin which was destined for its advantage; you fill your heart with bitterness on an occasion when charity is exercised towards you; and, very far from correcting your fault, according to the intention of the superioress, you commit several others by receiving the correction badly, by forming judgments, and sentiments of animosity, bitterness, and revenge against those whom you think the cause of you being corrected. How much better would you have done by humbly submitting to the correction, profiting by it, and renouncing all the suggestions of self-love! You would by that means have avoided many faults, preserved your heart in peace, edified your superioress and sisters by your humility ; you would, in fine, have sacrificed to God your touchiness of feeling, which would have been more agreeable to Him than if you had fasted and worn the cilice for a long time."

After chapter, she who has assisted at it should, first, lay at the foot of the cross the reproaches and humiliations which God has sent her, thank Him for them, and offer them to Him. Secondly if feelings of wounded self-love or bitterness arise, she should carefully combat and suppress them, and pray for her who is the object of them. Thirdly, let her examine whether the defects with which she is reproached really exist in her ; if she discovers them, let her take the resolution of combating and correcting them ; if she cannot perceive them, let her thank God for the favour He has done her in preserving her from them, and let her be more than ever guarded against them. Religious should never speak to any one of what takes place at the chapter of faults.

Those who look on the chapter of faults in this point of view, will repair to it in a spirit of lively faith, will conduct themselves as we have pointed out, and will certainly derive from it great spiritual advantage.

CHAPTER XII.

OF THE SANCTIFICATION OF OUR ACTIONS IN GENERAL.

SECTION I.—*Necessity of sanctifying our ordinary Actions.*

THE religious soul ought not only be animated with the interior spirit, and the desire of her perfection, in her spiritual duties: it should pervade her every action, even the most ordinary and common, which absorb more than half her life. The Apostle recommends that "whether we eat or drink, or whatever else we do, we should do all for the glory of God."

The life of the creature, according to Father Bellecius, is but a series and succession of actions recurring daily. If these are done with suitable perfection, they are acts of virtue; so that, if our actions are done with holy dispositions, our life becomes a succession of virtuous actions ; they form, as it were, so many links of a golden chain. For, according to the doctrine of the Council of Trent, to each virtuous action performed by a just soul, corresponds a degree of sanctifying grace ; and to each degree of such grace, corresponds a degree of heavenly glory, which will endure for ever. It thence follows that our daily actions, done with perfection, are like a golden chain, the links of which are formed of so many degrees of grace in this life, and glory in the other, united together with a marvellous connexion. Each day, you perform at least twenty different actions: these actions amount to one hundred and forty in the week, and in the month to six hundred and twenty. If these actions are done with perfection, they acquire for us six hundred and twenty degrees of glory for eternity.

Now, one single degree of such grace and glory is so priceless a treasure, that to procure this one degree, the devils would suffer a thousand times all the torments of hell; and, if the saints in heaven were capable of regret, it would be for having lost one single degree of glory. And we, miserably blind as we are, continue to regard as trifling the inestimable and for ever irreparable loss of so many degrees of grace and glory! But at death and judgment, we shall think differently of this irremediable wrong we are now doing to our souls.

The religious soul who does not apply herself to perfect her ordinary actions, not only deprives herself of many advantages, but also causes herself great injury. The first injury she does is to prepare for herself a less joyful death. Oh, how will this thought torment her at the gate of eternity! "As a religious, I was bound, under pain of mortal sin, to tend to the perfection of my state ; to satisfy this obligation I had within reach a most easy and efficacious means, which was simply application to perform well my daily actions ; according to all spiritual writers, this is the shortest and most secure means of arriving at perfection. I have known this truth, nevertheless I have neglected to conform my conduct to it. I might have lived holily ; I could have done so with much facility, by arising from languor in my daily duties, by employing the means prescribed to execute them perfectly, and by often renewing my intention. I could easily have performed my duties perfectly. Nothing else was required of me ; it was only requisite to act differently from what I did. But, oh, detestable sloth! I have increased my pains in purgatory, by those same actions for which, had I done myself a little violence, I should have been elevated to the sublime throne of glory, occupied by that sister, now one of the elect, who lived with me. Others have done their actions perfectly; animated by their example, I proposed doing the same. I even began. Oh! why did I not persevere? hurried away by a disgraceful inconstancy, I have abandoned the good commenced, I have neglected the high perfection to which God called me.

"I can now recall the weariness, misery, and disgust which, during the course of my life, accompanied my ordinary actions; what regrets and repugnances had I not to endure! And, oh! what glory might I not have acquired, had I made good use of these difficulties! But labouring, toiling, day and night, I have laboured in vain! Wearying myself without merit, and for simple vanity, I have exhausted my strength, ruined my health, shortened my life, and instead of meriting reward, I have accumulated debts for which I must satisfy the divine justice."

Such, at death, will be the reflections of a soul who, during life, allowed precipitation and negligence to mingle with her actions. Be on your guard, that at your last moment you may not be obliged to utter this sad lamentation: "Alas! I have done little good, and this little I have not done well! My life has been but a succession of defects, with which the devils have surrounded me to present me to my judge."

The second injury the religious exposes herself to in not perfecting her ordinary actions, is a more rigorous judgment. After death her actions alone will accompany her to the tribunal of Jesus Christ, that "each one may receive what is due to the good or bad works she did, whilst clothed with the body." There she will not be asked whether she were called to distinguished employments, or had performed conspicuous deeds, but how she has fulfilled her obligations and performed her actions; it will not be examined with what facility she accomplished the duties imposed on her, but with what sanctity: in a word, her daily actions will be the matter of this examen; "for the Son of Man will render to each according to her actions."

The third injury that imperfect actions cause the religious soul is a longer and severer punishment. Oh! how terror-struck will you be when, after judgment, you will find that for so many actions and labours you have merited punishment in place of recompense! that those actions which so often caused you to take complacency in self, and to prefer yourself to others, are in the eyes of God, on account of the imperfect manner in which they were done, but fuel for the flames of an expiatory fire! How would you then desire to have done them? But, alas! it will be too late! Wishes will then be useless. If you are wise, take great care in time. Could a soul from purgatory return to this world, how perfectly would she not accomplish her actions! You will be guilty of an unpardonable cruelty towards yourself, if you do not now do what this soul would, and one day you will bitterly lament so culpable an omission.

SECTION II.—*Of Purity of Intention in our ordinary Actions.*

We belong to God by many titles. We belong to Him by title of creation; He has made us what we are. We belong to Him by acquisition; He has purchased us with the price of the blood of His only Son, according to the Apostle: "You are no longer your own, you have been bought with a great price." We belong to Him by our own free choice; we chose Him as master the day of our baptism, and vowed to serve but Him alone. Lastly, by the vows of religion, we have given ourselves to Him in a still more intimate manner ; for by this act, we have renounced all dominion over liberty, our will, and our faculties: we have immolated them all to God. We are then the property of God ; we are, if I may use the expression, the field of God, a field over which He has the most perfect, the most absolute, and the most inalienable dominion. But the field should fructify for its master. We should then fructify for God, that is to say, we should consecrate to Him all our faculties; to withhold anything from Him would be theft; the only end of all our thoughts, words, and actions should be His glory and the accomplishment of His will.

This fidelity in directing our actions to God is called by ascetics purity of intention: and this alone, with divine grace, renders our works agreeable to God, meritorious and worthy of recompense. In truth, however good, useful, or praiseworthy, an action may be in itself, if God, to whom we owe all, and from whom we can snatch nothing without injustice, be not the object of it, how can it be agreeable to Him, and by what right do we demand any recompense? What answer should we make to a dishonest servant who, being engaged in our service, not only robbed us of the time and care he owed us, but even expected our praise and recompense for deeds he had performed in favour of our very enemies and rivals?

With what intention should our actions be performed, in order to render them agreeable to God, and worthy of recompense? The actual intention, by which we would have God continually present to the mind, with an ever-conscious desire of pleasing Him in each action, would be perfect and desirable; but it is not possible to the creature, on account of her feebleness; nor is it even necessary. It is enough to offer our actions to God in the morning, and to maintain the general intention of acting in everything for His glory; this is called the virtual intention. Nevertheless, we ought, as far as possible, to practise the actual intention; by renewing our offering in frequent aspirations to God, and by often purifying our intention: because, if we do not exercise ourselves in a continual vigilance, the virtual intention will easily be impaired, or perhaps will disappear completely, to give place to some other intention which will insidiously creep into our soul. The virtual intention is impaired by the spirit of routine and tepidity; it is vitiated by vainglory, self-love, and pride; it is even annihilated by these several feelings, when they gain the ascendant in the heart.

It is the opinion of the Saints, that self-love is the most dangerous and subtle of these enemies; we ought consequently to be on our guard against it. St. Gregory says that vainglory is like a robber, who first craftily insinuates himself into the company of a traveller, pretending to go the same way he does, and afterwards robs and kills him, when he is least on his guard, and when he thinks himself in greatest security. I confess, says this great Saint, in the last chapter of his Morals, that when I examine my intention, even when I am writing this, it seems to me I have no other desire but to please God. But notwithstanding, while I am not on my guard, I find that a certain desire of pleasing creatures insinuates itself, and it seems to me I feel some vain satisfaction for having, perhaps, done it well. And in any case, what I perceive clearly is, that I do not feel actuated by an intention as pure as at the beginning; for I know that I undertook it, at first, with the best intention, and with the view of pleasing God alone; and now I see that a thousand other considerations intrude themselves, and render my intention less pure and upright. It is, continues the Saint, like what occurs at our meals. In the beginning we eat from necessity; but sensuality so cunningly insinuates itself, that what we began in order to supply absolute necessity, and to preserve our life, we continue on account of the relish and pleasure we feel in eating.

Experience often shows us something like this in our most holy actions; we begin with the best motives, afterwards vanity glides in. We desire to please creatures, and to be esteemed by them; and when we fail of gaining this human end, it seems as if we lost courage, and did everything with regret.

We ought then to propose to ourselves but the glory of God as the end of our actions, and follow the advice of the Apostle, already quoted; "Whether you eat or drink, or whatever else you do, do all for the glory of God." In order that nothing may vitiate or destroy this intention, it is well frequently to purify and renew it.

Section III.—*Of retiring to Rest, and of Sleep.*

We ought, says M. Tronson, to be very careful in acquitting ourselves well of the action of retiring to rest. First, on account of the sad consequences which may arise when this action is not well done. Secondly, because it is difficult to perform it well. Thirdly, because it is the last action of the day, and may be the last of our lives.

First, on account of the fatal consequences of this action, when not well done. We pass nearly one-third of the day in bed; now this precious time we absolutely lose when we fail to make good and holy use of it. If we continue in this negligence during our entire lives, we lose irreparably the third part of it. What a serious loss, and with what care should we not labour to avoid it when we know the inestimable value of time!

But we lose much more than the third of the day when we do not sanctify our repose; let us see how this is. There is so close a connexion between retiring to rest and rising, that the greater number rise as they went to bed. For, in truth, if we go to sleep with our minds engaged with vain and worldly thoughts, we rise next morning with the same thoughts. If, on the contrary, when retiring, we are occupied with God, if we only take sleep and the repose of the night to repair our strength, to do the will of God and to please Him, we will rise only to accomplish His holy will, and to employ our strength in His service.

During the day, the thoughts which come into the mind do not ordinarily make deep impressions, because they are but passing, and succeed each other in rapid succession; but at the moment of retiring, as the soul is in a more tranquil state, and closes the door against all exterior objects, the idea of the things which occupy it at that time remain profoundly impressed: these thoughts return with facility at the moment of awaking; and as on these thoughts depends the good use of a great part of the day, we may say that she who does not go to rest in a Christian and religious manner, exposes herself to the loss not only of the time devoted to repose, but also of the greater part of the day.

Besides, it is difficult to be free from temptations during sleep, if we retire to rest without placing ourselves under the protection of God, and without having any Christian end in view; and although then we are not conscious, and therefore not in a state of sinning from any illusions which may occur, nevertheless, we awake sometimes; we feel now and then not quite asleep; we see the temptation, perceive it so as to apprehend it, but cannot use our reason so as to combat and get rid of it: and these moments are full of danger. What then is the remedy? It is, when retiring to rest, to place ourselves in the arms of our Heavenly Father; so that, as He provides for all our wants during the day, He may protect us during sleep. They neglect to use this precaution who do not retire to rest in a Christian manner; their souls resemble a city without garrison or defence, where the soldiers are all asleep, and where there is no sentinel on guard.

Secondly, we should be most careful to sanctify this action, because it is one of the most earthly, and merely animal, of the day. Just as massive stones require great exertion to raise them from the earth, so do we require great efforts to elevate this action to God. It is so much the more difficult to give the necessary attention to it, because the soul, dissipated by the occupations and exercises of the day, seeks but rest from labour, and repose; and the religious, in place of thinking that this repose is one of her principal occupations, yields to it without being animated with any Christian disposition; and even sometimes when she would wish to perform it in a holy manner, she is so overpowered by drowsiness, as to be incapable of any distinct act of the will.

The third reason, which should lead us to sanctify our repose, is that it is the last action of the day, and it may be the last of our lives.

It is the last action of the day; consequently we should consecrate it to God more fervently than our other actions. For if we begin the day by Him we should also conclude it by Him, according to these words of Holy Writ: "I am the first and the last, the beginning and the end." Besides, this last action, if well done, may repair the defects of the others; and, on the contrary, if imperfectly done, may tarnish the merit of every preceding action.

It may be the last act of our lives; how many retire to rest and never again rise, but pass from the natural sleep to the sleep of death! If death surprise us in our other duties, we may have a moment for reflection and repentance; but in sleep it is impossible. What a state to appear before God, and to undergo His judgment! Those who do not retire to rest in a pious, Christian manner, incur this risk.

How then are we to sanctify sleep? We are to regulate the exterior and interior.

As to the exterior, there are three principal virtues which should accompany it: exactness, modesty, and silence. Exactness, by being in bed at the hour appointed; and having our candle extinguished, as the rule ordains, which is the expression of the will of God. Modesty, which should be very great; we should undress in the presence of God, and our guardian angel, with as much reverence as we would do in the presence of those persons who would inspire us with most respect; in sleeping our attitude should be conformable to the strictest decorum, and we should always be entirely covered. In fine, the most exact silence, if from circumstances we are in the same cell or apartment with another; we should never utter a word that could be deferred to another time.

As to the interior sentiments with which we should perform this action. In undressing, let us adore Jesus Christ at the moment of taking His repose, and let us be penetrated with the sentiments with which He was animated, namely, sentiments of penance and sacrifice.

In going to bed, we may adore our Lord in the mystery of His death and sepulture, considering our bed as a coffin, our sheets as winding sheets, and our sleep as an image of death, of which we shall one day be the victims. When going to sleep, let us adore the eternal repose that God takes in Himself, and which He takes and will for ever take in His saints; or that which Jesus Christ Himself took whilst on earth. We should partake of the repose of sleep, because such is the will of God, because He has subjected us to this necessity, and in order that we may repair our strength to labour for His glory.

If it happens that we awake from time to time during the night, we may gently and without effort renew some of these holy thoughts, or think of the mysteries of religion, implore the mercy of God, the protection of Mary, &c.

SECTION IV.—*Of Rising, and the Manner of sanctifying it.*

M. Tronson says, when we do not sanctify this first action of the day, we offend God, injure ourselves, and give the devil an advantage over us.

We offend God, by depriving Him of an action which belongs to Him, since we are His by so many titles, and we should only fructify for Him, as the field becomes fruitful for its owner; we offend Him, because we place something created, which is a nothing in His eyes, in competition with Him; and inasmuch as He is very jealous of the first fruits.

We injure ourselves, because, as we have said before, we ordinarily spend the day as we commenced it; if we begin it by distractions and sloth, we shall continue it in the same way. The reason is, that on our awaking from sleep the passions are more deadened, the imagination more disengaged, the mind more at liberty, the soul more calm and tranquil, and the thoughts which then take possession of our minds make strong and durable impressions. Such thoughts, say the Fathers, are like a stone which is cast into still water: it forms circles which increase and multiply without number; circles which would be soon effaced in a running stream. During the day, when the soul is agitated and excited by the different objects which present themselves, when the passions are alive, thoughts do not make such lively impressions, but those which come in the calm and repose of awaking, make deep impressions which are with difficulty effaced. St. John Climacus relates that a great servant of God said, that he judged of the whole day by the morning, and that he knew how he would spend it by the way he commenced it.

Lastly, by not sanctifying our rising, we give the devil an advantage over us ; for we generally spend the day as we commenced it, and the greater part belongs to Him who occupied the beginning: so that, if the devil snatches it from us by sloth, dissipation, or levity, we shall find it rather troublesome to divest ourselves of our subtle enemy, in our actions during the day. St. John Climacus remarks, that the devils use every effort to rob us of the first moments of the day; and depute one of their number to watch our waking, to occupy our first thoughts, and hinder us from consecrating them to God.

We should then sanctify it outwardly and inwardly.

Outwardly, by observing punctuality, diligence, and modesty.

Punctuality, by rising immediately when the signal is given, without anticipating or deferring a moment.

Diligence, by dressing promptly, in order to be ready for prayer at the appointed signal, and not be obliged to arrange our dress on our way to the choir but to leave our cell fully dressed.

Modesty, by shunning every attitude which would not be becoming: a pious author says, that the faithful soul regards her body as a sacred vessel which has the honour of containing Jesus Christ, or as the temple of the Holy Ghost; and treats it with the respect due to it in this double quality.

In order to sanctify this action interiorly, we may make a few considerations on awaking and dressing.

On awaking. Our actions should be done in honour of those of Jesus Christ, or in union with them: so in this one we may propose to ourselves to honour three mysteries of the Son of God, uniting our intentions to His, and entering into the dispositions He had in each of these mysteries.

The first is the Incarnation. As our Lord, in this mystery, came forth in a manner from the bosom of His Father, where He reposed, to embrace a painful and laborious life, so by awaking, we come forth from our repose, to enter on a life of pain and labour. Let us honour the dispositions of our Lord in this circumstance, and conform ours to them; these dispositions should be adoration, gratitude, love, and oblation.

The second mystery in honour of which we may consecrate our awaking, is the awaking of Jesus Christ. He awoke like us, in order to sanctify in His person our awaking, by meriting for us grace, and showing us the dispositions we should have to sanctify it. Besides the four dispositions we have just indicated, and which were ever in His Heart, there are two others, which were conspicuous in His awaking; the first was an ardent desire to procure the glory of His Father; the second, to destroy the empire of the devil and of sin: dispositions which we should nourish in our hearts daily, even from our awaking.

Lastly, the third mystery of Jesus Christ which we may consider, is that of His Resurrection, of which our awaking is the image. In effect, we arise from our bed, which is a figure of the grave; we awake from sleep, which is an image of death, to resume a new life; now in the Resurrection, we find two dispositions to which we should conform. The first disposition of Jesus Christ is an estrangement and separation from every creature: He separated Himself from the world; we should separate our thoughts and affections from it. The second disposition of Jesus Christ is to retire into the bosom of His Father; like Him, we should remain hidden in God.

Whilst we dress ourselves, we may honour Jesus Christ assuming our mortality, and enter into the sentiments with which He was penetrated in this mystery; sentiments of penance for our sins, and submission to the will of God.

To these two sentiments, we may add two others; the one of thanksgiving, for the garments which have been given to us to preserve us from the inclemency of the weather. How many poor creatures in the most severe winter have not sufficient covering, and who, perhaps, have not offended God as often as we have. The other sentiment is an ardent desire of being invested with the grace of an innocent heart.

SECTION IV.—*Of our Meals.*

Taking our meals is an action of such a nature, that it requires all our application to perform it well; and if we are not particularly attentive and vigilant, we run the risk of never doing it in a Christian manner. Thus, when the great apostle warns us to refer to God all our actions, he specifies this in particular: "Whether you eat or drink, or whatever else you do, do all for the glory of God." He speaks in a general manner of our other actions, but he refers particularly to that of eating and drinking, to make us understand how careful we should be to perform it well.

The Church also shows us the importance we should attach to this action, by the prayers that it makes us recite before beginning it. Why so many prayers for an action so common? We do not find that it has prescribed anything similar for our other actions.

What renders the sanctification of our repasts important, is because this action is of a lower order, and perilous; and nevertheless necessary and frequent.

First, this action is important, because of its inferior nature. Man, who by nature is so greatly raised above other corporeal creatures, and by grace is exalted above the angels, and associated with God, by the participation of His divine nature, is so lowered by the action of eating, that he is abased beneath his condition, and rendered similar to the brute creation. Now, the inferiority of this action increases its importance; for the lower and more earthly it is, the more careful must we be to exalt, sanctify, and elevate it to God, to whom all our actions are to be referred.

Again, this action is important because it is surrounded by dangers. When we are obliged to expose ourselves on a stormy and dangerous sea, or to penetrate into regions difficult of access, where on all sides are precipices, we comprehend the necessity of great vigilance, and we use every means of escaping these dangers; now, the action of which we are treating is full of shoals and encompassed with danger; danger before meals, danger during meals, and danger after meals.

Danger before meals, by the immoderate desire of food; this leads to impatience, murmuring, sadness, anger, and many other emotions, which arise in the heart on this occasion; it is difficult to govern this desire when violent. St. Gregory says, that the disorders into which we fall, in consequence of this desire, are sometimes more criminal than the faults we commit in eating. This action is accompanied with danger, or rather with dangers, so manifold that few persons escape them all. St. Thomas specifies two kinds in particular; the first regards the food we take, too great delicacy in our choice or selection of food, or being too particular about the way in which it is dressed; also gluttony, taking more than necessary, &c. The others concern the action itself, as eating with too much precipitation and eagerness.

Lastly, this action is followed by danger, because the body having acquired new strength, is more impetuous in its movements, and it is more difficult to subject it; the body is an insolent slave, that we never treat well, but it revolts; becoming strong, it crushes the spirit beneath its weight, and renders it almost incapable of elevating itself to God.

This action is so necessary and frequent that it is another reason why we should attach great importance to it. When danger is great, frequent, and difficult to be perceived, provided it is not necessary, we have no reason to fear. And why? Because we can escape. But what is truly lamentable is, when danger is necessary and inevitable. And this is the case in the matter of which we are speaking; we are obliged to eat to preserve life, and God commands us to do so.

To sanctify the action of eating, it is necessary to place ourselves in Christian dispositions before, during, and after meals.

Before meals. The custom of our Lord, of the Apostles, of the primitive Christians, and of the universal Church, teaches us never to partake of food without having first addressed our prayers to God. We should conform to this custom with pious exactness; and, before going to table, ask of God two things which the Church suggests in the formula it prescribes. The first, that He would deign to bless us; the second, that He would bless the food we are going to take. We ask God to bless us, that we may not take nourishment from a carnal motive, but in a spirit of faith; to repair our strength, that we may be able to glorify Him. We ask Him to bless the food of which we are about to partake, that being sanctified by this benediction, instead of being an occasion of temptation and sin, it may sanctify and lead us to Him by gratitude and love.

During meals, we must try, according to the advice of the Saints, to nourish and occupy our souls with some pious thought. The most laudable and holy meditation we could have, would be to think of Jesus Christ taking His nourishment, or giving Himself for the nourishment of His creatures. Let us consider Jesus Christ taking His food. The dispositions of our Divine Redeemer during this action were obedience, frugality, penance, modesty, and a spirit of sacrifice. Let us place ourselves in the same dispositions; let us take our meals to obey God, and not the desires of sensuality; with frugality, not giving way to eagerness; in a spirit of penance, remembering that it was by eating that man lost original justice; in a spirit of mortification, taking what is least pleasing to the palate; in a spirit of sacrifice, immolating to God our desires and natural avidity.

We may unite ourselves to Jesus Christ giving Himself as food to His creatures, in the Holy Eucharist, or constituting the nourishment of the blessed in heaven: and from time to time we may elevate ourselves to Him by short and loving aspirations; adoring Him from this double point of view, and desiring this two-fold nourishment which will transform and render us divine, whilst earthly nourishment renders us material.

After our meals, we should thank God for the food He has given us, beg Him to pardon the faults we have committed, and beseech Him to grant that the strength we have derived from nourishment, may be employed in His service, and for His greater glory.

Section V.—*Of Recreation.*

Père Marin says that there exist few religious orders in which all intercourse with our neighbour and exterior relaxation are entirely forbidden. In the religious profession, as elsewhere, there are certain hours in which the sisters can converse together, to unbend the mind, and maintain mutual union and charity; and to this time we may apply the words of Scripture: " There is a time to laugh."

We are permitted to rejoice in it innocently; and it would be an unreasonable thing to assist at recreation with as serious an air as we would have in the refectory, or at chapter. Nor would it be just to require the young to have at that time as much gravity as the more advanced. What would make a novice or young professed laugh very much, would scarcely cause a mother or senior sister to smile. The old should not repine at the gaiety of the young, when it is within bounds, nor the junior be offended at the cold indifference of the senior, who cannot laugh at what amuses them so much. They should bear with each other in a spirit of meekness and charity; and each should act in such a manner, at recreation, that it may correspond to the end for which it has been instituted; which is, to unbend the mind, that they may afterwards apply more willingly to recollection, and thus maintain all hearts in strict union.

Let us add, continues the same author, that recreation should be regarded as an exercise of the community, to which each religious should repair through a principle of charity and regularity. In truth, it is much more edifying to see all the sisters cordially rejoice together, than making separate parties. Those private recreations always denote some division, or at least that some do not sympathise with the others, and have not sufficient charity and virtue to bear with their conversation. I would prefer seeing the religious at the hour of recreation innocently rejoice with their sisters, than through a misplaced desire of retreat retire alone to their cells, or through mistaken devotion employ this time in lecture or meditation. Each exercise in religion has its fixed hour; and this, not to gratify the desire of any one in particular, but that they may render to all their sisters what they owe to them: and if the particular employment of any one, or obedience, do not call her elsewhere, charity and her rule oblige her to rejoice in the Lord with her sisters.

In recreation there is a certain excess to be avoided. Père Bourdaloue observes, that in our conversations with our neighbour many abuses creep in. From these we cannot better guard ourselves than by following these three general rules.

First. That our conversation should always be accompanied with a religious modesty and a wise reserve.

Second. That it should be useful and solid.

Third. That charity should reign in it, and that we

should banish from it everything contrary to the spirit of peace and union.

Our conversation should always be accompanied with religious modesty. As there are certain rules of worldly decorum for persons in the world, so in religion there are rules of religious decorum for those engaged in that holy state; and with regard to conversation, it is certain that a thousand things which would not be at all blameable in worldlings, would be very unsuitable, and even reprehensible, in religious. To religious may be specially applied the advice of the Apostle to the primitive Christians: " Let your modesty be known to all." It appears in the countenance, in the deportment, in the gesture, in the tone of voice, in our expressions, and in the whole exterior. Modesty is neither affected nor studied; affectation and modesty never go hand in hand. Without constraint or effort, it avoids certain haughty airs, precipitate motions, affected gesture, bursts of loud speaking and laughter, expressions and words too familiar. It is a well known maxim, " that from the abundance of the heart the mouth speaketh," and we find the heart diffuses itself by means of the tongue; we may thence conclude that a religious, too lively and worldly in her conversation, is dissipated in her inward soul. A recollected soul, who keeps herself everywhere in the presence of God, and acts for God, never abandons herself to her natural vivacity; she is straightforward and affable, without exterior dissipation; she is neither morose nor melancholy; but in the midst of her joy and the demonstrations she gives of it, she loses nothing of that seriousness which should temper it. She never maintains a sad and mournful silence, nor does she seek to have the whole conversation to herself, and to domineer over her sisters; she says simply what she thinks, and leaves to each one leisure to explain herself, being always more ready to listen than to speak. How many faults should we avoid, did we form ourselves on such a model, and if we never forgot the Christian and religious respect we owe to each other.

Our conversation should be solid and useful; this does not mean that it should be always on spiritual or pious subjects, although this would be very desirable amongst religious; but after all, as religion affords these hours of recreation to unbend and relax the mind, it also allows a little more liberty at this time, and we are not forbidden to introduce subjects which are not so elevated or important; this toleration is reasonable and at times necessary.

But it would not be at all suitable for religious to converse only on trifles, or to hold only vain and childish discourses; if they only spoke of the affairs of the world or what passed in it, as if they assembled to content curiosity, and to hear worldly reports and rumours; if in their recreations there was not a word of God, nor with reference to God; if when any subject was brought forward that had a spiritual tendency, the conversation fell away, and the sisters testified disgust or weariness. Such conduct as this would certainly not be in accordance with the sanctity of the religious profession.

Our conversation should be charitable, without giving offence to any one. The Apostle has said, "that he who does not sin by his tongue is a perfect man;" we may say so more especially, with regard to charity. It is great perfection and rare virtue never to wound it in our conversation; even in religious houses, it is one of the most common and dangerous stumbling-blocks we have to fear. Charity is impaired in different ways:—

First, by the natural impatience and sourness of certain hasty and passionate tempers, who cannot express themselves on any subject in a gentle manner; we can scarcely speak to them, without exposing ourselves to a disagreeable answer: and it is in vain that we take all possible precautions; we shall always have many repulses to sustain on their part.

Secondly, charity is wounded by those contentions and disputes in which both parties become heated; this proceeds from two sorts of characters very annoying in the intercourse of life: the first are of a contradictory disposition, and the other obstinate; whence it results that the former, through a spirit of contradiction, form difficulties about everything that is said to them; and the latter, through obstinacy, never yield, nor acknowledge they are deceived.

Thirdly, jests wound charity; both when we are too free in using them, or too sensitive in receiving them.

Fourthly, rash judgments, or murmurs, either against superiors, or those who are charged with any office in the community; or against particular persons.

Fifthly, it is wounded by detraction; and religious on this point require to be as much on their guard as persons in the world.

To sanctify recreation, we must offer it to God, and make frequent ejaculatory prayers.

SECTION VI.—*Of Chapters and Assemblies which take place in Convents to deliberate on the Affairs of the Community.*

By chapters we mean those assemblies which take place in convents, either at fixed periods, or at times appointed by the superioress. They are of two kinds; those appointed to arrange the spiritual and temporal affairs of the establishment, and those for fraternal correction. Of the latter we have elsewhere treated under the head of Chapter of Faults; it is, therefore, of the former we are now to speak.

Lay sisters are not admitted to those chapters in which the temporal or spiritual affairs of the community are transacted. Even all the choir nuns are not allowed to be present; only those who have attained the number of years prescribed after profession can assist at them, take part in the deliberations, and give their votes.

Vocal religious (as those are called who have a deliberative vote) should bring to these chapters, when they are convoked, general dispositions in harmony with their holy state. In these assemblies, as in every other action, they should be penetrated with a spirit of faith; considering that the glory of God is concerned in the function they fulfil. They should offer it to Him, and discharge it with a view of pleasing Him.

They should be animated by the spirit of profound humility; being careful not to exalt themselves in their hearts, either over those sisters who have not a deliberative vote, or over those who sit in council with them; mistrusting their own lights, they should banish the spirit of contention and attachment to their own views, and avoid all witty repartees and offensive words in the discussions which may be necessary to clear up the points in deliberation.

The Vocals, in these chapters, should be penetrated before God with the importance of the affairs submitted to their deliberation. The most important which can be proposed to them are the election of the superioress or of the different officials; the admission of postulants to the habit, and of novices to profession.

The Election of the Superioress.—There is nothing more important than the choice of a superioress for the convent she is to govern. In a word, the superioress is the soul of the community at the head of which she is placed; if she has the requisite dispositions, she will maintain and increase the religious spirit, where it is in vigour; she will reanimate it, if it has been weakened; and she will revive it, if it has been destroyed. She will be an anchor of salvation for the community confided to her, and for each in particular. But if she have not the requisite qualifications, what evils may she not entail on the whole community?

Nothing, therefore, is more important than the choice of a superioress, for those whose duty it is to make the selection; for, says Collet, the wrong a superioress would do who had not the spirit of her state and the requisite qualifications, is to be imputed to those who elected her, when they could have foreseen it.

How, then, are the Vocals to proceed to this important choice? The Abbe Desvillars says, that " as the time of the election approaches, the sisters must begin by a more regular and mortified life, to obtain guidance from the Holy Spirit in so delicate a matter. They should often invoke His assistance and light; after the example of the Apostles, who assembled to elect from amongst the disciples, one who was to take the place of the traitor Judas in the apostolate. They should pray fervently that God would make known to them her whom He has chosen: they must consult God alone, not flesh and blood; they should be perfectly disengaged from every bias of human feeling, from every prejudice and prepossession.

"It sometimes happens," continues the same author, "that they give their vote because the person in question is a relative, one whom they love, and who, in her office, would act as they would wish; although they are perfectly convinced she has not the requisite qualifications to discharge her office before God. To give a vote from such motives as these would be sinful; because it would not be the glory of God or the good of religion they would seek, but their own advantage.

If often happens that we are convinced a certain sister has all the qualities necessary to fulfil an office; but we do not give her our vote, because we nourish a secret dislike to her, or we fear her regularity. By this conduct, we deprive religion, as far as depends on us, of a subject of great value, and we shall have to render a terrible account to God, for the good she would have done, and which she will not do, because we have deprived her of the occasion of doing it.

What then should a Vocal do who wishes to act irreproachably in so delicate a matter? Having put aside all human feelings, having consulted God alone, and the good of the community, she should give her vote to the person whom she believes, after serious reflection, qualified to fulfil the important office; and if succeeding events prove that she was deceived in her choice, she is not responsible before God; because, in giving her suffrage, she had Him alone in view, and she adopted all the precautions suggested by prudence, in a matter of such importance.

In convents where the principal officials are elected, the Vocals should attach the same importance to such a choice as to that of superioress, and proceed to it with the same spirit of faith, the same precautions, and the same detachment.

The Admission of Postulants to the Habit.—The step which the postulant takes, the day on which she assumes the religious dress, is not irrevocable, since she does not bind herself by any vows. However, it is the first advance into the sanctuary; she approaches nearer to God; although she does not unite herself to Jesus Christ indissolubly, still she openly manifests her intention of doing so; and if her assuming the habit were not the expression of this intention, she would be guilty of base hypocrisy. The Vocals, then, should only admit to the habit those in whom they perceive marks of a vocation, not indeed certain, but probable; it would be as wrong for them to admit a person in whom they discovered no marks of a vocation, as to reject one whose vocation was undoubted.

The Admission of Novices to Profession.—This is an action of the highest importance, and one which may involve the Vocals in a fearful responsibility, if they do not use the necessary precautions, and are not animated by upright intentions. During the accomplishment of this duty, we may say they are suspended between two precipices, in both of which danger is to be apprehended. If, by an imprudent vote, they reject a person with a true vocation, and again plunge her into the perils of the world, against which God willed to shelter her by conducting her to religion, will they not have to answer one day for their imprudence and her ruin, if, unhappily, she goes astray and is lost? If, on the contrary, they imprudently admit a person who has no vocation, and who, consequently, may become for the community not only a burthen, but also an object of scandal, or even a source of danger and ruin, what account will they not have to render?

The Vocals should therefore prepare themselves for

this important vote with the same spirit of faith, and the same prudence, that we have spoken of before: they should guard against natural sympathies and natural aversions, having in view only the glory of God, the good of the community, and their own salvation.

This vote is of such importance that she, who would be guided by passion or caprice, would evidently be guilty of a serious fault.

How are the Vocals to procure the light necessary to guide them in giving their votes? By prayer, and by the wise reflections they will make at the foot of their crucifix.

When there is a question of the reception of postulants to the habit, or of novices to profession, the Vocals, seeing them but seldom, as the novitiate is separated from the community, may, in all safety, form their judgment on the accounts given them by the superioress and mistress of novices, and vote accordingly. If they are led into error, the fault would be in no way visited on them.

CHAPTER XIII.

OF THE TRIALS OF THE INTERIOR LIFE.

It is written in the Holy Scripture that God tries those whom He loves, and experience proves to us that He acts thus towards those souls upon whom He has designs of perfection; those whom He calls to the religious life should expect similar trials. In treating of prayer, we touched on this important subject; but as trials do not exist in that exercise alone, we will speak of them here in a more extended and general manner.

Section I.—*Of Interior Pains in general.*

After the soul has been for some time favoured with divine consolations (for God generally consoles her in the beginning to encourage her in the way of perfection), " it happens," says Père Nouet, " that God withdraws from her by a secret design of His providence, and dries up the source of her spiritual delights."

Then the understanding, which was accustomed to enjoy the light of God, finds itself in thick and painful obscurity, having no longer the liberty of acting, nor the pleasure of receiving the rays which come to it from the Father of lights; it seems to it that it has become blind, so destitute is it of good thoughts; and this privation of sight, added to its feebleness, is a source of great suffering.

The will, which before had such sweet affections, or at least so great strength and vigour in embracing good, however contrary to its inclinations, seems no longer able to form a single desire of virtue, and remains in an extreme dryness, languor, and insensibility.

The memory remembers nothing; or, if it has any remembrance of God, or of the graces it has received, this only serves to embitter its grief and augment its regret for being deprived of them.

The inferior appetite feels great trouble and strong aversion to the practices of virtue and mortification, which it conceives to be too difficult and contrary to nature: thence it yields to wearisome sadness, which abates its courage, and changes into bitterness the sweetness it before experienced.

The soul thus desolated, seeing herself reduced to so painful a state that she can neither use her memory for remembering, her understanding for meditating, nor her will for producing affections to good, sometimes becomes so frightened, that she looks on herself as abandoned by God: imagining it is all her own fault; that she has committed some great sin of which she is not aware; that it may be a mark of reprobation; or that all which hitherto passed between herself and God is illusion. The devil, seeing her pains, and trying to fish in troubled water, takes occasion to attack her by different temptations, to make her fall into his snares. He awakens her passions anew, inclining her on the side of sensible things, raising in the inferior part of the soul, where his power chiefly lies, many subjects of disgust, which render her so sad and fretful that she can hardly support herself.

He tempts her to despair, persuading her that there is no longer any remedy; that having abused too many of the graces of God, she has merited an eternal confusion by her infidelity; he tempts her to blaspheme and murmur against God, as though He were cruel and merciless to her.

He importunes her with a thousand horrible thoughts, and with doubts against faith, to make her lose patience and tranquillity of mind. Agitated by so many waves which incessantly beat against her, and penetrated with such acute pain, she is sometimes so affected by her own sufferings as to pity herself. At other times she seeks support and consolation in the advice of her director, who saddens her more than he consoles her; in books of piety and exercises of devotion, which weary her; in penances, fasts, watchings, and mortifications, which exhaust the little strength remaining to her, and kill the body without curing the soul.

Sometimes she is even reduced to such an extremity, that not finding any remedy, and feeling herself oppressed with sadness, she feels, as it were, forced to complain to our Lord of His rigour. It seems to her that she reproaches Him for His severity, and says to Him with Job: "Oh, how cruel art Thou become to me!" A thousand dark and distressing thoughts pass through her mind in succession, or sometimes all at once, to overwhelm her.

At one moment she offers herself to suffer to the end of the world; and the next, she begs some consolation; another time she would wish, if it were possible, to be reduced to nothing and even to be plunged into hell; in a word, her spirit undergoes a thousand caprices, and says many things which would be so many blasphemies, if her will took part in them; if they were not rather expressions of the pain she feels than deliberate movements. But as these words come rather from the lips than the heart, they are in a manner excusable; at least they must not always be looked on as criminal, since the soul on reflection humbles herself immediately, and casts herself on God by a total acquiescence to His will.

Is it not plainly the love she bears Him which causes her pain? Not believing that she loves Him, she can have no rest; and this privation of love, which she imagines, would never overwhelm her thus, if she did not love Him.

The most dangerous temptation, and the one most prejudicial to troubled souls, who have the fear of God and their perfection at heart, is that which persuades them to examine themselves on the thoughts they have had, to see if they have consented to them or not. This examen is more injurious than the evil itself, because it throws the soul into great uneasiness, and hinders it from attending to God and to her duty. The pain the temptation causes is a sign she has not consented to it. And even if she were clearly to see she had been faulty, she should humble herself without trouble, tranquilly make an act of contrition, and without any vexation or bitterness; she should simply accuse herself of it, and then rest in peace without thinking more of it.

It is an artifice of the spirit of darkness to suggest to the soul who resists him these scrupulous examens, under pretext of greater purity of conscience, when he sees he cannot otherwise gain her consent. If he can once engage her in this labyrinth, he is not content with using stratagem with regard to present temptations: he places before her eyes her past life, embroiling her in many doubts, persuading her that she has not been sufficiently explicit in her past confessions, and, therefore, that she should repeat them. He seizes, above all, the time of communion and prayer to torment her, and make her lose the fruit of both; he entangles her in his meshes so skilfully and cunningly, that she can only escape by absolute submission of her own judgment, in allowing herself to be blindly conducted in paths so obscure. This is generally the most difficult point for her: for if she is told to pay no attention to those importunate temptations against faith and purity, or to be anxious about producing contrary acts, she takes that for a tacit consent; again, if she is told not to mind the scruples which arise concerning her past life or her present state, she imagines that those who conduct her do not understand her, and that assuredly she is obliged, under pain of mortal sin, to have an elucidation of the matter.

She goes even farther, and imagines that neither the superioress nor the confessor can dispense her from the commandments of God and of the Church; and that the precept of confession being one of the most important, she cannot acquit herself of it properly, if she does not reflect on herself incessantly;

although she derives no other profit from this than to say a multitude of useless things, which are often even ridiculous and unworthy of the sacrament.

If any one believed her, they would allow her to speak always of herself and her pains; than which nothing could be more injurious to her, because it would strengthen her trials and prevent the operation of God in her soul. This arises from weakness of mind, accompanied by secret pride and self-love, covering itself with a mantle of humility; thinking she practises this holy virtue in saying many things very abject, either in confession or in the declaration she makes of her state. She is, however, miserably deceived: true humility would be submission of judgment.

Behold a sketch of what passes in souls who are afflicted with interior pains. Not that a soul feels all these trials at once; aridity is not always universal either as regards the pains or the duration; it may be almost continual, or it may come from time to time.

These trials have their degrees and intervals. If they are great in the beginning, they increase in proportion to their duration. At the same time there are some peaceful moments in which God communicates to the soul much sweetness; after which she experiences great sufferings, which are also followed by interior communications, intimate in proportion to the length of time and fidelity with which she has suffered. When she is suffering, it seems to her she could never again have any content; and when she is in consolation, she thinks she will never again be in pain.

However, God does not always act thus towards the souls whom He tries. To show He is absolute master, and that He has the key of heaven and hell,

He allows the same soul at the same time to have consolation and desolation, shedding extraordinary lights in the superior part of the soul, whilst the inferior part is immersed in agony by the excess of its pains.

The best advice that can be given to a soul in this state is to allow God to act: to receive, suffer, and support all that He does and all that He permits with an invincible patience and a perfect abandonment to His will; without thinking all is lost, when she feels extreme pain. Let her await the visitation of God with loving confidence. Let her not be weary or cast down, no matter what she suffers or what imperfection she discovers in herself; let her remember that the greatest friends of God, St. Teresa, St. John of the Cross, &c., have passed through these ordeals. Let her neglect nothing of what concerns obedience and the practice of virtue; let her acquit herself carefully of her office and of all that is assigned to her; after the example of Jesus Christ, who being in mortal sadness did not abandon His prayer at the customary hour, and like a good and vigilant pastor, left His prayer three times to visit and console His poor apostles dejected by languor, sadness, and want of courage. Let her imitate this great Model, and neglect nothing of what her duty prescribes exteriorly; as to the interior, let her be satisfied with appeasing her passions, without constraining herself to produce many acts or practices of devotion.

We have just seen that the state of privation and trial to which God sometimes permits souls to be reduced, gives rise to fears, uneasiness, and unfounded doubts; this uneasiness and these doubts are what we call scruples, and of them we will speak in the next section.

Section II.—*Of Scruples.*

A scruple is an unfounded doubt, or one that has very little foundation, which troubles and disquiets the conscience. It is a vain apprehension, an extravagant fear that there is sin, where in reality there is none; this causes much disturbance to the soul.

The symptoms of scruples may be reduced to four. First, to be ever changing in opinion for reasons of no moment, as to what is lawful or unlawful, in what we have done or are going to do. The second, is to indulge in minute and absurd reflections on the most trivial circumstances of our actions. The third, is to show much pertinacity of will and judgment, consulting many persons, thinking little of their advice, and still clinging to self-opinion. The fourth, to act with anxiety, a certain trouble which takes off the attention and discernment, which embarrasses the liberty and holds the soul captive.

We may assign three causes to scruples; the Divine permission, the human soul, and the spirit of darkness.

First, though we must beware of saying that God is in any sense the principle and author of our illusions; yet, from motives known to His Sovereign wisdom, He sometimes withholds the light which would dissipate them. By this withholding of light, God punishes certain souls, making them expiate their trivial faults and the disorders of their past life, and this penance is indeed as great as the roughest hair cloth.

We may add that God, by this means, represses in souls of distinguished merit, the pride arising from science and human talents; He rouses the fervour and zeal of tepid souls, and prepares some souls for the highest virtues; because this state humbles them, makes them lose confidence in self, places them in the way of meriting, by making them seek not the consolations of God, but the God of consolation. It is thus that St. Teresa and so many others have been raised to very high perfection; and if they are persons whom God destines for the direction of souls, He teaches them, by their own experience, how they should guide others.

To know if scruples thus come from God, it is useful to examine what motive gives rise to them, and what effects they produce. When they come from God, they arise from a great fear of offending Him; and although this fear is immoderate, it springs from a good foundation, which is charity. The effects produced by scruples which come from God are, a more sensible horror of sin, a careful avoiding of occasions, a perfect reformation of the past, and more generous efforts to advance in virtue.

These scruples do not generally last very long. When God sees that His elect souls are well purified, He dissipates, according to His promise, the storm which agitates them, making them enjoy a profound calm. These persons, to be cured of their scruples, should apply themselves to know what God demands of them, and do it generously.

Secondly, scruples may be from the human soul itself. They often arise, say the holy Fathers, from a cold melancholy temperament, one naturally disposed to fear and doubt; or from a phlegmatic constitution, fond of ease, impatient, abhorring the least difficulty; or from a morbid state of the imagination, which, owing to great vivacity, receives impressions from all the objects which present themselves to it, and is disturbed by them; or from levity of mind, which changes opinion with every breath of wind; or from subtlety of spirit, which is too artful in forming difficulties, and too easily troubled when they are to be resolved; or, lastly, from a littleness of mind, which can only consider things to a certain extent, which always takes a one-sided view of matters, which cannot discern between good and evil, between mortal and venial sin, between temptation and consent.

To all these causes may be added others, such as immoderate austerities which weaken the mind, the society of scrupulous persons, ignorance, reading (without understanding) books which go too deep for us; or, again, mere superficial reading, &c.

In some persons scruples arise from pride. They abound in their own sense and judgment: this produces conceitedness and difficulty in submitting; sometimes they wish to appear clever, make distinctions and difficulties about everything, &c.

Persons whose scruples arise from themselves, are distinguished by a profound melancholy, an excessive timidity about everything, useless and vexatious subtlety; an obstinacy and conceitedness which which makes them ever revert to their first ideas, and hinders the best advice from entering their minds: whence results a great indocility, which does not allow them to yield to truth.

Thirdly, scruples may come from the spirit of darkness. This cruel enemy of salvation carefully observes the state of souls; if he perceives that one is carried to relaxation, he urges her to adopt many works of supererogation, in order that she may fancy herself devout, and that she may not think of her culpable negligence in her essential duties. Such a person teases herself with scruples about objects of mere devotion, while she neglects her indispensable duties.

If, on the contrary, the devil finds a soul rigidly exact in her duties, and naturally inclined to practices of piety, he suggests to her a greater number to overload her, and thus cause her to perform them negligently, that he may afterwards throw her into trouble about her want of faithfulness.

At other times he endeavours to shake the firmness of a timorous soul, troubling her imagination in such a manner, that it presents but gloomy thoughts to the understanding; he fills her with vain fears and perplexities, making her fear she had consented to the bad thoughts which came into her mind, or to the impressions which she felt.

We know at once the scruples which are from the devil by the darkening effect they produce in the soul. They chill its ardour in pursuit of good, inspiring it even with disgust, representing to it its evils as incurable, inspiring despair, and leading it to deny itself trifling things, as though they were grievous, and on the contrary to allow itself to do without remorse what is criminal.

For scruples there are general and particular remedies; general, which suit all kinds of scruples; particular, adapted to particular kinds and characters.

The general remedies may be reduced chiefly to four.

First, humble and fervent prayer. The scrupulous soul needs great confidence in God; she should regard Him as a tender father who wishes to save all His children. In the height of her disturbance, she should recur rather to God than to her director; it is prayer made with faith, confidence, and abandonment to the mercy of God, and not confession, which cures the scrupulous soul.

Second, entire and blind obedience to her confessor. The scrupulous soul should choose a good confessor, and when she has found such, she should be perfectly submissive to him, and place unlimited confidence in his opinion. In place of seeking to guide herself by her own lights, she must feel the absolute necessity of submitting to the advice which is given to her. Without this, no remedy could avail her.

Third, she must shun idleness. Nothing is more useful to the scrupulous than occupation. Manual works, when painful, are often a better remedy than any advice that could be given. Exterior works of charity, for example, withdraw the mind from self and its sad reflections, to apply it to objects of compassion; the scrupulous soul, in her leisure moments, should never be alone. It would be desirable if then she could have the society of sensible persons, solidly virtuous, of a cheerful turn, not to talk about her distress, but to learn from them to acquit herself cheerfully of her duties, and to get out of her silly and dangerous train of thought.

Fourth, she is to despise annoying thoughts, and distract herself from whatever may trouble her. A scrupulous soul who listens to her scruples and reflects on them, finds a thousand occasions of being troubled about nothing. She is frightened by an imaginary fear of sinning in all she does, and although she has observed that this is vain and foolish, still she accustoms herself to fear where there is no danger. The sovereign remedy, when the scruple begins to make itself felt, is to let it pass quietly, and despise it; to renew your confidence in God, and determine to follow the advice of your confessor.

As to particular remedies, each director can apply what is suitable to his penitent, and each penitent should manifest a docile spirit in following the instructions given her.

CHAPTER XIV.

There is no position on earth so advantageous for salvation, nor any state so holy, in which we do not encounter some shoals, against which we are in danger of being thrown, and of being shipwrecked; for which reason the Saviour recommended so often to His Apostles, and in their persons to all those who have their salvation at heart, to watch and pray without ceasing.

Those who vow themselves in religion to the interior life should be guarded against three principal shoals, which we will indicate in the following sections; tepidity, the abuse of grace, and illusions.

Section I.—*Of Tepidity.*

We must be on our guard not to confound the state of desolation and trial of which we have spoken with tepidity. The state of dryness is a kind of weakness and impotence which sometimes takes possession of a soul all of a sudden, and independent of her will; and so paralyses it, that it seems incapable of applying to spiritual things. The soul afflicted with it is frightened; she is grieved, she laments, and makes every effort to recover her primitive fervour. It is, say spiritual writers, a state of violence in which the soul suffers, but which brings no detriment to her innocence. God permits that she should pass through this ordeal, to purify her, and to detach her from sensible consolations; and He often acts thus even towards His greatest friends.

Tepidity is very different; it is the consequence and punishment of voluntary infidelities, or rather, it is infidelity itself, bound in a manner to the will, by the force of habit, and which benumbs, depraves, and inspires it with horror for the accomplishment of duty, and gives it an attraction for torpor and inaction. The tepid soul does not bewail her state, as does the soul desolated by aridity: she loves and is pleased with it. Let us look on the fearful portrait of tepidity traced for us by an eminent spiritual writer.

"I understand," says he, "by the state of tepidity, a state of languor in the service of God; a state in which, to tranquillise ourselves on our faults, we say to ourselves, if we do not all the good we should do, at least we do not much evil; if we transgress the rules, we do not infringe on our vows; if we have not great virtue, neither have we great defects. I mean that division of the heart, in which we wish to give to God what is of precept, and to reserve to ourselves what is of counsel;—in which we still love our duty, but in which we also love our convenience;—in which being content to be neither better nor worse, neither perfect nor criminal, we would neither advance nor recede in the path of virtue. I mean that spirit of relaxation, that voluntary languor, that habitual indolence, that culpable inactivity, those continual negligences,—those constant infractions of rule. I mean that state in which we form good resolutions to-day, and to-morrow violate them,—in which we occasionally make some efforts and immediately relax; in which we are incessantly falling into the same irregularities, and in which we believe ourselves victorious because we are not conquered in essential points. In a word, I mean by tepidity a determination in the conduct to pass lightly over common and ordinary faults, to commit them without concern, to multiply them without remorse, to speak without circumspection, to murmur without scruple, to complain without consideration; to live without recollection, to pray without attention, to confess without amendment, to communicate without fervour, and to act thus without being troubled, because we do not see any other evil in it than that of deriving no fruit from all. That is what I mean by a state of tepidity."

How displeasing this state is to God, He Himself has declared in the most explicit manner. The tepid soul, He says in Holy Scripture, has become so insupportable to Him, that she provokes Him to a kind of vomiting. He does not yet reject her, but He begins to do so by withdrawing from her. Thus tepidity is a beginning of reprobation. And if tepidity in a simple Christian is revolting in the sight of God, what must it be in a religious? The religious is by her profession obliged to tend to perfection; and she who is tepid is crouching amid her imperfections without making any effort to arise from them. God lavishes on her His choicest and most abundant favours, to enable her to attain the perfection of her holy state; and she resists, despises, and perpetually abuses them, thus drawing down on herself the indignation of God. These few reflections suffice to show us clearly the danger of the state of tepidity, but what will make it still more evident is, that the soul in this state is not affected by it, but remains in it without remorse, because, instead of thinking of the evil she has done or the good she should do, she thinks only of the evil she has not done, and of the little good she has done. Instead of comparing herself with those in religion who are more fervent and regular than herself, she compares herself with those who are less so; because this comparison flatters and deceives her. She says to herself, with the confidence of the Pharisee, that she has not the defects which such or such a sister has. Hence it comes that serving God with this deplorable negligence and remissness, she renders herself a flattering testimony as if she fulfilled all justice.

O state infinitely dangerous, since, according to the oracle of the Holy Ghost, a state still worse, that of sin, would be preferable! It would be better for some souls, says Bourdaloue, to fall into mortal and grievous sin than into this state; for they would not long support the remorse of such sin. Humbling, alarming them by its enormity, it would soon force them to a perfect conversion; whereas the state of tepidity causes them neither reproach nor uneasiness. All spiritual writers have agreed that it is more difficult to arise from a life of tepidity, than from a life of sin and licentiousness.

But whence does tepidity generally spring? One of its great causes is, facility in omitting spiritual exercises; prayer, lecture, communion, examens of conscience, practices of penance and mortification. The least business withdraws us from them; the least impediment is a pretext for exemption for them, or at least for deferring them, which is often the same as omitting them.

A second cause is the negligence with which we discharge our duties. We do not begin at first by omitting our duties, but by performing them tepidly and negligently. We live like the rest of the community; we conform to the general routine; but without recollection and without an interior spirit. We are in habitual dissipation; now is it to be imagined that amid the sea of troubles in which the soul is plunged, and the diversity of objects which distract us, our zeal for perfection will not gradually be quenched, and in the same proportion we shall not slacken our pace and fall away?

The third and essential cause of tepidity, although

the most remote, is, despising little things; by this it is that we begin to degenerate. Instead of remembering that there is nothing little in the service of God and in the worship due to Him; that perfection does not consist so much in great as in little things; that it is greater to be faithful in small things that in great; in fine, that small things lead to greater; instead of reflecting well on these truths, we grow weary of little observances, we look on them as only fit for beginners, we are not careful about them; thus we descend step by step to the abyss of tepidity.

We may now inquire what are the remedies for tepidity. As tepidity is a numbness which keeps the will inactive, or leads it to neglect of duty, it follows, that to cure the will of this species of infirmity, it must be awakened and excited by some striking reflections.

Let the tepid soul consider the greatness of the God she serves. Let her consider what God is to her, and what she is to God. God is to her, her Master, her Sovereign, her Judge, her Creator; how then does He merit to be served? She is to God, His servant, His slave, His creature; how in these qualities should she serve Him? Considerations such as these, St. Paul used, to excite the primitive Christians to fervour. "I conjure you," said he to them, "to walk in the ways of God, in a manner worthy of God." Excellent rule, infallible remedy for tepidity; to think, speak, act and live in a manner worthy of God.

Let the tepid soul consider how the great ones of this world are served. The conduct of worldlings is for religious a continual lesson, and they should blush in comparing themselves to those courtiers whom interest or ambition attaches to princes and kings. Let the tepid soul humble herself and be confounded at seeing how little zeal she has for God, while the slaves of the world testify so much ardour in the service of mere mortal lords.

Let her reflect that each action she does or is about to do in religion may procure for her an inestimable recompense. These actions are the work of God; according as she will have executed them more or less holily, will she be rewarded more or less abundantly. They may merit for her an eternal recompense. Such holy thoughts, and others like them, each day and each moment inflame with a fresh ardour the fervent religious of the same order and community, whose virtues she daily witnesses, and whom she ought to propose to herself as models.

Practically speaking, the most effectual means to awaken the tepid religious from her supineness, is to destroy its causes, and oppose to them opposite principles; contraries are cured by contraries. For example, to resume all the exercises of piety, the omission of which has been so full of harm; to be henceforward exact and assiduous in the discharge of them; to fail in nothing, not even the smallest duties or the most trifling rules; surmounting all difficulties, overcoming all repugnances, willing, if necessary, to serve God during her whole life without consolation or unction, too happy if He deigns again to receive her, even on those terms.

Section II.—*Of the Abuse of Grace.*

God lavishes on souls who consecrate themselves to Him in religious life, the most abundant and various graces. Exterior graces: how many prayers, meditations, examens, spiritual lectures! How many moving exhortations, useful advices, wise counsels, charitable admonitions, holy examples! How many visits to Jesus Christ in His temple, masses heard, mortifications practised! How many directions, confessions, absolutions, communions! Interior graces: what bright rays of light, holy impressions, pious motions, encouraging consolations, salutary remorse! God leads the religious soul, as it were, by the hand, with all the solicitude of a tender mother, and opens to her His treasures with boundless generosity.

These abundant graces are so many talents which God entrusts to the religious soul; talents which she is strictly obliged to render fruitful, because she is only the depository of them. She should use them according to the designs of Him who distributes them, and to whom afterwards she must render an account. And what use would God have her make of them? He says to her:—"Deny thyself, take up thy cross, and follow Me. Be holy, because I am holy. Be perfect, as your Heavenly Father is perfect." Hence, the graces the religious soul receives are the materials destined to construct the edifice of her sanctity and perfection; an edifice which is to be lofty in proportion to the means entrusted to her.

It is of faith, says Bourdaloue, that God will call us to account for all the graces which we have received, and which we continually receive from him; for these graces are talents He entrusts to us, and which He would have us improve to our advantage. They are not graces for which He demands no return, but funds of a debt which we contract with God: and this is to be understood of all sorts of graces, of what nature soever they may be. It is likewise of faith that the more graces we receive, the greater account we shall have to render; for each grace, by the use we are bound to make of it, ought to fructify in us, and render to God a degree of glory. " Thou hast given me five talents," said the good servant to his master; "behold, five others I have gained and added to them."

This fidelity in rendering fruitful the graces that we receive, merits for us each day additional graces: according to these words of the Gospel:—" Because you have been faithful over a few things, I will place you over many." A thought truly encouraging! " Be grateful for the least graces," says the author of the " Imitation," " and you will merit to receive greater. Have a high esteem for the smallest, and let the least considerable be most precious to you. Since He who gives is infinitely great, He communicates His greatness to all His gifts; thus nothing which comes from the hand of so great a God can be small."

These are the dispositions in which a religious should be with regard to the gifts of God, whether they are interior or exterior, great or small, hidden or brilliant, consoling or crucifying. She should receive them with humble gratitude, carefully turning them to her spiritual profit, and being most exact that not the least portion of them be lost through her negligence.

Many abuse in a fearful manner the graces lavished on them in the holy state of religion. Some, by not turning them to sufficient profit. Such souls live in an alternate succession of co-operation and infidelity; they are even more frequently indocile than faithful to grace, and remain in a low degree of virtue, weak, crawling, and degenerate; and after many years they find they have not corrected a single vice, nor overcome a single passion.

There are others who derive absolutely no profit from the graces lavished on them. After ten, fifteen, perhaps twenty years, or even more, during which time they were bound to tend towards perfection, they have not advanced a step. They are as liable to vanity, as susceptible, as immortified, as they were in the beginning; they are as great enemies to obedience, poverty, self-denial, recollection, regularity, silence, &c., as they were the first day. Those means of sanctification and perfection, which have sanctified thousands of religious souls, have not produced in them the least change.

We tremble sometimes for those in the world, on whom God bestows great fortunes, and whom He raises to high honours. Alas! we ought rather to tremble for ourselves, after so many blessings, not temporal, but spiritual, and of greater worth, that God has bestowed on us, and for which we must account at the day of judgment.

Our Lord Jesus Christ wept over Jerusalem, at the consideration of the innumerable graces with which that city had been enriched, and which it had abused. He was melted to compassion at the sight of the calamities which were to befall it. Have we not reason to shed tears over the woes in store for such ungrateful and prodigal souls? To them are addressed those fearful oracles of the Gospel: "Take from the slothful servant the talent he buried in the earth, and give it to one who will profit by it. Cast him into the exterior darkness, where there will be weeping and gnashing of teeth. Cut down the barren fig-tree, why doth it cumber the ground?"

"Oh! how guilty," says Pere Marin, "is a religious who accustoms herself to neglect inspirations, good desires, and who does not profit by the exterior means she has of becoming sanctified! What can her life be called but a series of infidelities and resistance to the Holy Spirit? It is from this that the insensibility of many proceeds; this pernicious habit of neglecting graces leads us, in fine, to make such little account of them, that we even sometimes despise them; faith is weakened, the idea of virtue is effaced from the mind, the heart becomes almost like an impenetrable buckler, on which neither the loving invitations of Jesus Christ, nor His threats, make any impression, when thus hardened. Terrible state of a soul, which a long habit of abusing grace has conducted to this insensibility! Deplorable, that on considering a spouse of Jesus Christ in this state, we have no other language to address her in than that of the prophet Jeremias, when he sat on the ruins of Jerusalem, weeping bitterly for the destruction of that great and magnificent city. If a religious recognise in this sad picture her own character, she should no longer remain hardened, but endeavour to return to God immediately, by sincere repentance; lest death surprise her in this sad lethargy, and lest she experience the threat God makes in Scripture to souls so often unfaithful: "You have despised My advice, and have neglected My reprehensions. I also will laugh in your destruction, and will mock when that shall come to you which you feared."

SECTION III.—*Of the Illusions of the Interior Life.*

Tepidity and the abuse of grace are not the only quicksands against which souls may be shipwrecked in the interior life; there are many others of which we cannot speak here; we will merely specify some under the general title of illusions. Those who desire more ample instruction on this important point, may very profitably read the excellent treatise of Pere Guillore on "The Secrets of the Interior Life;" of which we will now analyze a few considerations in this present section.

There is nothing more common, says this Father, than illusions, and we often see a number of persons who aspire to the interior life become the victims of them.

There are two kinds of illusions: one, that of deceitfulness and real hypocrisy; the other, into which we fall through error.

As to deceitful illusions, we will say but one word: they are usually found in certain persons, who, making profession of the interior life, have merely the show of it.

Some of these enter on the interior life, fathoming and measuring it with a proud spirit. This life seems to them great, noble; and not satisfied with the beaten path, they aspire to the most sublime. They only think of themselves in this research; and occupy themselves with vain complacency, caused by the pretended beauty of their interior soul, and the sublimity of their conceptions

Others engage in the interior life through a spirit of vanity; they see that this life is highly approved of, that there are few persons more esteemed than those who pass for interior persons, and that what they say is esteemed as a message from heaven. This reputation, which they ambition and prefer to every other, determines them and leads them on.

Others again are more subtle; they erect themselves as great spiritualists, and assume all the language and brilliant ideas such persons should have; but it is only to serve their own ambitious projects. Their spirituality is a veil with which they hide their secret intention of insinuating themselves and of arriving at their end; that is to say, honours and employment in the community.

It is difficult to cure these sick persons, because their evil is voluntary   All that can be done is to unveil their deceit: they must cure themselves by practising humility, candour, and sincerity, without which they will never have more than the mere mask of the interior life.

The second class of illusions proceeds from error and ignorance. Some imagine that the interior life consists in a complete estrangement from all society, and from all contact with their fellow-creatures, even from those who are, like themselves, vowed to the service of God in the same monastery. They are gloomy, sad, dreamy, severe, inaccessible; this is an illusion. The interior life excludes dissipation, but not useful or necessary intercourse, nor those recreations prescribed by rule, nor cordiality in our dealings with others, nor spiritual joy.

They fancy to themselves that the interior life is incompatible with exterior duties; they complain of the multiplicity of their occupations, they murmur about them, and ask to be relieved from them: if they cannot obtain this, they are troubled, annoyed, and even go so far as to desire to change their Order, that they may enter into one more perfect, and to devote themselves entirely to contemplation; this is an illusion.

We must neither desire, nor seek offices; but we must accept and retain them when obedience lays them on us: we are merely permitted to make some respectful remonstrances, when we believe the employment with which we are charged is beyond our strength, or hurtful to our spiritual advancement. When superiors do not deem it proper to relieve us of it, we should consider their decision as an order from heaven, ask the graces necessary for our state, then banish every other desire, being careful to make no complaint or murmur, but apply ourselves to unite recollection to our exterior occupations, as did St.

Catherine of Sienna, St. Francis of Sales, St. Vincent de Paul, and a multitude of others, who admirably allied the interior life with the most distracting and multiplied occupations. A religious who, contrary to obedience, wishes to change her office or employment, is like a sick person who wishes to change her bed; this change will not cure her. Let her apply herself to die to self; if she has not the courage to do so, she will never become an interior person.

They cannot suffer the least contradiction, the least reprehension; humiliations horrify them, they complain of the trouble and agitation they experience, they are annoyed at everything. "How can we live with such persons?" they exclaim; "how become interior under such a superioress? One can expect from her only contradictions, reproaches, and humiliations; one could never possess one's soul in peace with her and be united to God!" This is a gross illusion. Attachment to one's own will and judgment, susceptibility and pride, are the greatest obstacles to the interior life. As long as we do not surmount these, it is impossible to attain to it. And how acquire those virtues if we are neither contradicted, despised, nor humbled, and if we cannot suffer to be so? Thus the Saints, who had at heart their spiritual advancement, sought, through preference, superiors whom they believed best qualified, by their firmness and vigour, to assist them to die to self: and they solicited as a favour to meet with trials and humiliations. Those who sincerely desire to become interior, should freely have recourse to the same means; otherwise they will never attain their end.

Others foolishly fancy to themselves that the interior life is a life of spiritual consolations, in which the soul, sweetly united to God, is continually inebriated with delight, with celestial joys; is sheltered from every trial, aridity and temptation; this is another illusion. She who only seeks sweetness, joys, and consolations, seeks herself rather than God. The truly interior soul receives with humility consolations when it pleases the divine goodness to give them to her; but she knows also how to renounce herself, to carry her cross, and follow her Divine Master through the difficult and thorny paths by which He leads her; she seeks but Him alone, and provided she finds Him, she is happy. Knowing that He tries those whom He loves, she looks with the eyes of faith on the trials He sends her as favours, and blesses the hand that strikes.

The enemy of salvation has recourse to a thousand other stratagems to ensnare souls: "He transforms himself into an angel of light," according to the saying of the Apostle; he inspires them with a fatal confidence in their own wisdom, and distrust in the counsels and advices of superiors and directors; he fills them with disgust for their most sacred duties, and with zeal for particular practices and works of supererogation; he dazzles their eyes by a deceitful light, fills them with treacherous consolations, and by false revelations hurls them into an abyss of pride. Of all illusions this is the most dangerous, and the most difficult to cure; and when the soul is thus ensnared, it is almost a miracle to rescue her; the devil has closed against her the ordinary ways of return, which are the inspirations of grace, to which she has become insensible, the wise counsels of superiors and directors, against which he has prejudiced her and put her on her guard.

There are many other kinds of illusions, into a detail of which our space will not allow us to enter. The most efficacious remedy to get rid of every illusion is fidelity in laying all the secrets of the soul open to a wise director, and docility in following his advice.

CHAPTER XV.

OF SOME WORKS OF CHARITY WHICH ARE UNITED IN SEVERAL RELIGIOUS ORDERS TO THE PRACTICES OF AN INTERIOR LIFE.

SECTION I.—*Of the Instruction of Youth.*

HAVING thus traced for persons consecrated to God the path which conducts to the perfection of their holy state, we will now address to them a few counsels and reflections, proper to guide and encourage them in the principal works of charity, in which they may be employed, conformably to the institute they have embraced.

The occupation to which religious communities are in most cases devoted, is the instruction of youth. Nothing can be more important than this work; not only for those who are the objects of it, but for society at large. It is one of the most meritorious of works.

Nothing can be more important than the instruction of youth. First, for those who are the objects of it, because on the education and training they receive in their early years, depends the rest of their lives; it is in youth man is formed to good or evil, and accustoms himself to either.

"The brain of children is soft," says Fenelon, "it hardens daily; as to their mind, it knows nothing; all is new to it. This softness of the brain causes everything to be easily impressed on it, and the impression it receives from sensible objects is very lively. We must hasten, then, to write in their brain whilst the characters can be easily formed; but we must select the images we wish to engrave on it, for into a receptacle so small and so precious we should place only the best of things. At that age, we should only imprint in the mind what we wish to remain there for life. The first images, engraven whilst the brain is soft, and when nothing has yet been inscribed on it, are the most lasting. Those images are hardened in proportion as age dries the brain; thus they become ineffaceable. Do we not daily hear it said, I have taken my bent, I have been brought up this way, I am too old to change; besides, do we not feel a singular pleasure in recalling the impressions of our youth? Are not our strongest impressions formed at that age? Does not all this prove that early impressions and habits are the strongest?"

All that is said about the brain by the pious and learned Archbishop of Cambray, is applicable to the heart. It is in youth we must sow the first seeds of Christian virtues, and extirpate the fatal and vicious inclinations, which begin to develope; for, says the Holy Ghost, the habit of vice or virtue which man has contracted in his youth will accompany him to his old age. Thus a careful education, over which prudence, wisdom, and virtue preside, contribute most powerfully to form the mind and heart of young persons, and to preserve them from many dangers.

It is equally important to adorn the mind of young persons with useful knowledge. Nothing is more neglected, says Fenelon, than the education of girls. As for girls, it is said, it is not necessary to make them learned; if they know how to manage their households and obey their husbands without reasoning. It is not proper to engage them in studies which take them out of their sphere of action. It is not the business of women either to govern the state, to carry on war, or to enter the sacred ministry; they may therefore dispense with certain extended points of knowledge which concern policy, military art, jurisprudence, philosophy and theology. Generally speaking, the greater part of mechanical arts are not suited to them. They are formed for moderate exercises; their bodies, as well as their minds, are weaker than those of men. Nature has given them industry, delicacy, and economy to fit them for the quiet ordering of domestic life.

The weaker they are, the more important it is to fortify them. The ignorance of a girl is the cause of the weariness that afflicts her, since she knows not how to occupy herself usefully. When she arrives at a certain age, without having applied herself to any solid occupation, she can neither acquire taste nor value for it. Whatever is serious appears to her dull: whatever requires continued attention fatigues her; the propensity to pleasure, so strong in youth, the example of persons of the same age, who are plunged in amusements, all contribute to make her dread a life of regularity and industry. In this state, what will she do?

There you behold a great void, which we cannot hope to fill up with anything solid; frivolity must take its place. In this state of inactivity, a girl gives herself up to idleness, which is a languor of the soul, and an inexhaustible source of weariness. She accustoms herself to sleep one-third more than is necessary for the preservation of health. This long sleep serves only to weaken her, to make her more delicate, more exposed to bodily infirmities; whereas a moderate degree of sleep, accompanied by regular exercise, renders a person gay, vigorous and robust: this constitutes the perfection of the body, without speaking of the advantages which the mind draws from it. Such languor and idleness, joined to ignorance, give rise to a pernicious sensibility, and a desire for worldly amusements. It also excites an indiscreet and insatiable curiosity.

Persons who are instructed and employed in serious occupations, have generally but a moderate degree of curiosity. What they know makes them hold in contempt many things of which they are ignorant. They see the inutility and folly of the greater part of those things which little minds, who know nothing, and who have nothing to do, seek with avidity.

On the contrary, girls ill instructed, and not accustomed to application, have a wandering imagination. For the want of solid nourishment for the mind, their curiosity leads them to objects which are vain and dangerous. Those who have wit often become conceited, and read books which nourish their vanity; they become passionately fond of romances, plays, fiction, and tales of imaginary adventure, in which profane love is set forth. These render their minds visionary, by accustoming them to the strained sentiments of romantic heroes; they are even spoiled by this for the world; since extravagant sentiments, generous passions, and wild adventures, which the authors of romance invent to give pleasure, have nothing to do with the motives which govern human actions, and decide human conduct; nor with the usual course of human disappointments.

A poor girl, full of the tender and of the marvellous, which has charmed her in all she has read, is astonished at not finding in the world persons who resemble her heroes; she would wish to live like those imaginary princesses, who, in romances, are always charming, always adored, always above every care. What distaste for her to descend from a heroine to the mean details of domestic management?

Thus, the absence of a solid and religious education exposes a young girl to indolence, softness, and all the other evils which spring from these fertile sources. Would that these evils injured herself alone! But society at large becomes the victim; and for this reason, we have said, the education of young girls is a work of the highest importance.

Secondly, for society. The world, continues the author already quoted, is not a phantom; it is an assemblage of families; and who can regulate these families with a care more exact than females, who, with their natural authority and assiduity in their houses, have also the advantage of being naturally careful and attentive to minute things—industrious, insinuating, and persuasive? Can men hope to have any happiness in life, if their closest connexion, which is that of marriage, be turned to bitterness? What will become of children, who are eventually to form the human race, if their mothers spoil them in their early years?

Behold, then, the occupations of women, which are not less important to the public than those of men; since they have a house to regulate, a husband to render happy, and children to educate well. Virtue is of no less importance to women than to men. Ah! is it not women who destroy or build up houses, who rule the detail of domestic duties, and who decide all that is most intimately connected with the human race? A judicious woman, industrious and religious, is the soul of her house; she regulates all, not alone the temporal affairs, but even the spiritual. Men, with all their public authority, cannot by their deliberations establish any effective good, if women do not aid them in executing it.

We must also consider the good which women may produce when they are well educated, and the evil which they cause to the world when they have not such an education as inspires them with virtue. It is certain that the bad education of women produces more evil than that of men, since the disorderly conduct of men often arises, either from the bad education they receive from their mothers, or from the passions with which they are inspired by other females in a more advanced age. There is nothing, then, more important than the education of young persons; both for themselves and for society, of which they are members. It is a work most meritorious for those who devote themselves to it.

In fact, instruction, if it had no other end than human knowledge, would not be without recompense before God, who recompenses with liberality even a glass of cold water given in His name. These sciences enlighten and enlarge the soul, replenish it with useful knowledge, hindering it from sitting down in idleness, or from being amused with dangerous trifling. Teaching them cannot be otherwise than a meritorious work.

The instruction which is given to young girls in religious communities, has an end more sublime than human sciences. Its great object is the science of God and of religion, the science of morality and of Christian virtues; its great object is to teach the way to heaven by teaching the way to true happiness here below, a happiness which is found in virtue alone. Many of those who are instructed in these homes of piety would elsewhere have learned but vanity, perhaps even immorality, and would thus have found death in what should have been to them a source of life. Others, if they had not been received and instructed in these homes, would have been deprived of all instruction, and remaining in idleness, would have become the disgrace of their families, and the scourge of society.

Thus the spouses of Jesus Christ, by procuring for young persons a solid and Christian education, snatch them from almost inevitable ruin, and merit more the title of mother of those to whom they consecrate their care, than the parents who have given them birth; for the latter gave them but a temporal and perishable life, whilst these procure for them a life eternal and blessed.

What merit do not the spouses of Jesus Christ acquire by this spiritual maternity? Is it not said by spiritual writers: "He who has saved the soul of his brother has, by that means, secured the salvation of his own?" What then will it be for those who have procured the salvation of many souls? Is it not again written, that "those who instruct others into justice, shall shine as stars for all eternity?" The education of youth is a true apostolate, and if, according to the consoling language of a father of the Church, the Apostles and their successors are to appear before the God of recompence, followed by the nations they have converted to the faith, may we not also say that the holy religious who devote themselves to the instruction of youth will appear before Jesus Christ, followed by their innumerable pupils, who will present them to God as their deliverers and mothers in the faith? Behold, Lord! will they exclaim, those who have inspired us with a horror of vice and a love of virtue; behold those to whom we owe the happiness of having known, loved, and served Thee. Had it not been for them, we should be rejected from Thy face. Give to them, O Lord! the hundred-fold for which we are indebted to them; surround them, according to Thy promise, with as much glory as they have procured for each of us! What can be more consoling than such a thought?

Let it not be said that the trouble taken in the instruction of young persons is useless, and that the greater number do not profit by it. If but one alone profited by it, would it not be something to save one soul? Besides, the precious seed which is sown in the heart of youth sooner or later bears the fruit of salvation. Those who, led away by passion, abuse it for the moment, will profit by it afterwards when the passions become calm. A still more consoling truth is this; that God, in His infinite goodness, not only recompenses our success, but even our unsuccessful efforts. The more painful are the efforts we make, and the less consoling, the more abundant is His reward.

SECTION II.—*Of some Defects we should carefully avoid in the Instruction of Youth.*

Certain defects, capable of paralysing all the care we take to form youth to virtue and knowledge, glide sometimes into education; it is most necessary to preserve ourselves from them. We will here mention a few which seem the most prominent and ordinary.

Religious instructresses should be guarded against natural antipathy and natural sympathy.

Amongst young persons, there is nothing more diverse than the gifts of nature, both in soul and body. Nature has been prodigal to some, sparing to others; and to others, again, has been so stinted as to seem to have set a brand upon them. Then, all have not an origin equally honourable, are not equally endowed with the gifts of fortune, and have not equal recommendations. What a fertile source of sympathy and antipathy for our feeble nature, which is carried to admire, love, and favour what is beautiful and attractive, and to regard with indifference, contempt, and hatred what is mean, poor, and defective! If we add to this, the caprice and inconstancy of our tastes and sympathies, we shall readily acknowledge that a mistress who only consulted vitiated nature, and who only followed her natural inclinations, would be exposed to fall into deplorable mistakes, and to render useless and unfruitful all the efforts she would make to instruct and form to virtue the young persons confided to her. If she wishes to attain the sublime end she has proposed to herself, she must divest herself of all her prejudices, of all natural sympathy and antipathy, elevate herself above the flesh and the senses; she must have in view that God alone whom she desires to glorify, and the souls whom she desires to conduct to salvation, without paying any regard to the gifts of nature, talents, fortune, birth, &c. If, of those confided to her care, there should be one more specially the object of her zeal than another, it should be the one in whom she discovers the greatest defects, vices, and miseries; this is the lost sheep after which she should run, like the Good Shepherd, that she may lead it back to the fold; this is the one that will merit for her the most brilliant crown.

Mistresses must avoid too great familiarity with their pupils. Undoubtedly they should love them in God, and for God, and allow them to have free access to them; they should never allow an air of pride or haughtiness to appear in their manner which would close against them those hearts into which they should have free access, in order to implant the precious seeds of virtue. But at the same time they must avoid all familiarity which would be of a nature to lessen the respect due to them, or would be contrary to religious modesty, or awaken in the heart affections too human; consequently, they should neither give nor receive any token of too sensible an affection; this advice is of great importance.

Mistresses should avoid not less carefully all rigor and excessive severity towards their pupils. Fenelon counsels them never to assume an austere or imperious air, which would make children tremble; in those who govern it is often only affectation and pedantry, for children are usually even too timid and bashful. You would close their hearts and lose their confidence, without which you cannot hope they will derive any fruit from your instructions. Make them love you, let them be unreserved towards you, and let them not fear your knowing their defects; never appear astonished or irritated at their bad inclinations; on the contrary compassionate their weakness. Sometimes this inconvenience may ensue, that they will be less restrained by any fear: but on the whole, confidence and frankness are more useful than rigorous authority.

Besides, authority would not find its place, if confidence is not great. You must always begin to treat children with an open, gay, and familiar manner, but without meanness; which will enable you to discover their natural inclinations, and to know them thoroughly. When from authority you bring them to observe all your rules, you will not have attained your end; all will be but restrained formality, and, perhaps, even hypocrisy; and in place of inspiring them with a love of virtue, you will give them disgust for it.

If the Wise Man recommended parents (and this may equally be applied to instructresses), "to keep the rod ever raised over children;" and that he has said, "that a father who plays with his children will afterwards weep;" it is not that he blames a gentle and patient education: he only condemns those weak and inconsiderate parents who flatter the passions of their children, and who, during youth, permit them all manner of excesses. A child who as yet only acts from fancy, and to whose mind things present themselves in a confused and entangled manner, hates study and virtue, because she hates the person who speaks to her of them. Thence arises that sombre idea of piety, which she retains all her life; and this is often all that remains of a strict education.

Instructresses should carefully avoid punishing a child in the first movement of indignation or impatience they may feel, or while the child is agitated by passion.

"Never," says Fenelon, "reprove a child in her first angry emotion, nor in yours;" if you do it in yours, she will perceive you are governed by humour and impatience, not by reason and friendship; you will lose your authority beyond recovery. If you reprehend her in her first emotion, her mind will not be sufficiently free to acknowledge her fault, to overcome her passion, and to feel the importance of your advice. It is even exposing the child to lose the respect she owes you. Watch every moment, even though it should be during some days, to correct properly. Do not tell the child her fault, without adding some means by which she may get the better of it, which will encourage her to do so; for we should avoid the discouragement which comes from dry instruction. If we find a child somewhat open to reason, I believe it may be well to encourage her insensibly to ask us what are her faults; it is a means of pointing them out without distressing her: and never tell her many at a time.

It is to be considered that children have weak

heads, that their age renders them, as yet, alive only to pleasure, and that we often demand from them an exactness and seriousness of which even we are incapable. We make a dangerous impression of weariness and sadness on their temperament, by speaking to them always of words and of things which they do not understand; no liberty, no enjoyment, always lessons, silence, restrained posture, correction, and threats.

But though we can hardly hope to succeed always without employing fear with ordinary children, whose dispositions are hard and indocile, we must not have recourse to it till we have patiently tried all other means. It is necessary, however, always to make childen understand how much we demand of them; what will make us satisfied with them: for joy and confidence must be their ordinary disposition, otherwise we shall darken their minds and oppress their spirits; if they are lively, we irritate them; if they are gentle, we render them stupid. Fear is like those violent remedies which we employ in extreme maladies; they drive out the disease, indeed, but with injury and exhaustion. The mind led by fear is always the weaker for it.

We must not, on the other hand, always threaten without punishing, lest we give them a contempt for our menaces. We should, however, chastise them less than we threaten; in chastisement, the pain should be as light as possible, but accompanied by all the circumstances which may affect the child with shame and remorse. For example, show her all you have done to avoid this extremity; appear to her afflicted by it; speak before her to others of the misfortune of those whose want of a proper feeling makes it necessary to chastise them; withdraw from her your usual marks of friendship, until you see she has need of consolation; make this chastisement public or secret,

according as you shall judge that it will be most
useful to the child, either to cause her a great degree
of shame, or to show her that you will spare her from
it. Reserve this public shame as a last resource; make
use sometimes of a sensible person to console the child,
who may say to her what you could not then say yourself; who will recover her from her false shame, who
will dispose her to return to you, and to whom the
child, in her first emotion, can open her heart more
freely than she would be able to do to you. But above
all things, do not let it appear to the child that you
demand from her unnecessary submission; endeavour
to induce her to condemn herself, and to do it with a
good grace, that it may only remain for you to soften the pain she may feel. Every one must apply
these general rules to particular wants. Grown persons, and surely children, are not always in the same
mind: what is good to-day, may be dangerous to-
morrow; a conduct invariably uniform cannot be useful. We ought never, in any case, to strike children.

Mistresses should not allow their pupils plays too
boisterous or exciting. Games too dissipating, or
causing too great excitement of mind, ought to be
avoided. When we are not spoiled by any great diver-
sions, and when we are possessed by no ardent passion, we easily find pleasure. Health and innocence
are its true sources; but those who have had the misfortune to accustom themselves to violent, exciting
pleasures, lose the taste for those of a more moderate
kind, and weary themselves in a restless pursuit after
such as serve only to dissipate the mind.

We spoil our taste for pleasure as for food; we
accustom ourselves to high-flavoured dishes, till those
which are simple and unseasoned become flat and
insipid. Let us, then, fear those great emotions of
the mind, which lead to weariness and disgust; but

above all, they are to be feared for children, who can less resist their feelings, and are always seeking. Let us give them a taste for simple things: it does not require much in a repast to nourish them, or great preparations in an entertainment to give them pleasure. With that temperance, which constitutes the health of the body and mind, we always feel a sweet and moderate joy; we neither require public shows nor expense to enjoy ourselves; a little game which we invent; reading; a work which we undertake; a walk; an innocent conversation, which refreshes after labour, makes us feel a purer joy than the most delightful music.

Simple pleasures are less lively, less keenly felt, it is true; they give an equal and lasting joy, without leaving any hurtful impression; they are always beneficial; whereas other pleasures are like adulterated wines, which please at first more than the natural, but which afterwards ruin the health; the temperament of the mind is spoiled as much as the taste by the research after lively and studied pleasures.

Mistresses must avoid flattering or spoiling children who have an agreeable exterior. Often, says Fenelon, the pleasure we derive from pretty and engaging children spoils them; they are encouraged by it to speak all that enters their minds, and of things of which they have no distinct knowledge. The effect of which is that there remains with them for life the habit of judging with precipitation, and of speaking of things of which they have no clear idea; which produces an ill-formed character of mind.

The entertainment we derive from children produces another bad effect on them; they perceive that we notice them, that we observe all they do, and that we hear them with pleasure; they are thus accustomed to believe that everybody is occupied with them.

At that time of life, while they are applauded, and experience no contradiction, they are apt to form chimerical hopes, which prepare infinite disappointments for life. I have seen children who believed we spoke of them every time we conversed in secret, because they had observed we frequently spoke of them; they fancied that everything in them was extraordinary and admirable. Children should be watched and guarded without perceiving it. Show them that it is from friendship, and from the need they have of your aid, that you are attentive to their conduct, and not from admiration of their talents.

Children know little, and should not be excited to talk; but as they are ignorant, they have, consequently, many questions to ask. It is sufficient to answer them carefully, and sometimes to add little comparisons, in order to render your meaning clearer to them. If they judge of things without understanding them, it may be well to embarrass them by putting some new questions which will make them feel their fault, without rudely confounding them; at the same time they should be made to feel, not by vague praises, but by some effectual mark of esteem, that they give more satisfaction when they doubt, and when they ask what they do not know, than when they decide correctly. It is the surest means of implanting in their minds a politeness mixed with true modesty, and a contempt for such contests as are so common amongst young persons of little education.

Mistresses must be very careful never to allow any two of their pupils to become too intimate; and at recreation, play, or conversation, it is not well that they should be separated into groups. Many of those young persons have witnessed much bad example; consequently their heart is corrupted, and they are plunged in a depravity of manners, unknown even to persons of a more advanced age; it would be difficult to conceive how very dangerous it would be for their companions who have preserved their innocence, to have much intimacy with them. One single licentious conversation would suffice to inflict a wound, which would be most difficult to heal, which often bleeds for the entire life, and, in many cases, leads to the eternal ruin of the soul. What a misfortune if a young person, whose virtuous parents placed her in a community, as in a safe refuge for her virtue, a port wherein she was to be sheltered from passion, should there have her innocence shipwrecked! What responsibility for the mistress to whose care she was confided!

To avoid so great a calamity, mistresses should never lose sight of their pupils, should carefully watch their conversations, gestures, attitudes, and reprehend with severity all that bears the appearance of sensuality, levity, or that would indicate anything trenching upon vice.

Section III.—*Of the Method which may be successfully followed in the Instruction of Youth.*

Mistresses must try by every means that prudence will suggest to gain the affection and confidence of their pupils. "Gain first the affections of the people," wrote St. Francis Xavier to his fellow-labourers in India, "and then you will do what you please with their souls." This eminently wise advice is most important for the instructors of youth; if they possess their pupils' affections, they will form them to virtue with wonderful ease. Fear will never replace charity;

it makes slaves: but charity gives docile and devoted children. The confidence of children is gained especially by the spirit of justice and impartiality; by prudence, discretion, by zeal and devotedness, by assiduity in providing for their spiritual and temporal wants, and by perfect disinterestedness.

The principal end of religious instructresses being to form their pupils to Christian virtues, they should employ every means of rendering virtue agreeable to them. Let wisdom show itself but at intervals, and always with a smiling face.

If a child receives a dark and sullen view of virtue, all is lost; your labour is vain. Make children remark whatever amiable or accommodating qualities worthy persons have; their sincerity, their modesty, their disinterestedness, their fidelity, their discretion, but, above all, their piety, which is the source of all the rest. If any one amongst them have any repulsive quality, say that piety does not give these faults, but that it takes them away when it is perfect, or, at least, softens them. After all we must not obstinately persist in making children fond of persons who may be good and pious, but whose exterior is disagreeable.

Though you may watch over yourself, continues the pious Archbishop of Cambray, that nothing may be seen in you but what is good; yet, you must not expect the child will never find any fault in you: she will frequently discover even your lightest faults. Saint Augustine tells us, that he had remarked from infancy the vanity of his masters about their studies. It is most important you should know your faults as well as the child will know them, and that you desire your best friends to point them out to you. Generally, those who govern children, pardon nothing in them, though they pardon everything in themselves. This excites in the children a spirit of criticism and bad feeling; consequently when they discover any fault in their mistresses, they are delighted, and feel only contempt for them.

Avoid this unhappy result; fear not to speak of those defects which are visible in yourself, and of those which may have escaped you in presence of the child. If you see her capable of understanding reason on this point, say that you would give her the example of correcting her faults, as you can correct yours. By this means you will draw instruction from your faults, and edify the child by encouraging her to correct her defects; and you will avoid that contempt and dislike which your faults might otherwise cause her to feel for you.

Mistresses ought to inspire their pupils with a horror of vice, prudently laying before them the devious paths of the wicked. It is necessary to make them remark at an early age the impertinence of certain vicious and unreasonable persons, whose characters can claim no respect. We should show them how much those persons are despised, how much they deserve to be so, and how miserable they are, who follow their passions, and who do not cultivate reason. You may thus, without accustoming them to sarcasm, form their taste and make them alive to true propriety of conduct. You should not abstain from pointing out to them generally such kinds of defects, for fear it may open their eyes to the weakness of those whom you would wish them to respect: for we cannot hope, nor would it be just, to bring them up in ignorance of the state of the case on this point. On the other hand, the surest means of keeping them to their duty is to persuade them that they must bear with the defects of others, and that they must not even judge of them rashly; that defects often appear greater than they are; that they are made up for by good qualities; and that, as nothing is perfect on earth, we ought to admire what has the least imperfection.

Children must be encouraged in their studies and labours. It is necessary to find out every means of rendering agreeable to the child those things you exact from her; and should you have anything painful to enjoin, make her understand that the pain will be followed by pleasure. Always show her the utility of what you teach her. Make its usefulness appear in regard to her intercourse with the world, and the duties of her station. Without this, study will appear to her a toil without object, fruitless, and full of difficulties. Of what use is it, she will say to herself, to learn all these things, of which no one speaks in conversation, and which have nothing to do with our daily occupations? It is, therefore, necessary to give her a reason for all the things you teach her. You should say to her, it is to make you more capable of doing what you will one day have to do; to form your judgment, and to accustom you to reason well on all the duties of life. You should always give to children a solid and agreeable end to the objects you hold out to their view, in order to encourage them in their work; and never insist on subduing them by dry and absolute authority.

We run the risk of discouraging children, if we never praise them when they do well. Though praises are to be feared on the score of vanity, we must endeavour to make use of them to animate children, without turning their heads. We see that St. Paul employs them often to encourage the weak and to soften correction. It is true, in order to render them useful, we must adapt them so as to take from them all appearance of exaggeration and flattery, and at the same time, attribute all the good to God as its source. We can also reward children by innocent games, in which some little industry has a share; by a recreative walk, or some small present, which will be a sort of prize; as prints, pictures, medals, maps, or ornamented books.

We should have recourse to history, above all to sacred history, to instruct children. Children have a passionate fondness for ridiculous tales; we see them continually transported with joy or shedding tears, at the recital of adventures which we relate to them. Do not fail to profit by this inclination. When you see them disposed to hear you, relate to them some short and pretty story; but choose some fables that will be ingenious and innocent. Represent them for what they are, and develope the moral they contain. As to heathen fables, it is better that a girl should be always ignorant of them, because, generally speaking, they are immodest, and full of absurdities. If you cannot keep them totally ignorant of these, inspire, as much as possible, a horror of them. When you have finished telling one story, wait till the child shall ask you for another; her thirst for them being thus awakened, and her curiosity excited, relate certain chosen histories, but in a few words; connect them together, and put off from day to day the relation of the sequel, in order to hold the child in suspense, and to give her an impatience to know the end; animate your recitals with a lively and familiar tone; make all your characters speak. Children who have lively imaginations will believe that they see and hear what you tell them. For example, relate to them the history of Joseph; make his brothers speak like savages, Jacob like a tender and afflicted father; when Joseph himself speaks, let him take pleasure in being master of Egypt, in keeping himself unknown to his brothers, to excite their fear, then, finally, to make himself known to them. This simple representation, joined to the wonders of the history, will charm a child, provided we do not overload her with such kinds of recitals, but leave her to wish for more, and promise them as a kind of reward, when the child is good; nor must we ever give them the appearance of being a lesson.

We should endeavour to give children more taste for sacred history than for any other; not by telling them that it is more interesting, which probably they would not believe, but by making them feel it without telling them. Make them observe how important, how unparalleled, how full of marvel, how rich in natural pictures, noble, and life-like they are. Those of the Creation, of the fall of Adam, of the Deluge, of the call of Abraham, of the sacrifice of Isaac, of the vicissitudes of Joseph, of the birth and flight of Moses, are not only fitted to awaken the curiosity of children, but in discoursing to them on the origin of religion, its foundation is established in their mind.

This method of instruction, employed with discernment, has produced wonderful effects wherever it has been employed; we can generalise it as far as is necessary and prudent.

Section IV.—*Of the Care of the Sick.*

In order to make this book adapted to the general and particular wants of various congregations, we will add some reflections on care of the sick to which the sisters who attend hospitals are devoted.

There is nothing more pleasing to God than the care of those who are sick and in pain; and it is that charity which is the principle of it, which, above all, renders it pleasing to Him. Charity, according to the Holy Scriptures, is the fulfilling of the law, it is the mantle which covers the multitude of our sins, and obtains our pardon; it is it which, on the day of final retribution, is to obtain for us favour before God, who has promised to be merciful to those who have exercised mercy. In a word, works done through charity are, in the sight of Jesus Christ, of so great price, that He has promised to regard as done to Himself, what we do to His suffering members.

Charity in the care of the sick is exercised in two ways; in assisting them in their corporal infirmities, and in providing for their spiritual wants; that is to say, in trying to gain them to God, aiding them to profit by their sickness, and disposing them to die well.

First, to assist the sick in their corporal infirmities. Jesus Christ has promised, as we have said before, to consider as rendered to Himself the services we render to the miserable. The religious in the hospital, if she wishes it to be so with the service she renders to the sick confided to her care, must accustom herself to consider Jesus Christ under those rags of poverty, and it is to Him she is to tender her good offices. This consideration will inspire her with respect and tenderness for the sick, will redouble her assiduity and attention to them. Her exterior will breathe meekness, compassion, and tenderness for the afflicted; she will avoid speaking to them with bitterness or severity, and if necessary to reprehend them, she will do it in a spirit of meekness and charity. She will support with an admirable equality of soul the defects of the poor, their rudeness, their complaints, their murmurs, and their impatience, expecting nothing but ingratitude from the majority. She will attach herself particularly to those who are most difficult to please, most annoying, most burthensome; remembering always that it is Jesus Christ she serves, Who commands us to return good for evil.

The greatest care of the religious attending the hospital should be to conquer her repugnance and delicacy, never testifying, if possible, any horror even for the most disgusting sores; seeking in preference the sick, from whom there is something to suffer, either from their temper, or from the nature of their sickness.

Secondly, the religious of the hospital should procure spiritual assistance for the sick. The time of sickness is favourable to labour efficaciously for the souls of the poor; sickness, which has mostly silenced the passions, death, which hovers near, preach to them eloquently of the vanity of all things here below, and renders them more tractable and docile to the lessons of religion.

The religious should profit by this moment to insinuate herself into their hearts; and, to attain this, she must compassionate their sufferings and try and alleviate them in every possible way: then gently open their eyes to the miseries of their souls, the malady of which is more serious, and may have infinitely worse consequences than that of the body. She should speak to them of the goodness and boundless mercy of God, who is ever ready to pardon the sinner when he returns to Him; who seeks him, and as it were runs after him, as the Good Shepherd does after the stray sheep. Make the sick person understand that his sickness is perhaps a merciful stroke of Divine Providence, which often smites the body to heal the soul; show him how amiable and consoling religion is, how sweet it is to be able to say that God has pardoned us.

It is well not to insist too much the first time, above all when you perceive the sick person is annoyed and irritated; but you must from time to time return to the subject, and pray fervently for those poor souls who are frequently loaded with many mortal sins. When you see the sick persons dejected by anguish and pain, encourage them to suffer patiently, reminding them that by this means they can expiate their sins, and merit heaven. Show them that you serve them joyfully, and that your only trouble is not to be able to relieve them as much as you would wish. Thus a holy and tender compassion, frequent visits, familiar and religious conversations, some edifying anecdotes appropriate to their position, will sweeten their pains, dilate their hearts, and gain them to God. How many souls now in heaven owe their salvation to the good sentiments with which such holy religious inspired them!

When the religious has had the happiness to cause the sick person to open his heart to her, and has determined him to put his conscience in order, she should ascertain whether he is properly instructed in the mysteries of religion, in the manner of approaching the sacraments, especially the sacrament of Penance. If she find him sufficiently instructed, she should induce him to confess as soon as possible; if he is not, and if death is fast approaching, she should try to instruct him, and to put him in a condition to make a good confession, before presenting him to the minister of reconciliation.

Even when the disease is not mortal, the religious should take care not to neglect the conversion and instruction of the sick confided to her care. She should use every means to gain them to God, to instruct and confirm them in the practice of good, so that when they again return to the world, and are exposed to the occasions of sin, they may persevere in virtue.

Several sisters serving hospitals are not cloistered. Those even who live enclosed are obliged, in the accomplishment of the work to which they are devoted, to have much intercourse with the world. Thus it is absolutely necessary for them, if they would preserve the spirit of their holy state, to live in continual interior mortification, in union with God, and to animate every action with lively faith. They should be guarded against all natural antipathy and sympathy for the sick; they must act from supernatural views, and with the greatest impartiality; watch assiduously over their senses and their heart in the care they give those of a different sex; in a word, they should try to be in the midst of the world as if they were not there.

THE END.

Printed by MOORE AND MURPHY, 2, Crampton-quay, Dublin.

www.ingramcontent.com/pod-product-compliance
Lightning Source LLC
Chambersburg PA
CBHW030118240426
43673CB00041B/1321